S0-DTD-829

Teach Yourself
Windows® NT 4

VISUALLY™

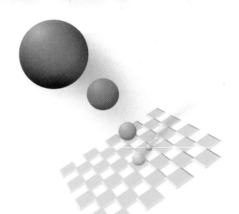

IDG's **3-D Visual**™ Series

IDG BOOKS

From
maranGraphics™

IDG Books Worldwide, Inc.
An International Data Group Company
Foster City, CA • Indianapolis • Chicago • Southlake, TX

Teach Yourself Windows® NT 4 VISUALLY™

Published by
IDG Books Worldwide, Inc.
An International Data Group Company
919 E. Hillsdale Blvd., Suite 400
Foster City, CA 94404

Copyright© 1998 by maranGraphics Inc.
5755 Coopers Avenue
Mississauga, Ontario, Canada
L4Z 1R9

All rights reserved. No part of this book, including interior design, cover design, and icons, may be reproduced or transmitted in any form, by any means (electronic, photocopying, recording, or otherwise) without prior written permission from maranGraphics.

Library of Congress Catalog Card No.: 98-74205

ISBN: 0-7645-6061-1

Printed in the United States of America

10 9 8 7 6 5 4 3 2 1

Distributed in the United States by IDG Books Worldwide, Inc.

Distributed by Transworld Publishers Limited in the United Kingdom; by IDG Norge Books for Norway; by IDG Sweden Books for Sweden; by Woodslane Pty. Ltd. for Australia; by Woodslane (NZ) Ltd. for New Zealand; by Addison Wesley Longman Singapore Pte Ltd. for Singapore, Malaysia, Thailand, Indonesia and Korea; by Norma Comunicaciones S.A. for Colombia; by Intersoft for South Africa; by International Thomson Publishing for Germany, Austria and Switzerland; by Toppan Company Ltd. for Japan; by Distribuidora Cuspide for Argentina; by Livraria Cultura for Brazil; by Ediciencia S.A. for Ecuador; by Ediciones ZETA S.C.R. Ltda. for Peru; by WS Computer Publishing Corporation, Inc., for the Philippines; by Unalis Corporation for Taiwan; by Contemporanea de Ediciones for Venezuela; by Computer Book & Magazine Store for Puerto Rico; by Express Computer Distributors for the Caribbean and West Indies. Authorized Sales Agent: Anthony Rudkin Associates for the Middle East and North Africa. For corporate orders, please call maranGraphics at 800-469-6616. For general information on IDG Books Worldwide's books in the U.S., please call our Consumer Customer Service department at 800-762-2974. For reseller information, including discounts and premium sales, please call our Reseller Customer Service department at 800-434-3422. For information on where to purchase IDG Books Worldwide's books outside the U.S., please contact our International Sales department at 650-655-3200 or fax 650-655-3297.
For information on foreign language translations, please contact our Foreign & Subsidiary Rights department at 650-655-3021 or fax 650-655-3281. For sales inquiries and special prices for bulk quantities, please contact our Sales department at 650-655-3200. For information on using IDG Books Worldwide's books in the classroom or for ordering examination copies, please contact our Educational Sales department at 800-434-2086 or fax 317-596-5499. For press review copies, author interviews, or other publicity information, please contact our Public Relations department at 650-655-3000 or fax 650-655-3299. For authorization to photocopy items for corporate, personal, or educational use, please contact maranGraphics at 800-469-6616.

LIMIT OF LIABILITY/DISCLAIMER OF WARRANTY: AUTHOR AND PUBLISHER HAVE USED THEIR BEST EFFORTS IN PREPARING THIS BOOK. IDG BOOKS WORLDWIDE, INC., AND AUTHOR MAKE NO REPRESENTATIONS OR WARRANTIES WITH RESPECT TO THE ACCURACY OR COMPLETENESS OF THE CONTENTS OF THIS BOOK AND SPECIFICALLY DISCLAIM ANY IMPLIED WARRANTIES OF MERCHANTABILITY OR FITNESS FOR A PARTICULAR PURPOSE. THERE ARE NO WARRANTIES WHICH EXTEND BEYOND THE DESCRIPTIONS CONTAINED IN THIS PARAGRAPH. NO WARRANTY MAY BE CREATED OR EXTENDED BY SALES REPRESENTATIVES OR WRITTEN SALES MATERIALS. THE ACCURACY AND COMPLETENESS OF THE INFORMATION PROVIDED HEREIN AND THE OPINIONS STATED HEREIN ARE NOT GUARANTEED OR WARRANTED TO PRODUCE ANY PARTICULAR RESULTS, AND THE ADVICE AND STRATEGIES CONTAINED HEREIN MAY NOT BE SUITABLE FOR EVERY INDIVIDUAL. NEITHER IDG BOOKS WORLDWIDE, INC., NOR AUTHOR SHALL BE LIABLE FOR ANY LOSS OF PROFIT OR ANY OTHER COMMERCIAL DAMAGES, INCLUDING BUT NOT LIMITED TO SPECIAL, INCIDENTAL, CONSEQUENTIAL, OR OTHER DAMAGES. FULFILLMENT OF EACH COUPON OFFER IS THE RESPONSIBILITY OF THE OFFEROR.

Trademark Acknowledgments

maranGraphics Inc. has attempted to include trademark information for products, services and companies referred to in this guide. Although maranGraphics Inc. has made reasonable efforts in gathering this information, it cannot guarantee its accuracy.

All brand names and product names used in this book are trade names, service marks, trademarks, or registered trademarks of their respective owners. IDG Books Worldwide and maranGraphics Inc. are not associated with any product or vendor mentioned in this book.

FOR PURPOSES OF ILLUSTRATING THE CONCEPTS AND TECHNIQUES DESCRIBED IN THIS BOOK, THE AUTHOR HAS CREATED VARIOUS NAMES, COMPANY NAMES, MAILING ADDRESSES, E-MAIL ADDRESSES AND PHONE NUMBERS, ALL OF WHICH ARE FICTITIOUS. ANY RESEMBLANCE OF THESE FICTITIOUS NAMES, COMPANY NAMES, MAILING ADDRESSES, E-MAIL ADDRESSES AND PHONE NUMBERS TO ANY ACTUAL PERSON, COMPANY AND/OR ORGANIZATION IS UNINTENTIONAL AND PURELY COINCIDENTAL.

maranGraphics has used their best efforts in preparing this book. As Web sites are constantly changing, some of the Web site addresses in this book may have moved or no longer exist. maranGraphics does not accept responsibility nor liability for losses or damages resulting from the information contained in this book. maranGraphics also does not support the views expressed in the Web sites contained in this book.

Permissions

Apple
Courtesy of Apple Computer, Inc. Used with permission.

Imation
Travan is a trademark of Imation Corp. SuperDisk, The SuperDisk logo, and the compatibility symbol are trademarks of Imation Corp.

Smithsonian
Copyright # 1996 by Smithsonian Institution.

Spiegel
© Spiegel, Inc. Used with permission.

USA Today
Copyright, USA Today. Reprinted with permission.

Yahoo!
Text and artwork copyright © 1996 by Yahoo!, Inc. All rights reserved. Yahoo! and the Yahoo! logo are trademarks of Yahoo!, Inc.

The following companies have also given us permission to use their screen shots:
Discovery Channel Online
Flower Stop
Intel
Lycos
Minolta
MSNBC
Sunkist

©1998 maranGraphics, Inc.
The 3-D illustrations are the copyright of maranGraphics, Inc.

U.S. Corporate Sales	U.S. Trade Sales
Contact maranGraphics at (800) 469-6616 or Fax (905) 890-9434.	Contact IDG Books at (800) 434-3422 or (650) 655-3000.

Welcome to the world of IDG Books Worldwide.

IDG Books Worldwide, Inc., is a subsidiary of International Data Group, the world's largest publisher of computer-related information and the leading global provider of information services on information technology. IDG was founded more than 25 years ago and now employs more than 8,500 people worldwide. IDG publishes more than 270 computer publications in over 75 countries (see listing below). More than 90 million people read one or more IDG publications each month.

Launched in 1990, IDG Books Worldwide is today the #1 publisher of best-selling computer books in the United States. We are proud to have received eight awards from the Computer Press Association in recognition of editorial excellence and three from Computer Currents' First Annual Readers' Choice Awards. Our best-selling ...For Dummies® series has more than 25 million copies in print with translations in 30 languages. IDG Books Worldwide, through a joint venture with IDG's Hi-Tech Beijing, became the first U.S. publisher to publish a computer book in the People's Republic of China. In record time, IDG Books Worldwide has become the first choice for millions of readers around the world who want to learn how to better manage their businesses.

Our mission is simple: Every one of our books is designed to bring extra value and skill-building instructions to the reader. Our books are written by experts who understand and care about our readers. The knowledge base of our editorial staff comes from years of experience in publishing, education, and journalism - experience which we use to produce books for the '90s. In short, we care about books, so we attract the best people. We devote special attention to details such as audience, interior design, use of icons, and illustrations. And because we use an efficient process of authoring, editing, and desktop publishing our books electronically, we can spend more time ensuring superior content and spend less time on the technicalities of making books.

You can count on our commitment to deliver high-quality books at competitive prices on topics you want to read about. At IDG Books Worldwide, we continue in the IDG tradition of delivering quality for more than 25 years. You'll find no better book on a subject than one from IDG Books Worldwide.

John Kilcullen
President and CEO
IDG Books Worldwide, Inc.

IDG Books Worldwide, Inc., is a subsidiary of International Data Group, the world's largest publisher of computer-related information and the leading global provider of information services on information technology. International Data Group publishes over 276 computer publications in over 75 countries. Ninety million people read one or more International Data Group publications each month. International Data Group's publications include: Argentina: Annuario de Informatica, Computerworld Argentina, PC World Argentina; Australia: Australian Macworld, Client/Server Journal, Computer Living, Computerworld, Computerworld 100, Digital News, IT Casebook, Network World, On-line World Australia, PC World, Publishing Essentials, Reseller, WebMaster; Austria: Computerwelt Osterreich, Networks Austria, PC Tip; Belarus: PC World Belarus; Belgium: Data News; Brazil: Annuário de Informática, Computerworld Brazil, Connections, Super Game Power, Macworld, PC Player, PC World Brazil, Publish Brazil, Reseller News; Bulgaria: Computerworld Bulgaria, Networkworld/Bulgaria, PC & MacWorld Bulgaria; Canada: CIO Canada, Client/Server World, ComputerWorld Canada, InfoCanada, Network World Canada; Chile: Computerworld Chile, PC World Chile; Colombia: Computerworld Colombia, PC World Colombia; Costa Rica: PC World Centro America; The Czech and Slovak Republics: Computerworld Czechoslovakia, Elektronika Czechoslovakia, Macworld Czech Republic, PC World Czechoslovakia; Denmark: Communications World, Computerworld Danmark, Macworld Danmark, PC Privat Danmark, PC World Danmark, PC World Danmark Supplements, TECH World; Dominican Republic: PC World Republica Dominicana; Ecuador: PC World Ecuador; Egypt: Computerworld Middle East, PC World Middle East; El Salvador: PC World Centro America; Finland: MikroPC, Tietoverkko, Tietoviikko; France: Distributique, Golden, Hebdo-Distributique, Info PC, Le Guide du Monde Informatique, Le Monde Informatique, Reseaux & Telecoms; Germany: Computer Partner, Computerwoche, Computerwoche Extra, Computerwoche Focus, I/M Information Management, Macwelt, PC Welt; Greece: GamePro, Multimedia World; Guatemala: PC World Centro America; Honduras: PC World Centro America; Hong Kong: Computerworld Hong Kong, PCWorld Hong Kong, Publish in Asia; Hungary: ABCD CD-ROM, Computerworld Szamitastechnika, PC & Mac World Hungary, PC-X Magazine; Iceland: Tolvuheimur/PC World Island; India: Information Systems Computerworld, PC World India, Publish in Asia; Indonesia: InfoKomputer PC World, Komputek Computerworld, Publish in Asia; Ireland: ComputerScope, PC Live!; Israel: People & Computers; Italy: Computerworld Italia, Computerworld Italia Special Editions, Macworld Italia, Networking Italia, PC Shopping, PC World Italia, PC World/Walt Disney; Japan: DTP World, HP Open World Japan, Macworld Japan, Nikkei Personal Computing, Open World Japan, OS/2 World Japan, SunWorld Japan, Windows World Japan; Kenya: East African Computer News; Korea: Hi-Tech Information/Computerworld, Macworld Korea, PC World Korea; Macedonia: PC World Macedonia; Malaysia: Computerworld Malaysia, PC World Malaysia, Publish in Asia; Mexico: Computerworld Mexico, Macworld, PC World Mexico; Myanmar: PC World Myanmar; Netherlands: Computer! Totaal, LAN Magazine, LanWorld Buyers Guide, Macworld, Net Magazine, Totaal! Beurskrant; New Zealand: Absolute Beginner's Guide, Computer Buyer, Computer Industry Directory, Computerworld New Zealand, MTB, Network World, PC World New Zealand; Nicaragua: PC World Centro America; Nigeria: PC World Nigeria; Norway: Computerworld Norge, Computerworld Privat (Datamagasinet), CW Rapport Norge, IDG's KURSGUIDE, Macworld Norge, Multimediaworld, PC World Ekspress, PC World Nettverk, PC World Norge, PC World's Produktguide, Windows World Spesial; Pakistan: Computerworld Pakistan, PC World Pakistan; Panama: PC World Panama; P. R. of China: China Computer Users, China Computerworld, China Infoworld, China Telecom World Weekly, Computer & Communication, Electronic Design China, Electronics Weekly, Game Camp, Game Soft, Network World China, PC World China, Popular Computer Weekly, Software Weekly, Software World, Telecom World; Peru: Computerworld Peru, PC World Profesional Peru, PC World Peru; Poland: Computerworld Poland, Computerworld Special Report, Macworld, Networld, PC World Komputer; Philippines: Computerworld Philippines, PC World Philippines, Publish in Asia; Portugal: Cerebro/PC World, Computerworld/Correio Informático, Dealer World Portugal, Mac*In/PC*In, Multimedia World Portugal; Puerto Rico: PC World Puerto Rico; Romania: Computerworld Romania, PC World Romania, Telecom Romania; Russia: Computerworld Russia, Mir PK, Sety; Singapore: Computerworld Singapore, PC World Singapore, Publish in Asia; Slovenia: MONITOR; South Africa: Computing S.A., InfoWorld S.A., Network World S.A., Software World; Spain: Computerworld Espa-a, COMUNICACIONES WORLD, Dealer World, Macworld Espa-a, PC World Espa-a; Sweden: CAP&Design, Computer Sweden, Corporate Computing, MacWorld, Maxi Data, MikroDatorn, Nätverk & Kommunikation, PC/Aktiv, PC World, Windows World; Switzerland: Computerworld Schweiz, Macworld Schweiz, PCtip; Taiwan: Computerworld Taiwan, Macworld Taiwan, PC World Taiwan, Publish Taiwan, Windows World; Thailand: Thai Computerworld, Publish in Asia; Turkey: Computerworld Turkiye, MACWORLD Turkiye, PC WORLD Turkiye; Ukraine: Computerworld Kiev, Computers & Software, Multimedia World Ukraine, PC World Ukraine; United Kingdom: Acorn User, Amiga Action, Amiga Computing, Appletalk, Computing, GamePro, Macworld, Network News, Parents and Computers, PC Advisor, PC Home, PSX Pro UK, The WEB; United States: Cable in the Classroom, CD Review, CIO Magazine, Computerworld, Computerworld Client/Server Journal, Digital Video Magazine, DOS World, Federal Computer Week, GamePro, InfoWorld, I-Way, JavaWorld, Macworld, Multimedia World, Netscape World Online, Network World, PC Entertainment, PC World, Publish, SunWorld Online, SWATPro Magazine, Video Event, WebMaster; Uruguay: PC World Uruguay; Venezuela: Computerworld Venezuela, PC World Venezuela; and Vietnam: PC World Vietnam.

Every maranGraphics book represents
the extraordinary vision and commitment of a unique family:
the Maran family of Toronto, Canada.

Back Row (from left to right): Sherry Maran, Rob Maran, Richard Maran, Maxine Maran, Jill Maran.

Front Row (from left to right): Judy Maran, Ruth Maran.

Richard Maran is the company founder and its inspirational leader. He developed maranGraphics' proprietary communication technology called "visual grammar." This book is built on that technology—empowering readers with the easiest and quickest way to learn about computers.

Ruth Maran is the Author and Architect—a role Richard established that now bears Ruth's distinctive touch. She creates the words and visual structure that are the basis for the books.

Judy Maran is the Project Manager. She works with Ruth, Richard and the highly talented maranGraphics illustrators, designers and editors to transform Ruth's material into its final form.

Rob Maran is the Technical and Production Specialist. He makes sure the state-of-the-art technology used to create these books always performs as it should.

Sherry Maran manages the Reception, Order Desk and any number of areas that require immediate attention and a helping hand.

Jill Maran is a jack-of-all-trades who works in the Accounting and Human Resources department.

Maxine Maran is the Business Manager and family sage. She maintains order in the business and family—and keeps everything running smoothly.

CREDITS

Author & Architect:
Ruth Maran

Technical Consultant:
Paul Whitehead

Conceptual Editor:
Wanda Lawrie

Project Manager:
Judy Maran

Editing & Screen Captures:
Roxanne Van Damme
Raquel Scott
Jason M. Brown
Janice Boyer
Cathy Benn
Michelle Kirchner
James Menzies
Frances LoPresti
Emmet Mellow

Layout Designer:
Treena Lees

Illustrators:
Russ Marini
Jamie Bell
Peter Grecco

Screens & Illustrations:
Jeff Jones
Sean Johannesen
Steven Schaerer

Indexer:
Raquel Scott

**Post Production &
Technical Consultant:**
Robert Maran

Editorial Support:
Michael Roney

ACKNOWLEDGMENTS

Thanks to the dedicated staff of maranGraphics, including
Jamie Bell, Cathy Benn, Janice Boyer, Jason M. Brown,
Francisco Ferreira, Peter Grecco, Jenn Hillman, Sean Johannesen,
Jeff Jones, Michelle Kirchner, Wanda Lawrie, Treena Lees,
Frances LoPresti, Jill Maran, Judy Maran, Maxine Maran,
Robert Maran, Sherry Maran, Russ Marini, Emmet Mellow,
James Menzies, Steven Schaerer, Raquel Scott,
Roxanne Van Damme, Paul Whitehead and Kelleigh Wing.

Finally, to Richard Maran who originated the easy-to-use
graphic format of this guide. Thank you for your inspiration
and guidance.

TABLE OF CONTENTS

PART 1: USING WINDOWS NT

Chapter 1

Getting Started

Chapter 2

Windows NT Basics

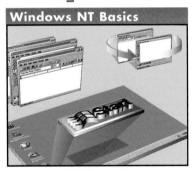

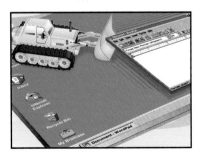

Chapter 3

Using WordPad

Chapter 4

Using Paint

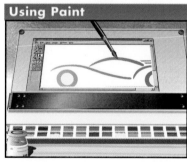

Chapter 5

View Files

TABLE OF CONTENTS

Chapter 6

Work With Files

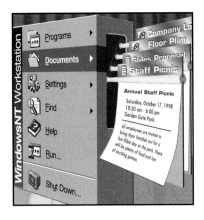

Chapter 7

Customize Windows NT

Chapter 8

Have Fun With Windows NT

Chapter 9

Work With Software and Hardware

TABLE OF CONTENTS

Chapter 10

Work on a Network

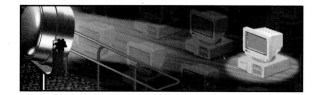

Chapter 11

Exchange Electronic Mail

Chapter 12

Browse the Web

PART 2: USING WINDOWS NT SERVER

Chapter 13

Manage User and Group Accounts

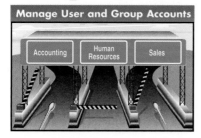

Chapter 14

Manage a Windows NT Server

CHAPTER 1

Getting Started

Read this chapter to find out how to use the mouse, start Windows NT and get help when you have a problem.

INTRODUCTION TO WINDOWS NT

**Microsoft® Windows NT®
is a program that controls
the overall activity of your
computer.**

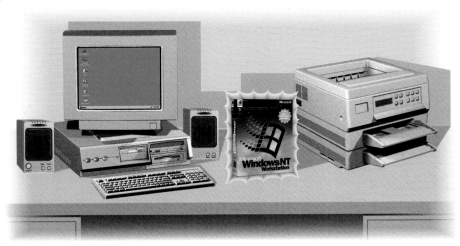

Windows NT ensures
that all parts of your
computer work together
smoothly and efficiently.

Work with Files

Windows NT provides ways to
organize and manage the files
stored on your computer. You
can open, sort, rename, move,
print, find and delete files.

Windows NT includes a word
processing program (WordPad)
and a drawing program (Paint)
to help you quickly start creating files.

Customize Windows NT

You can customize Windows NT
in many ways. You can add a
colorful design to your screen,
change the way your mouse
works and change the amount of
information that fits on the screen.

Have Fun with Windows NT

You can use Windows NT to play
games, view videos, record
sounds, listen to music CDs and
assign sounds to program events.

Work on a Network

Windows NT allows you to share equipment and information on a network. You can specify exactly who you want to have access to your printer and each folder on your computer by assigning permissions. You can assign permissions to individual users or groups of users on the network.

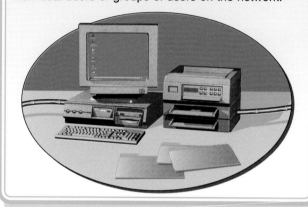

Exchange Electronic Mail

Windows NT allows you to exchange electronic mail with people on your network as well as people on the Internet. You can reply to, forward and print messages. You can also store e-mail addresses you frequently use in an address book.

Browse the Web

You can browse through the vast amount of information on the World Wide Web. Windows NT can display a specific Web page, keep a list of your favorite Web pages and search for topics of interest.

Use a Windows NT Server

Computers on a network can connect to a Windows NT server. The server can store all the information used by individuals on the network and control access to the network. There are many tools available to help manage a Windows NT server.

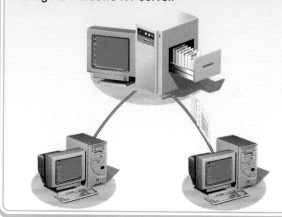

PARTS OF THE WINDOWS NT SCREEN

The Windows NT screen displays various items.

My Computer

Lets you view all the folders and files stored on your computer.

Network Neighborhood

Lets you view all the folders and files available on your network.

Inbox

Lets you send and receive electronic mail.

Internet Explorer

Lets you access information on the Internet.

Recycle Bin

Stores deleted files and allows you to recover them later.

My Briefcase

Updates files you worked with while away from the office.

Start Button

Gives you quick access to programs, files and Windows NT Help.

Taskbar

Displays a button for each open window on your screen. You can use these buttons to switch between open windows.

Title Bar

Displays the name of an open window.

Window

A rectangle on your screen that displays information.

Desktop

The background area of your screen.

USING THE MOUSE

A mouse is a handheld device that lets you select and move items on your screen.

When you move the mouse on your desk, the mouse pointer on your screen moves in the same direction. The mouse pointer assumes different shapes, such as ⌖ or I , depending on its location on your screen and the task you are performing.

Resting your hand on the mouse, use your thumb and two rightmost fingers to move the mouse on your desk. Use your two remaining fingers to press the mouse buttons.

MOUSE ACTIONS

Click

Press and release the left mouse button.

Double-click

Quickly press and release the left mouse button twice.

Right-click

Press and release the right mouse button.

Drag

Position the mouse pointer over an object on your screen and then press and hold down the left mouse button. Still holding down the button, move the mouse to where you want to place the object and then release the button.

START WINDOWS NT

Windows NT starts when you turn on your computer. You need to enter your user name and password to log on to Windows NT.

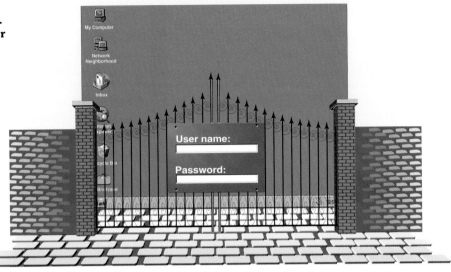

START WINDOWS NT

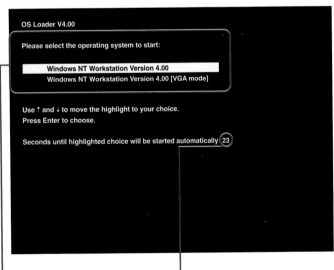

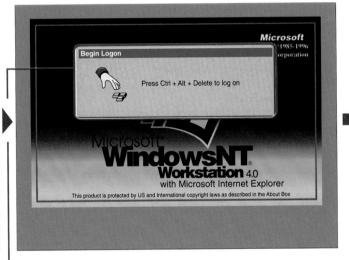

1 Turn on your computer and monitor.

■ Windows NT asks which operating system you want to start.

2 To start Windows NT in the normal mode, press the `Enter` key.

■ This area displays the number of seconds before Windows NT will automatically start the highlighted choice.

■ The Begin Logon dialog box appears.

3 To log on to Windows NT, press and hold down the `Ctrl` and `Alt` keys as you press the `Delete` key.

■ The Logon Information dialog box appears.

? **What is a domain?**

A domain is a group of computers on a network that are administered together. When logging on to Windows NT, you can log on to a domain on the network or your own computer. If you are not connected to a network, you will not be able to log on to a domain.

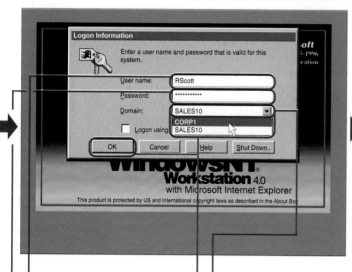

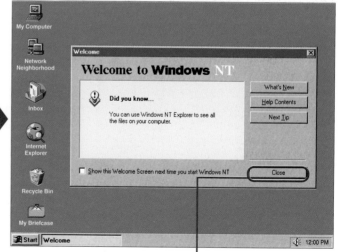

■ This area displays your user name.

Note: To enter a different user name, drag the mouse I over the current name until the text is highlighted. Then type a new name.

4 Click this area and type your password.

5 This area displays the domain you will log on to. To select a different domain, click this area.

6 Click the domain you want to log on to.

7 Click **OK**.

■ The Welcome dialog box appears.

8 Click **Close** to remove the dialog box from your screen.

LOG OFF YOUR COMPUTER

If you share your computer with others, you can log off so another person can use the computer.

Make sure you save your information and close your programs before logging off.

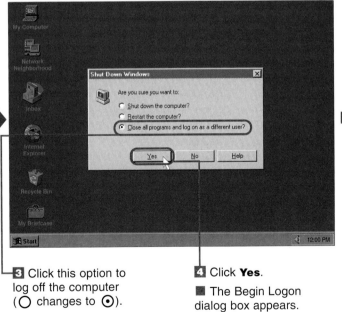

1 Click **Start**.

2 Click **Shut Down**.

■ The Shut Down Windows dialog box appears.

3 Click this option to log off the computer (○ changes to ⊙).

4 Click **Yes**.

■ The Begin Logon dialog box appears.

?

When a colleague uses my computer to log on to the network, why can't he access the same information that I can access?

The user name and password a person enters determines the type of access they are given on the network. If two people use the same computer but enter different user names and passwords, they may have different access to information on the network.

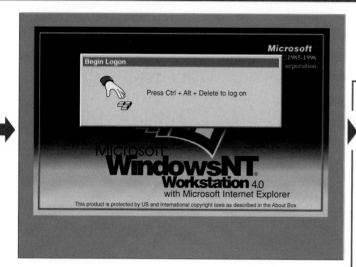

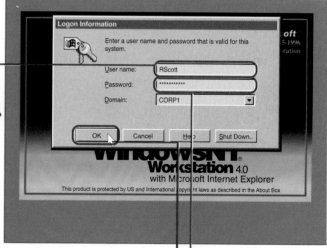

5 To log on as a different user, press and hold down the `Ctrl` and `Alt` keys as you press the `Delete` key.

■ The Logon Information dialog box appears.

6 To enter a different user name, drag the mouse I over the current name until the text is highlighted. Then type a new name.

7 Click this area and then type the password.

8 Click **OK** to log on to the network.

LOCK YOUR COMPUTER

If you are leaving your
desk for a short period
of time, you can lock
your computer so others
cannot access your
information.

LOCK YOUR COMPUTER

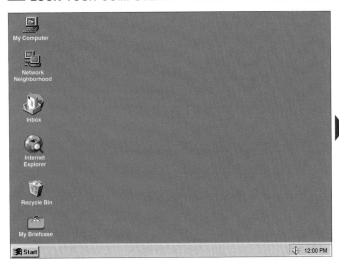

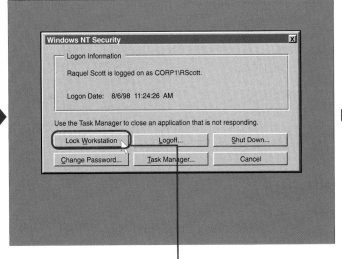

1 Press and hold down the
Ctrl and Alt keys as you
press the Delete key.

■ The Windows NT
Security dialog box
appears.

2 Click **Lock Workstation**.

Can I hide my information without locking my computer?

Yes. You can turn off your monitor or set up a screen saver to hide the contents of your screen. Hiding the contents of your screen will not prevent others from accessing information on your computer. To set up a screen saver, see page 134.

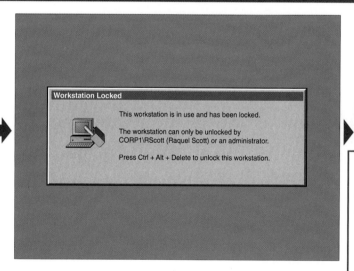

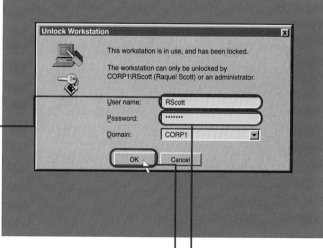

■ The Workstation Locked dialog box appears.

3 When you return to your desk and want to unlock the computer, press and hold down the `Ctrl` and `Alt` keys as you press the `Delete` key.

■ The Unlock Workstation dialog box appears.

■ This area displays your user name.

4 Type your password. An asterisk (*) appears for each character you type to prevent others from seeing your password.

5 Click **OK**.

GETTING HELP

If you do not know how to perform a task, you can use the Help feature to get information.

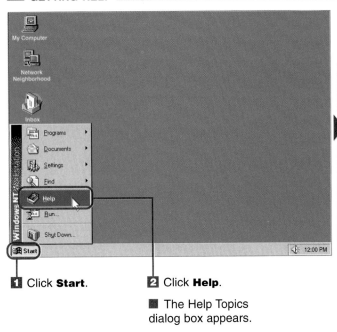

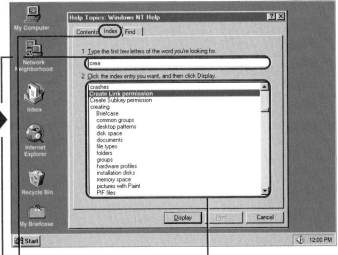

1 Click **Start**.

2 Click **Help**.

■ The Help Topics dialog box appears.

3 Click the **Index** tab to display an alphabetical list of help topics.

4 To search for a help topic of interest, click this area and then type the first few letters of the topic.

■ This area displays help topics beginning with the letters you typed.

Note: You can also use the scroll bar to scroll through the help topics.

How can I use the Help feature to find information?

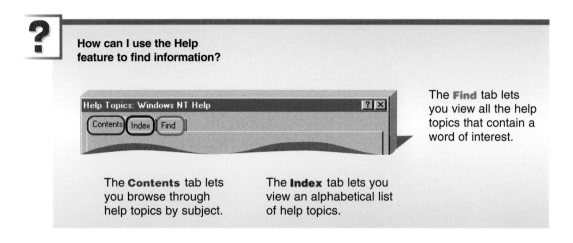

The **Find** tab lets you view all the help topics that contain a word of interest.

The **Contents** tab lets you browse through help topics by subject.

The **Index** tab lets you view an alphabetical list of help topics.

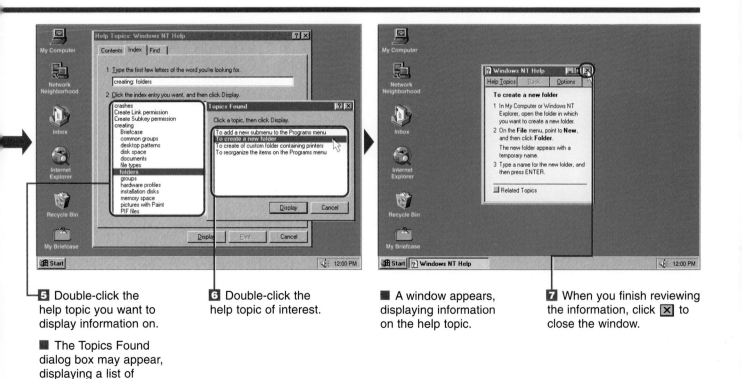

5 Double-click the help topic you want to display information on.

■ The Topics Found dialog box may appear, displaying a list of related help topics.

6 Double-click the help topic of interest.

■ A window appears, displaying information on the help topic.

7 When you finish reviewing the information, click ☒ to close the window.

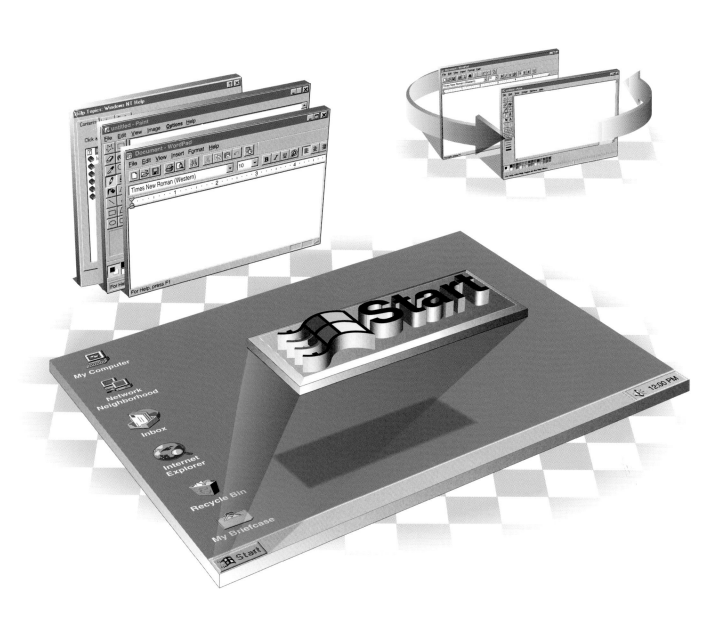

CHAPTER 2

Windows NT Basics

This chapter covers the basic skills you need to work in Windows NT. You will learn how to start a program, move and size a window, shut down Windows NT and more.

START A PROGRAM

You can use the
Start button to start
your programs.

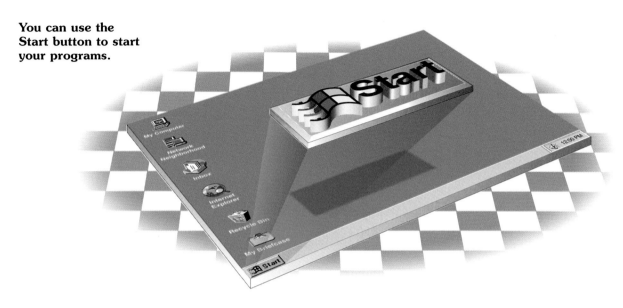

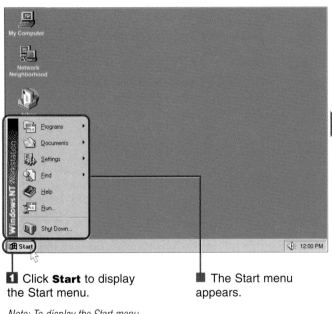

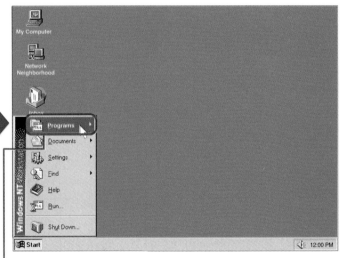

1 Click **Start** to display
the Start menu.

*Note: To display the Start menu
using the keyboard, press and
hold down the* `Ctrl` *key and
then press the* `Esc` *key.*

■ The Start menu
appears.

2 Click **Programs** to
display the programs
available on your
computer.

*Note: To select a menu item
using the keyboard, press the
key for the underlined letter
(example:* **P** *for* **P***rograms).*

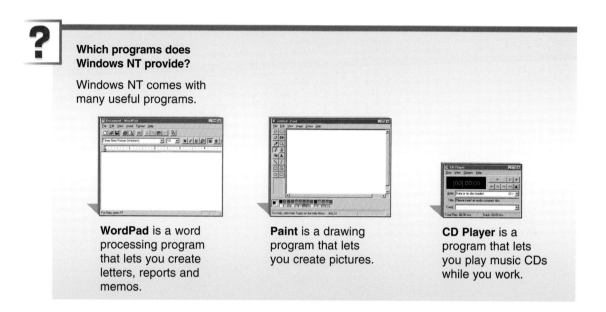

? Which programs does Windows NT provide?

Windows NT comes with many useful programs.

WordPad is a word processing program that lets you create letters, reports and memos.

Paint is a drawing program that lets you create pictures.

CD Player is a program that lets you play music CDs while you work.

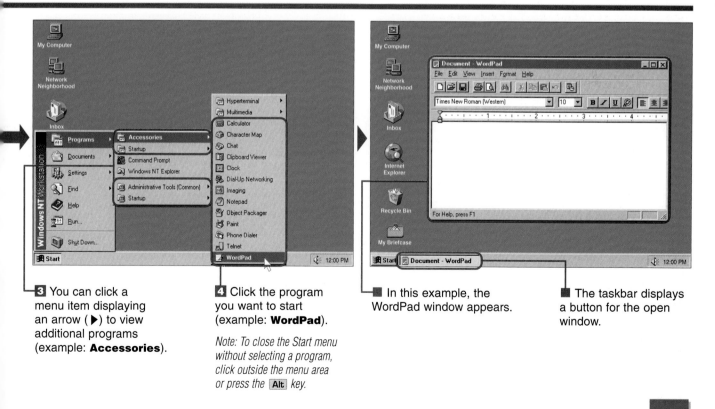

3 You can click a menu item displaying an arrow (▶) to view additional programs (example: **Accessories**).

4 Click the program you want to start (example: **WordPad**).

Note: To close the Start menu without selecting a program, click outside the menu area or press the **Alt** *key.*

■ In this example, the WordPad window appears.

■ The taskbar displays a button for the open window.

MAXIMIZE A WINDOW

You can enlarge a
window to fill your
screen. This lets you
view more of the
window's contents.

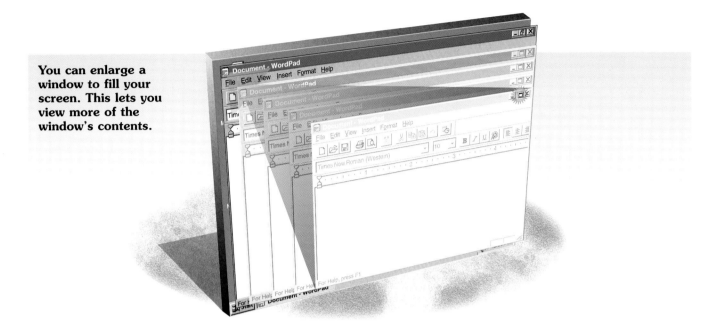

MAXIMIZE A WINDOW

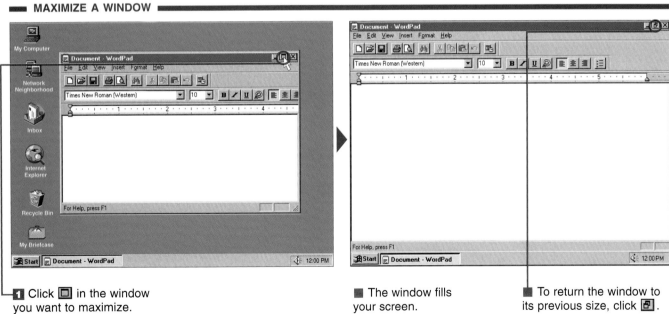

1 Click 🔲 in the window
you want to maximize.

■ The window fills
your screen.

■ To return the window to
its previous size, click 🔲.

MINIMIZE A WINDOW

If you are not using a window, you can minimize the window to remove it from your screen. You can redisplay the window at any time.

MINIMIZE A WINDOW

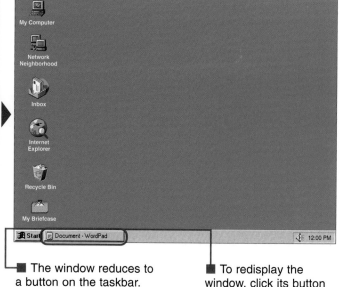

1 Click ▬ in the window you want to minimize.

■ The window reduces to a button on the taskbar.

■ To redisplay the window, click its button on the taskbar.

21

MOVE A WINDOW

If a window covers items on your screen, you can move the window to a different location.

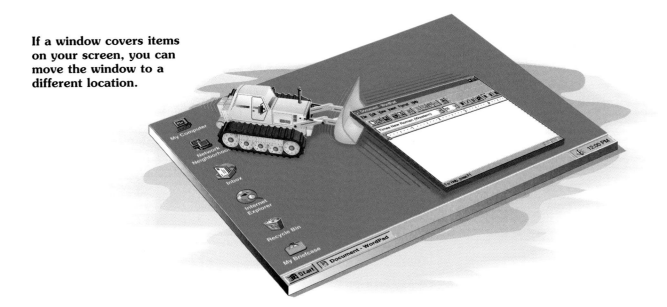

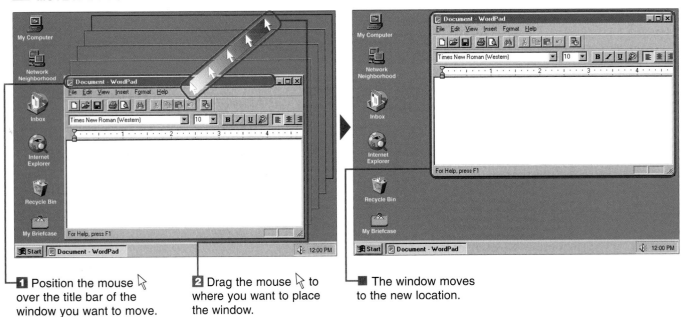

1 Position the mouse ⌕ over the title bar of the window you want to move.

2 Drag the mouse ⌕ to where you want to place the window.

■ The window moves to the new location.

SIZE A WINDOW

You can easily change
the size of a window
displayed on your
screen.

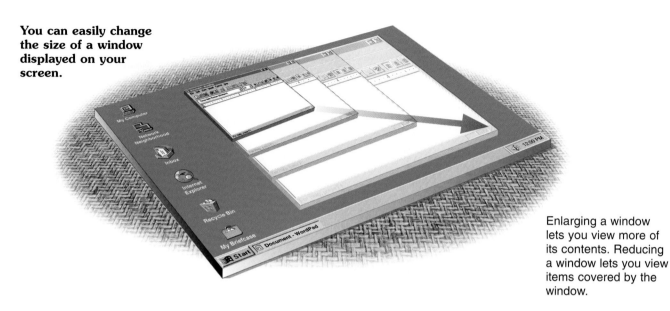

Enlarging a window
lets you view more of
its contents. Reducing
a window lets you view
items covered by the
window.

SIZE A WINDOW

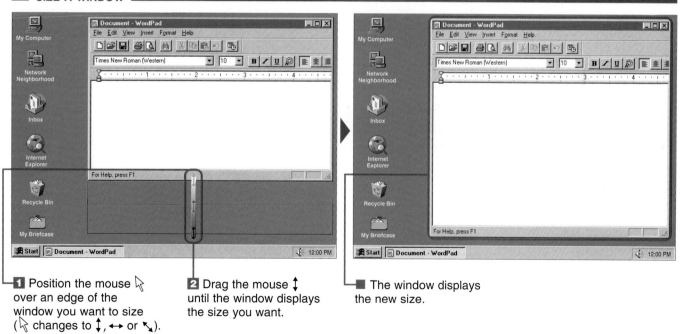

1 Position the mouse ⌖
over an edge of the
window you want to size
(⌖ changes to ↕, ↔ or ↘).

2 Drag the mouse ↕
until the window displays
the size you want.

■ The window displays
the new size.

SCROLL THROUGH A WINDOW

You can use a scroll bar to browse through the information in a window. This is useful when a window is not large enough to display all the information it contains.

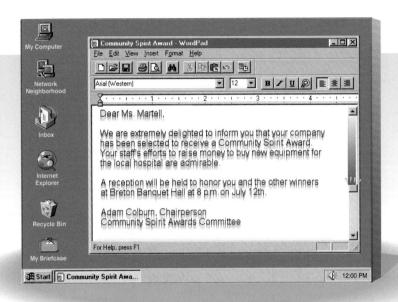

SCROLL DOWN

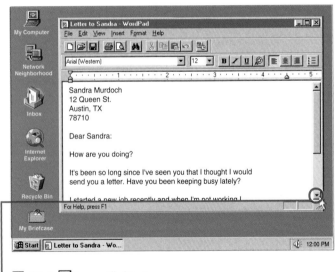

1 Click ▼ to scroll down through the information in a window.

SCROLL UP

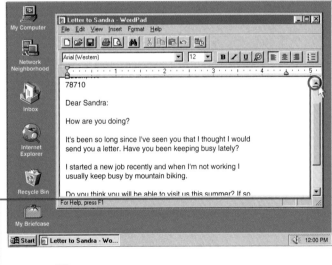

1 Click ▲ to scroll up through the information in a window.

? **Is there another way to use a mouse to scroll through a window?**

You can purchase a mouse with a wheel between the left and right mouse buttons. Moving this wheel lets you scroll through a window.

SCROLL TO ANY POSITION

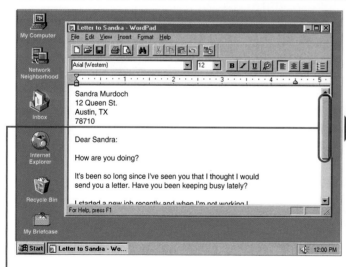

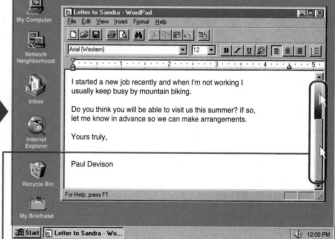

■ The location of the scroll box indicates which part of the window you are viewing. For example, when the scroll box is halfway down the scroll bar, you are viewing information from the middle of the window.

Note: The size of the scroll box varies, depending on the amount of information the window contains.

■ Drag the scroll box along the scroll bar until the information you want to view appears.

SWITCH BETWEEN WINDOWS

You can have more than one window open at a time. You can easily switch between all the windows you have open.

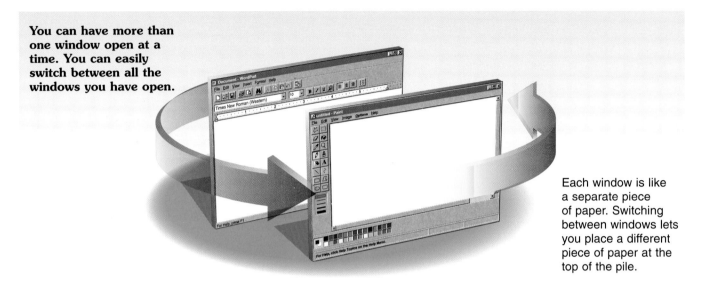

Each window is like a separate piece of paper. Switching between windows lets you place a different piece of paper at the top of the pile.

SWITCH BETWEEN WINDOWS

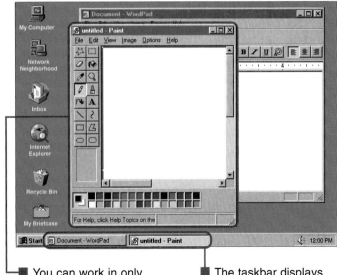

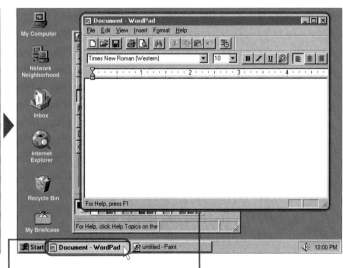

■ You can work in only one window at a time. The active window (example: Paint) appears in front of all other windows and displays a blue title bar.

■ The taskbar displays a button for each open window.

1 To display the window you want to work with in front of all other windows, click its button on the taskbar.

■ The window appears in front of all other windows. This lets you clearly view the contents of the window.

CLOSE A WINDOW

When you finish working with a window, you can close the window to remove it from your screen.

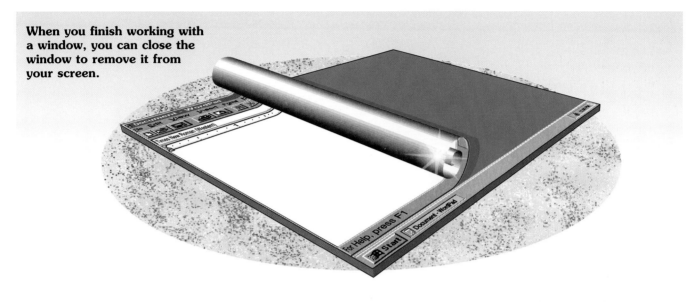

■ CLOSE A WINDOW ■

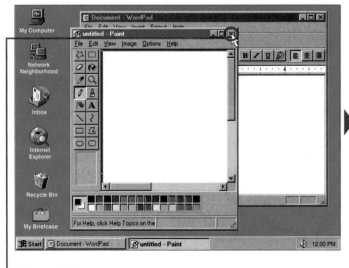

1 Click ☒ in the window you want to close.

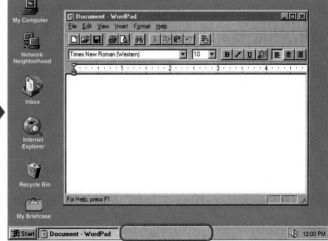

■ The window disappears from your screen.

■ The button for the window disappears from the taskbar.

ARRANGE WINDOWS

If you have several windows open, some of them may be hidden from view. The Cascade feature lets you display your open windows one on top of the other.

CASCADE WINDOWS

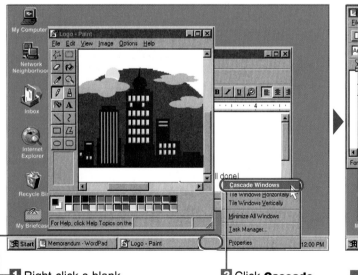

1 Right-click a blank area on the taskbar. A menu appears.

2 Click **Cascade Windows**.

■ The windows neatly overlap each other.

You can use the Tile feature to view the contents of all your open windows at once.

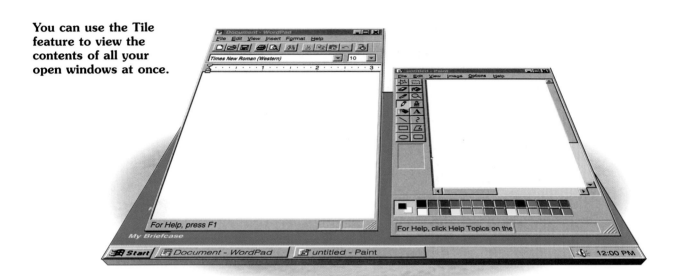

TILE WINDOWS

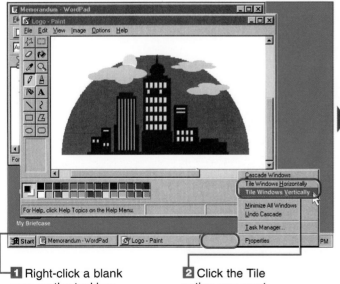

1 Right-click a blank area on the taskbar. A menu appears.

2 Click the Tile option you want to use.

■ You can now view the contents of all your open windows.

MINIMIZE ALL WINDOWS

You can instantly minimize all your open windows to remove them from your screen. This allows you to clearly view the desktop.

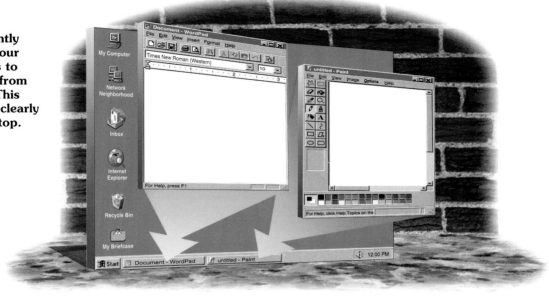

MINIMIZE ALL WINDOWS

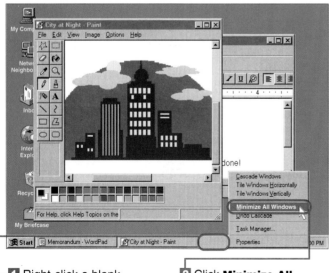

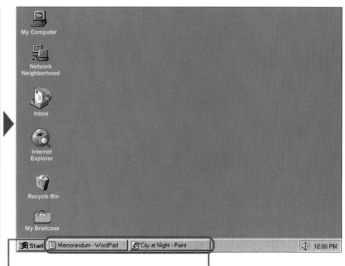

1 Right-click a blank area on the taskbar. A menu appears.

2 Click **Minimize All Windows**.

■ Each window minimizes to a button on the taskbar. You can now clearly view the desktop.

■ To redisplay a window, click its button on the taskbar.

SHUT DOWN WINDOWS NT

When you finish using your computer, shut down Windows NT before turning off the computer.

Make sure you close all open programs before shutting down Windows NT.

■ Do not turn off your computer until this message appears on your screen.

■■■ SHUT DOWN WINDOWS NT ■■■

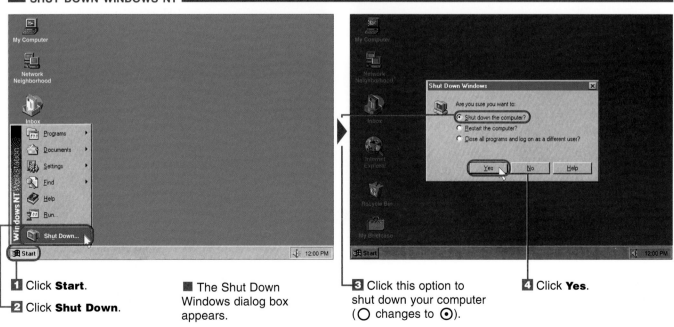

1 Click **Start**.

2 Click **Shut Down**.

■ The Shut Down Windows dialog box appears.

3 Click this option to shut down your computer (○ changes to ⊙).

4 Click **Yes**.

USING THE CALCULATOR

Windows NT provides a calculator you can use to perform calculations.

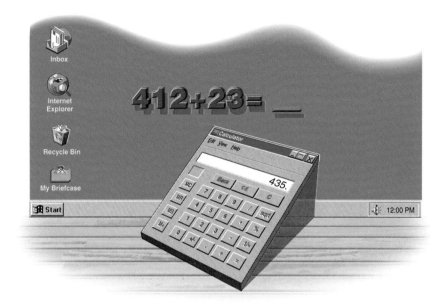

USING THE CALCULATOR

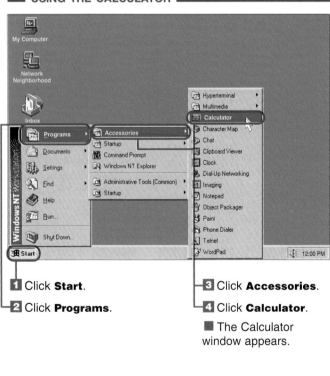

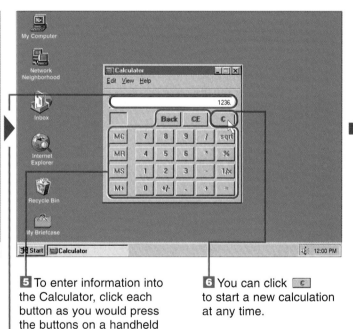

1 Click **Start**.

2 Click **Programs**.

3 Click **Accessories**.

4 Click **Calculator**.

■ The Calculator window appears.

5 To enter information into the Calculator, click each button as you would press the buttons on a handheld calculator.

■ This area displays the numbers you enter and the result of each calculation.

6 You can click [c] to start a new calculation at any time.

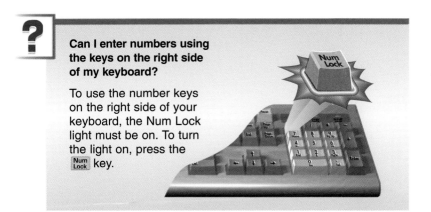

?

Can I enter numbers using the keys on the right side of my keyboard?

To use the number keys on the right side of your keyboard, the Num Lock light must be on. To turn the light on, press the Num Lock key.

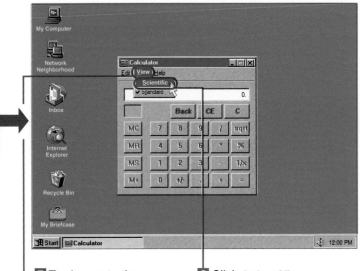

7 To change to the Scientific view of the Calculator, click **View**.

8 Click **Scientific**.

■ The Scientific view of the Calculator appears. You can use this view to perform more complex calculations.

Note: To return to the Standard view, perform steps 7 and 8, selecting Standard in step 8.

9 When you finish using the Calculator, click ☒ to close the Calculator window.

START A COMMAND PROMPT WINDOW

You can work with MS-DOS commands and programs in Windows NT.

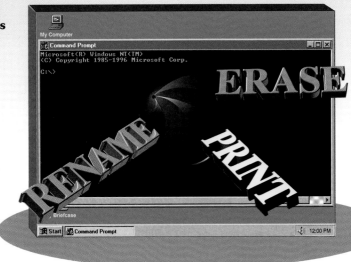

Some MS-DOS programs, especially games, will not work properly with Windows NT.

START A COMMAND PROMPT WINDOW

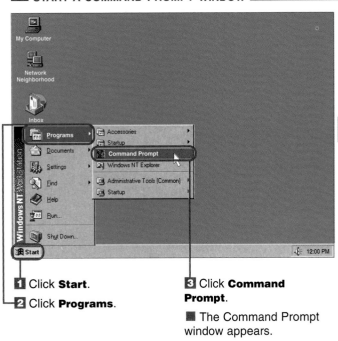

1 Click **Start**.

2 Click **Programs**.

3 Click **Command Prompt**.

■ The Command Prompt window appears.

■ You can enter MS-DOS commands and start MS-DOS programs in the window. In this example, we enter the **dir** command to list the contents of the current directory.

4 To fill the entire screen with the command prompt, hold down the `Alt` key and then press the `Enter` key.

How can I get help information for MS-DOS commands?

In the Command Prompt window, type **help** and then press the [Enter] key to display a list of MS-DOS commands that you can use.

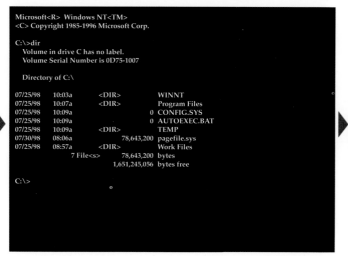

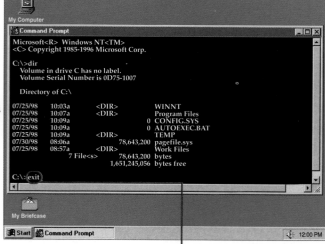

■ The command prompt fills the entire screen.

5 To return the command prompt to a window, hold down the [Alt] key and then press the [Enter] key.

■ The command prompt returns to a window.

6 When you finish using the Command Prompt window, type **exit** and then press the [Enter] key to close the window.

CHAPTER 3

Using WordPad

In this chapter you will learn how to use the WordPad program. WordPad allows you to create documents, such as letters and memos.

START WORDPAD

WordPad allows you
to create simple
documents, such as
letters and memos.

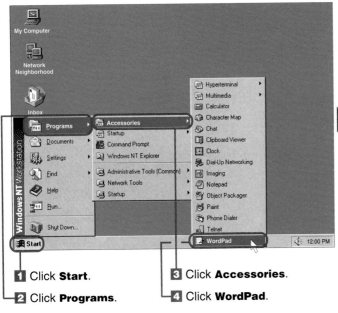

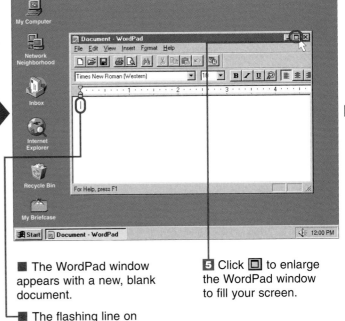

1 Click **Start**.

2 Click **Programs**.

3 Click **Accessories**.

4 Click **WordPad**.

■ The WordPad window
appears with a new, blank
document.

■ The flashing line on
your screen, called the
insertion point, indicates
where the text you type
will appear.

5 Click ☐ to enlarge
the WordPad window
to fill your screen.

?

Does WordPad offer all the features I need?

WordPad is a simple program that offers only basic word processing features. If you need more advanced features, you can purchase a more powerful word processor, such as Microsoft Word or Corel WordPerfect. These programs include features such as tables, graphics, a spell checker and a thesaurus.

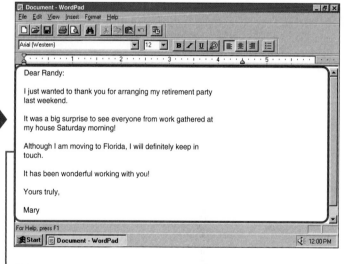

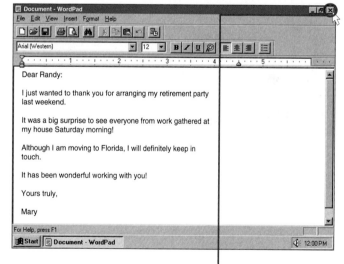

6 Type the text for your document.

■ When you reach the end of a line, WordPad automatically moves the text to the next line. You need to press the `Enter` key only when you want to start a new line or paragraph.

Note: To make the example easier to read, the font type and size have been changed. To change the font type and size, see pages 46 and 47.

When you finish using WordPad, you can exit the program.

1 Before exiting WordPad, save any changes you made to the document. To save your changes, see page 42.

2 Click ☒ to exit WordPad.

EDIT TEXT

You can add new text to your document and remove text you no longer need.

INSERT TEXT

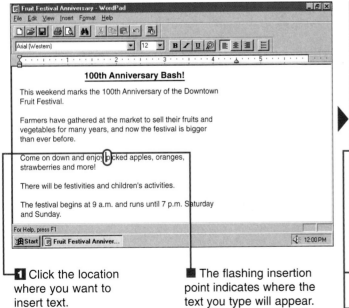

1 Click the location where you want to insert text.

■ The flashing insertion point indicates where the text you type will appear.

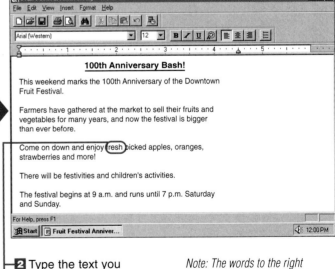

2 Type the text you want to insert.

3 To insert a blank space, press the Spacebar.

Note: The words to the right of the new text move forward.

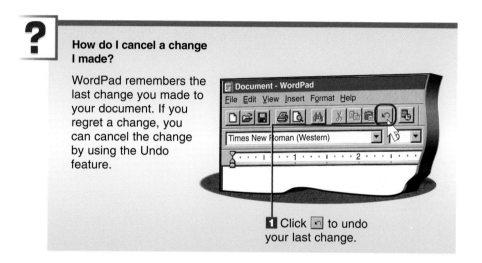

How do I cancel a change I made?

WordPad remembers the last change you made to your document. If you regret a change, you can cancel the change by using the Undo feature.

1 Click 🔄 to undo your last change.

DELETE TEXT

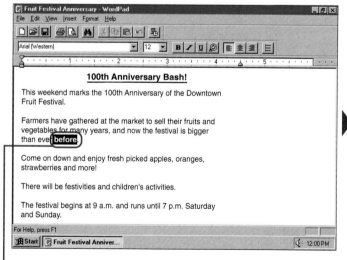

1 To select the text you want to delete, drag the mouse I over the text until the text is highlighted.

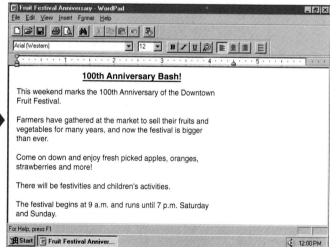

2 Press the Delete key to remove the text.

■ To delete one character at a time, click to the left of the first character you want to delete. Press the Delete key for each character you want to remove.

SAVE A DOCUMENT

You should save your document to store it for future use. This lets you later retrieve the document for reviewing or editing.

You should regularly save changes you make to a document to avoid losing your work.

■ **SAVE A DOCUMENT**

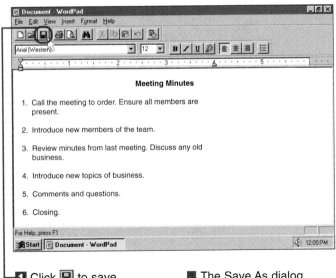

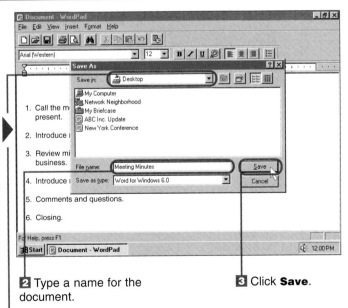

1 Click 🖫 to save the document.

■ The Save As dialog box appears.

Note: If you previously saved the document, the Save As dialog box will not appear since you have already named the document.

2 Type a name for the document.

■ This area shows the location where WordPad will store the document. You can click this area to specify a different location.

3 Click **Save**.

PRINT A DOCUMENT

You can produce a
paper copy of the
document displayed
on your screen.

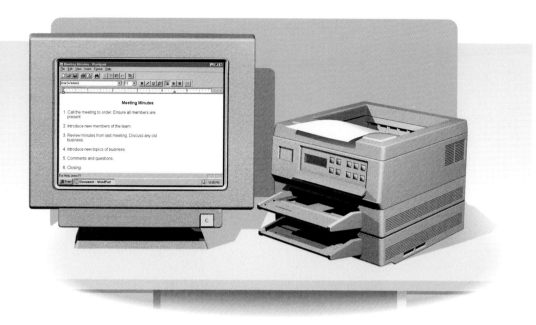

PRINT A DOCUMENT

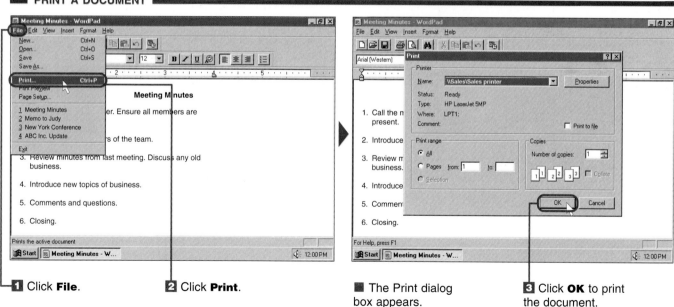

1 Click **File**.

2 Click **Print**.

■ The Print dialog
box appears.

3 Click **OK** to print
the document.

OPEN A DOCUMENT

You can open a saved
document and display the
document on your screen.
This allows you to view
and make changes to the
document.

OPEN A DOCUMENT

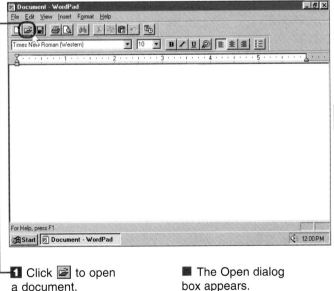

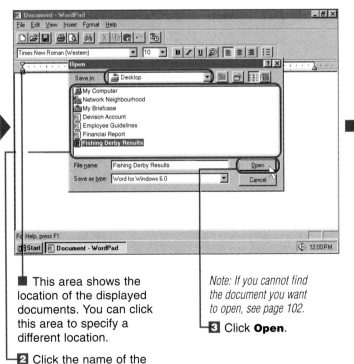

1 Click 🖿 to open
a document.

■ The Open dialog
box appears.

■ This area shows the
location of the displayed
documents. You can click
this area to specify a
different location.

2 Click the name of the
document you want to open.

*Note: If you cannot find
the document you want
to open, see page 102.*

3 Click **Open**.

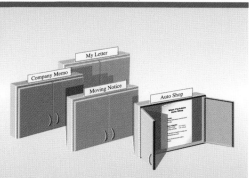

?

Can I work with two WordPad documents at the same time?

WordPad lets you work with only one document at a time. If you are currently working with a document, save the document before opening another. For information on saving a document, see page 42.

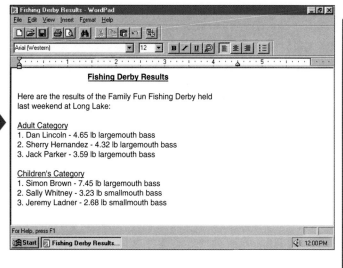

■ WordPad opens the document and displays it on your screen. You can now review and make changes to the document.

QUICKLY OPEN A DOCUMENT

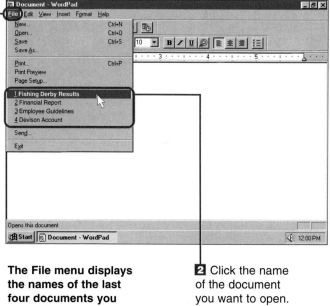

The File menu displays the names of the last four documents you opened.

1 To quickly open a document, click **File**.

2 Click the name of the document you want to open.

CHANGE FONT TYPE

You can enhance the appearance of your document by changing the design of the text.

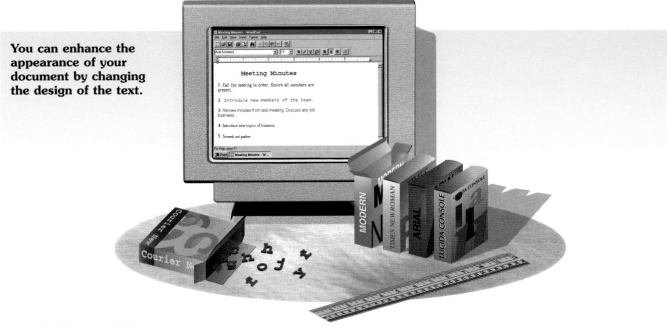

CHANGE FONT TYPE

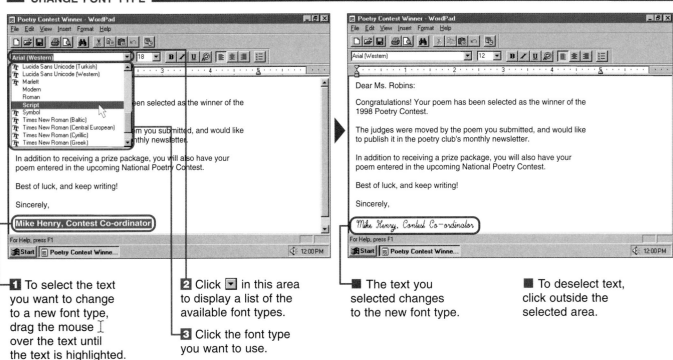

1 To select the text you want to change to a new font type, drag the mouse I over the text until the text is highlighted.

2 Click ▼ in this area to display a list of the available font types.

3 Click the font type you want to use.

■ The text you selected changes to the new font type.

■ To deselect text, click outside the selected area.

CHANGE FONT SIZE

You can increase or
decrease the size of
text in your document.

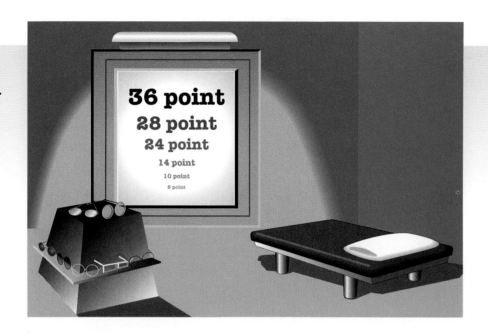

CHANGE FONT SIZE

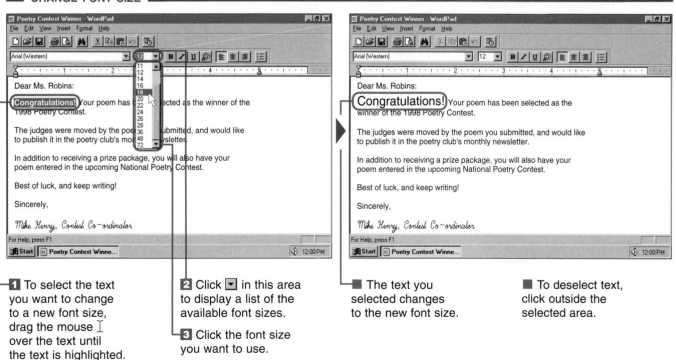

1 To select the text
you want to change
to a new font size,
drag the mouse I
over the text until
the text is highlighted.

2 Click ▼ in this area
to display a list of the
available font sizes.

3 Click the font size
you want to use.

■ The text you
selected changes
to the new font size.

■ To deselect text,
click outside the
selected area.

BOLD, ITALIC AND UNDERLINE

You can use the Bold, Italic and Underline features to emphasize important information in your document.

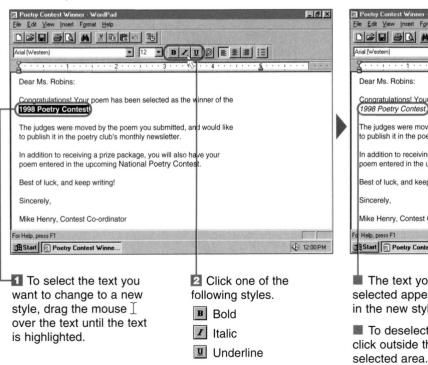

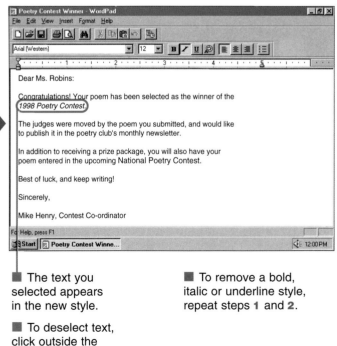

1 To select the text you want to change to a new style, drag the mouse I over the text until the text is highlighted.

2 Click one of the following styles.

B Bold

I Italic

U Underline

■ The text you selected appears in the new style.

■ To deselect text, click outside the selected area.

■ To remove a bold, italic or underline style, repeat steps **1** and **2**.

CHANGE ALIGNMENT OF TEXT

You can make your document look more attractive by aligning text in different ways.

CHANGE ALIGNMENT OF TEXT

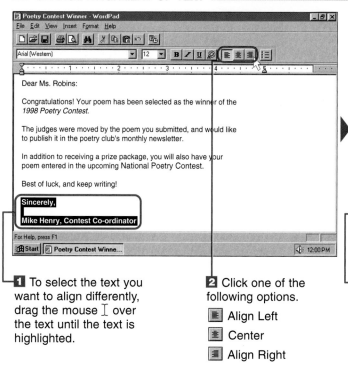

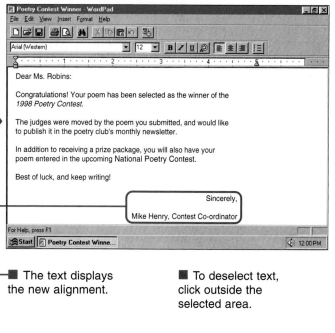

1 To select the text you want to align differently, drag the mouse I over the text until the text is highlighted.

2 Click one of the following options.

≣ Align Left

≣ Center

≣ Align Right

■ The text displays the new alignment.

■ To deselect text, click outside the selected area.

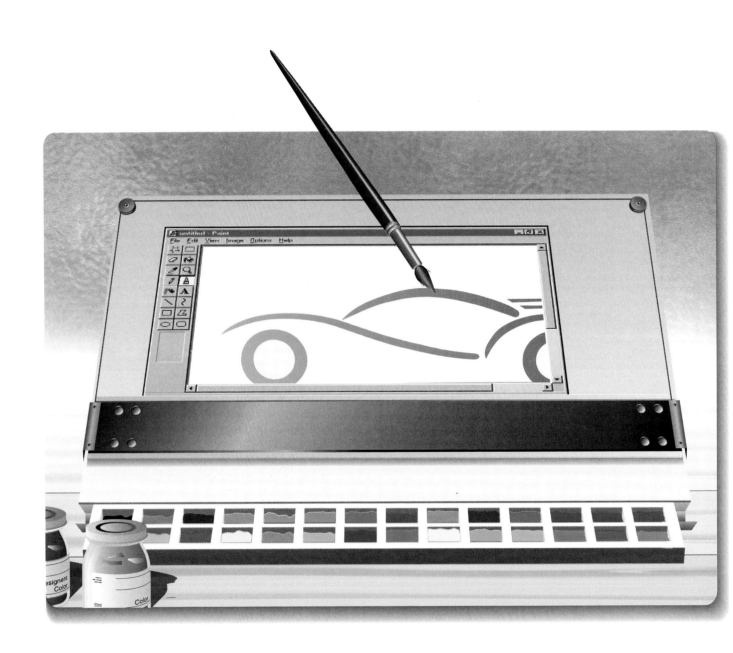

CHAPTER 4

Using Paint

This chapter shows you how to create, edit and save pictures using the Paint program.

START PAINT

You can use Paint
to draw pictures
on your computer.

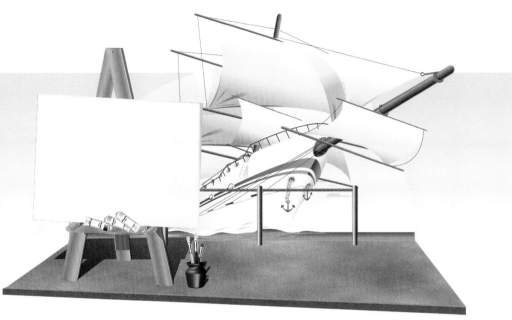

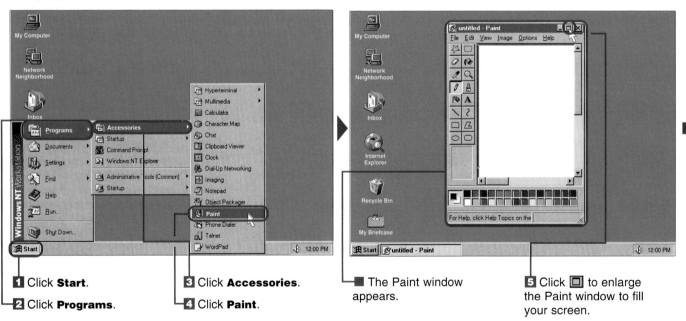

1 Click **Start**.

2 Click **Programs**.

3 Click **Accessories**.

4 Click **Paint**.

■ The Paint window
appears.

5 Click ▣ to enlarge
the Paint window to fill
your screen.

? **What can I do with the pictures I draw in Paint?**

You can place the pictures you draw in Paint in other programs. For example, you can add your company logo to a business letter you created in WordPad.

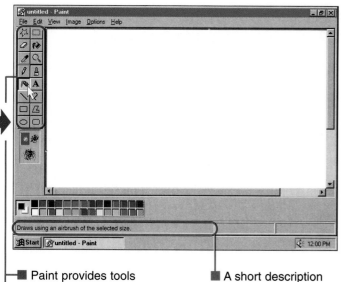

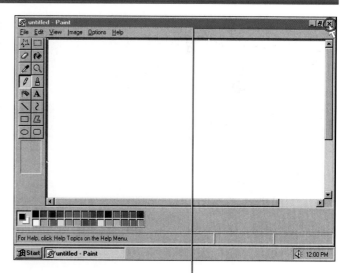

■ Paint provides tools that let you quickly perform tasks.

6 To display a description of a tool, click the tool (example: [✈]).

■ A short description of the tool appears in this area.

You can exit Paint when you finish using the program.

1 Before exiting Paint, save any changes you made to the picture. To save your changes, see page 61.

2 Click [✕] to exit Paint.

DRAW SHAPES

You can draw shapes
such as circles and
squares in various
colors.

■■ DRAW SHAPES ■■■■■■■■

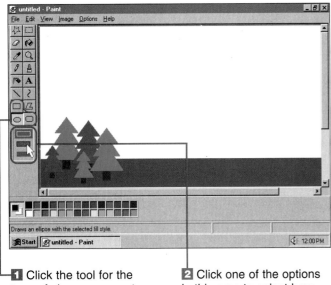

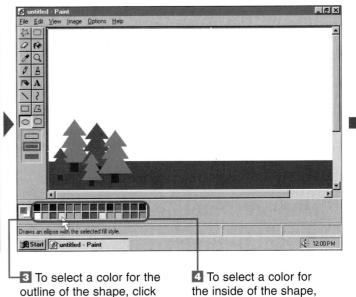

1 Click the tool for the
type of shape you want
to draw (example: ◯).

2 Click one of the options
in this area to select how
you want to draw the
shape.

*Note: For more information,
see the top of page 55.*

3 To select a color for the
outline of the shape, click
the color (example: ■).

4 To select a color for
the inside of the shape,
right-click the color
(example: ☐).

54

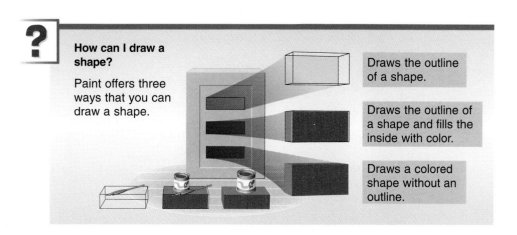

How can I draw a shape?

Paint offers three ways that you can draw a shape.

Draws the outline of a shape.

Draws the outline of a shape and fills the inside with color.

Draws a colored shape without an outline.

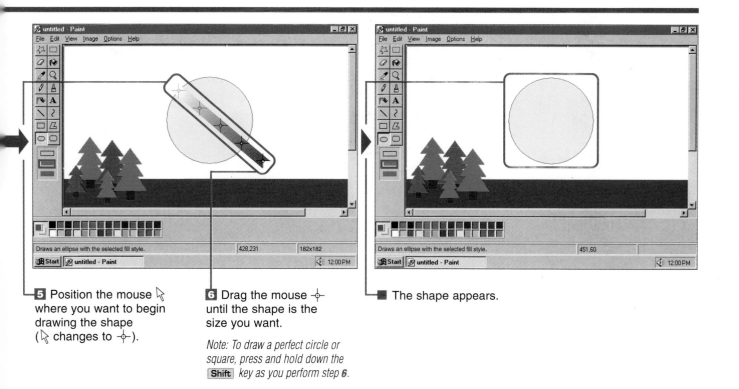

5 Position the mouse ⌖ where you want to begin drawing the shape (⌖ changes to ⊹).

6 Drag the mouse ⊹ until the shape is the size you want.

Note: To draw a perfect circle or square, press and hold down the Shift *key as you perform step 6.*

■ The shape appears.

DRAW LINES

You can draw straight, wavy and curved lines in various colors.

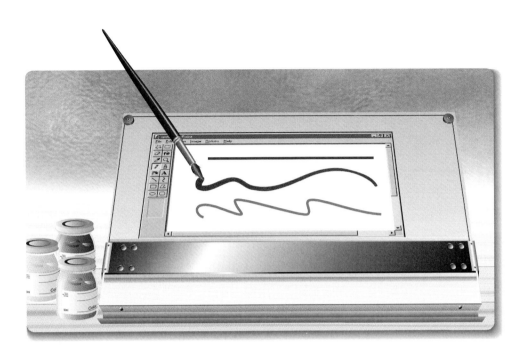

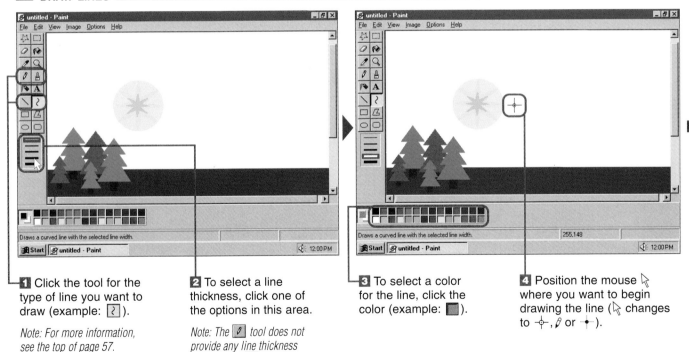

1 Click the tool for the type of line you want to draw (example: ⟨? ⟩).

Note: For more information, see the top of page 57.

2 To select a line thickness, click one of the options in this area.

Note: The ⟨∅⟩ tool does not provide any line thickness options. The ⟨A⟩ tool provides a different set of options.

3 To select a color for the line, click the color (example: ▣).

4 Position the mouse ⟨⟩ where you want to begin drawing the line (⟨⟩ changes to ⟨+⟩, ⟨∅⟩ or ⟨+⟩).

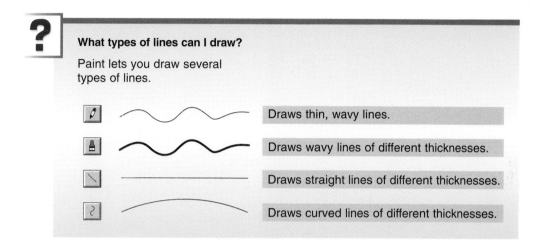

What types of lines can I draw?

Paint lets you draw several
types of lines.

Draws thin, wavy lines.

Draws wavy lines of different thicknesses.

Draws straight lines of different thicknesses.

Draws curved lines of different thicknesses.

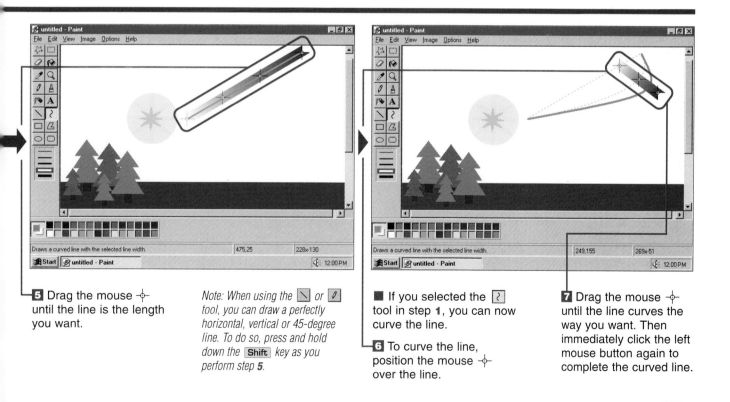

5 Drag the mouse ✛
until the line is the length
you want.

*Note: When using the ╲ or ✐
tool, you can draw a perfectly
horizontal, vertical or 45-degree
line. To do so, press and hold
down the* Shift *key as you
perform step 5.*

■ If you selected the ⟨
tool in step **1**, you can now
curve the line.

6 To curve the line,
position the mouse ✛
over the line.

7 Drag the mouse ✛
until the line curves the
way you want. Then
immediately click the left
mouse button again to
complete the curved line.

ADD TEXT

You can add text to
your picture, such as
a title or explanation.

ADD TEXT

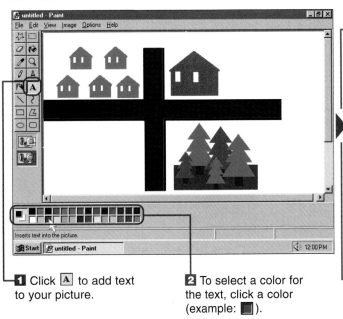

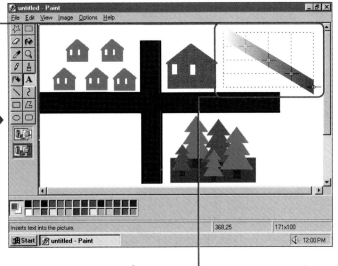

1 Click **A** to add text
to your picture.

2 To select a color for
the text, click a color
(example: ■).

3 Position the mouse
where you want to display
the top left edge of the text
(changes to +).

4 Drag the mouse +
to select the area where
you want the text to
appear.

■ A dotted box appears.

How do I display the Text Toolbar on my screen?

If the Text Toolbar does not appear when adding text to a picture, you can easily display the toolbar.

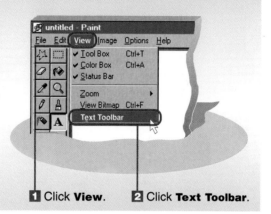

1 Click **View**. **2** Click **Text Toolbar**.

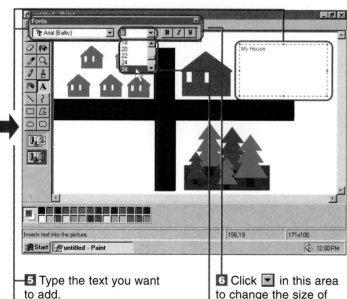

5 Type the text you want to add.

■ The Text Toolbar lets you change the appearance of the text. If the toolbar does not appear, see the top of this page.

6 Click ▼ in this area to change the size of the text.

7 Click the size you want to use.

■ The text appears in the new size.

8 When you finish changing the text, click outside the text box.

*Note: After you perform step **8**, you can no longer edit or change the appearance of the text.*

ERASE PART OF A PICTURE

You can use the Eraser tool to remove part of your picture.

When choosing a color for the eraser, select a color that matches the background color of your picture.

ERASE PART OF A PICTURE

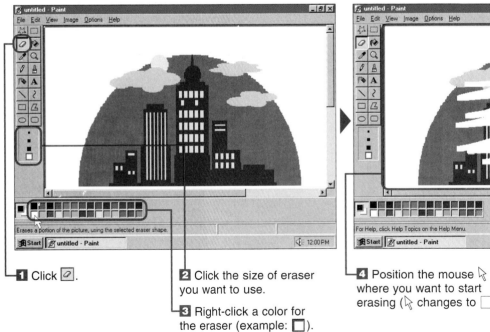

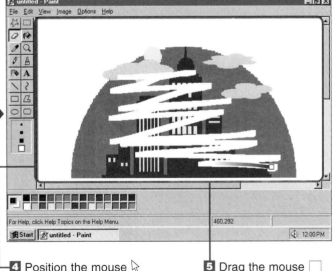

1 Click 🖌.

2 Click the size of eraser you want to use.

3 Right-click a color for the eraser (example: ☐).

4 Position the mouse � where you want to start erasing (� changes to ☐).

5 Drag the mouse ☐ over the area you want to erase.

Note: To immediately undo the change, press and hold down the **Ctrl** *key and then press the* **Z** *key.*

SAVE A PICTURE

You should save your picture to store it for future use. This allows you to later review and make changes to the picture.

You should regularly save changes you make to a picture to avoid losing your work.

■ SAVE A PICTURE ■

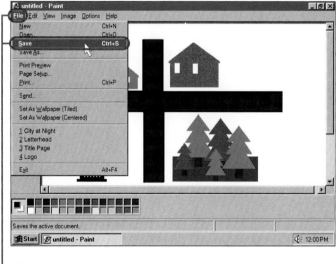

1 Click **File**.

2 Click **Save**.

■ The Save As dialog box appears.

Note: If you previously saved the picture, the Save As dialog box will not appear since you have already named the picture.

3 Type a name for the picture.

■ This area shows the location where Paint will store the picture. You can click this area to specify a different location.

4 Click **Save**.

OPEN A PICTURE

You can open a saved picture and display the picture on your screen. This allows you to view and make changes to the picture.

OPEN A PICTURE

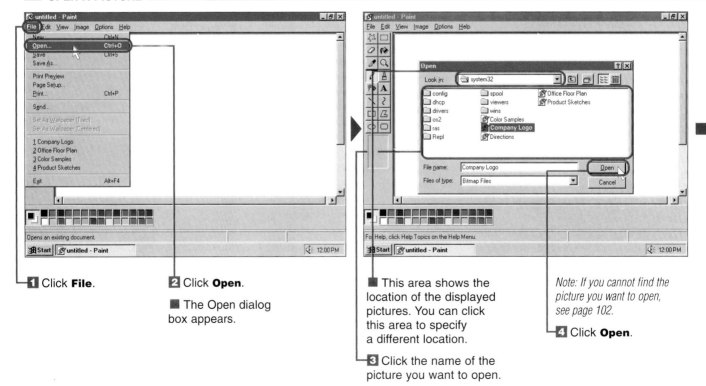

1 Click **File**.

2 Click **Open**.

■ The Open dialog box appears.

■ This area shows the location of the displayed pictures. You can click this area to specify a different location.

3 Click the name of the picture you want to open.

Note: If you cannot find the picture you want to open, see page 102.

4 Click **Open**.

Can I work with two pictures at the same time?

Paint lets you work with only one picture at a time. If you are currently working with a picture, save the picture before opening another. For information on saving a picture, see page 61.

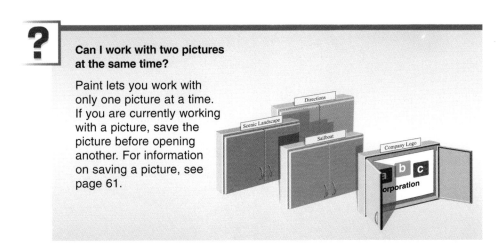

QUICKLY OPEN A PICTURE

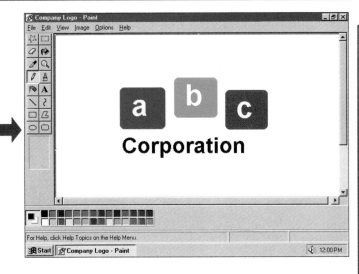

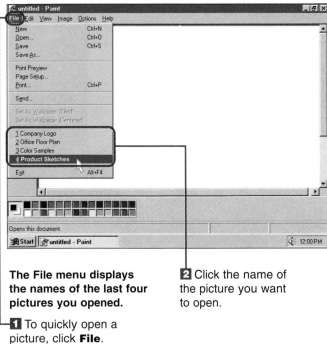

■ Paint opens the picture and displays it on your screen. You can now review and make changes to the picture.

The File menu displays the names of the last four pictures you opened.

1 To quickly open a picture, click **File**.

2 Click the name of the picture you want to open.

CHAPTER 5

View Files

This chapter teaches you how to view the files and folders stored on your computer. You will also learn how to change the way Windows NT displays items on your screen.

VIEW CONTENTS OF YOUR COMPUTER

You can easily view the folders and files stored on your computer.

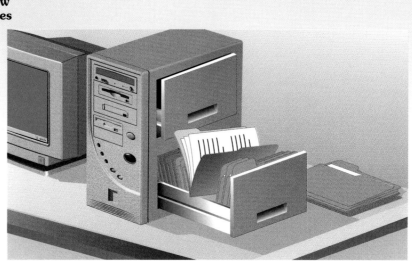

Like a filing cabinet, your computer uses folders to organize information.

■ VIEW CONTENTS OF YOUR COMPUTER ■

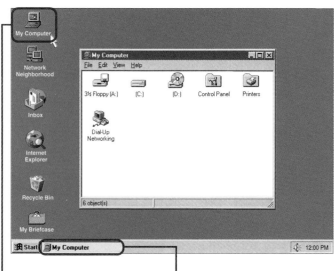

1 Double-click **My Computer** to view the contents of your computer.

■ The My Computer window appears.

■ A button appears on the taskbar for the open window.

■ These items represent the drives on your computer.

2 To display the contents of a drive, double-click the drive.

Note: If you want to view the contents of a floppy or CD-ROM drive, make sure you insert a floppy disk or CD-ROM disc before performing step 2.

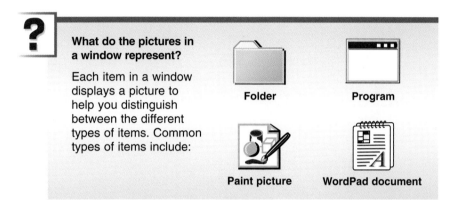

What do the pictures in a window represent?

Each item in a window displays a picture to help you distinguish between the different types of items. Common types of items include:

Folder

Program

Paint picture

WordPad document

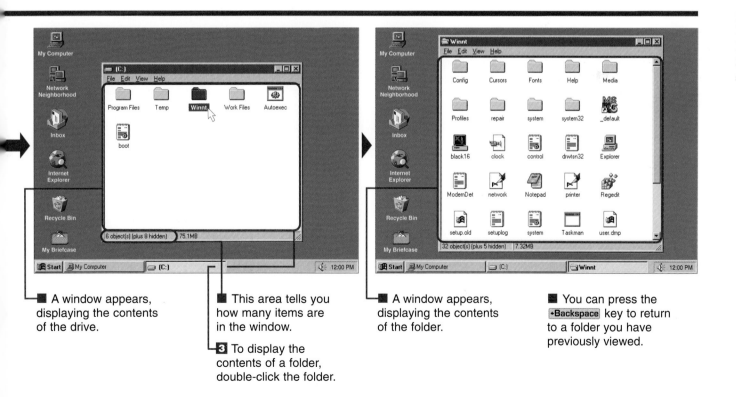

■ A window appears, displaying the contents of the drive.

■ This area tells you how many items are in the window.

3 To display the contents of a folder, double-click the folder.

■ A window appears, displaying the contents of the folder.

■ You can press the +Backspace key to return to a folder you have previously viewed.

CHANGE APPEARANCE OF ITEMS

You can change the appearance of items in a window. Items can appear as large icons, small icons or in a list. You can also display details about each item.

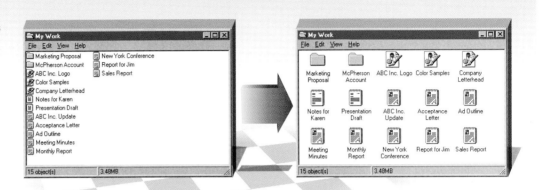

An icon is a picture that represents an item such as a file, folder or program.

CHANGE APPEARANCE OF ITEMS

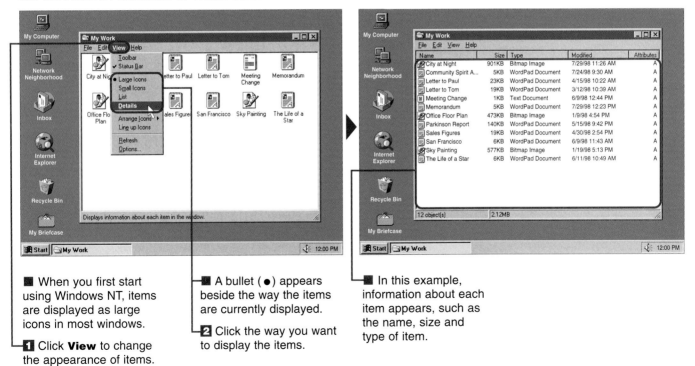

■ When you first start using Windows NT, items are displayed as large icons in most windows.

1 Click **View** to change the appearance of items.

■ A bullet (●) appears beside the way the items are currently displayed.

2 Click the way you want to display the items.

■ In this example, information about each item appears, such as the name, size and type of item.

68

SORT ITEMS

You can sort the
items displayed
in a window. This
can help you find
files and folders
more easily.

SORT ITEMS

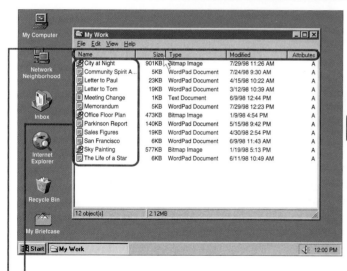

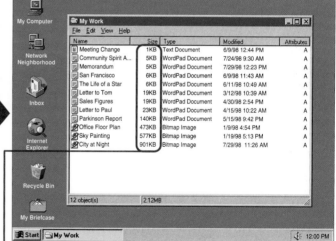

■ When you first start
using Windows NT, items
are sorted alphabetically
by name.

*Note: If the headings are
not displayed, perform
steps 1 and 2 on page 68,
selecting Details in step 2.*

■ In this example,
the items are sorted
by size.

■ To sort the items
in reverse order,
repeat step 1.

1 Click the heading for
the column you want to
use to sort the items.

ARRANGE ITEMS AUTOMATICALLY

You can have Windows NT automatically arrange items to fit neatly in a window.

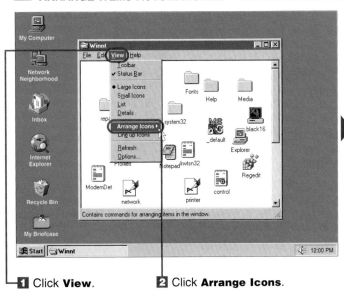

1 Click **View**.

2 Click **Arrange Icons**.

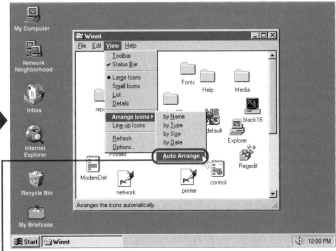

■ A check mark (✔) appears beside **Auto Arrange** when this feature is on.

3 Click **Auto Arrange** to turn this feature on.

*Note: If a check mark (✔) appears beside **Auto Arrange** and you want to leave this feature on, press the* **Alt** *key to close the menu.*

Why is the Auto Arrange feature not available?

The Auto Arrange feature is not available when items appear in the List or Details view. For information on changing the appearance of items, see page 68.

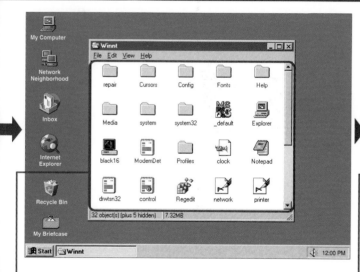

■ The items are automatically arranged in the window.

■ To turn off the Auto Arrange feature, repeat steps **1** to **3**.

■ When you change the size of a window and the Auto Arrange feature is on, Windows NT automatically rearranges the items to fit the new window size.

Note: To size a window, see page 23.

USING WINDOWS NT EXPLORER

Windows NT Explorer shows the location of every folder and file on your computer.

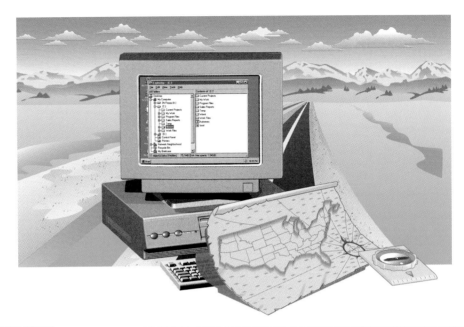

USING WINDOWS NT EXPLORER

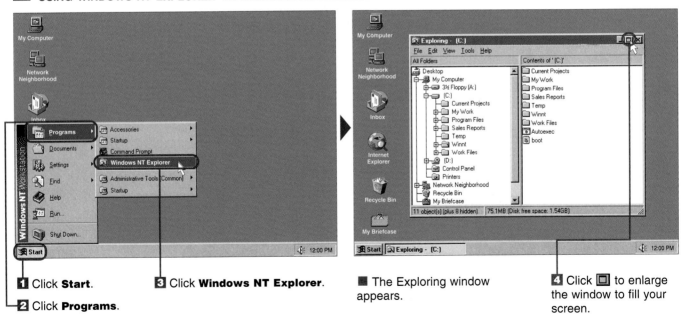

1 Click **Start**.

2 Click **Programs**.

3 Click **Windows NT Explorer**.

■ The Exploring window appears.

4 Click 🔲 to enlarge the window to fill your screen.

?

How can I work with files in Windows NT Explorer?

You can work with files in Windows NT Explorer as you would work with files in a My Computer window. For example, you can move, rename and delete files in Windows NT Explorer.

Note: For more information on working with files, see pages 78 to 115.

Windows NT Explorer   **My Computer**

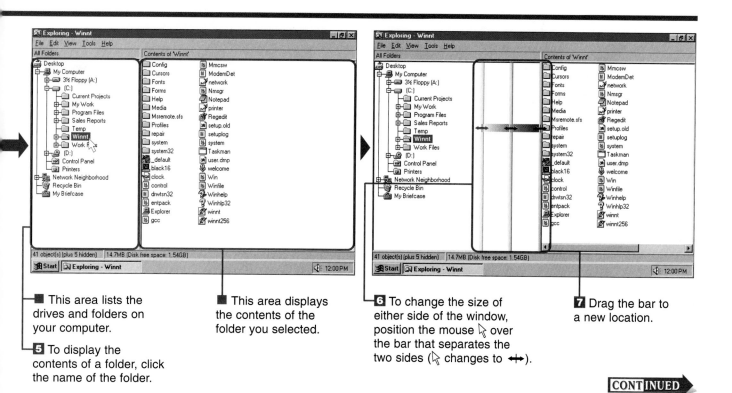

■ This area lists the drives and folders on your computer.

5 To display the contents of a folder, click the name of the folder.

■ This area displays the contents of the folder you selected.

6 To change the size of either side of the window, position the mouse ⌀ over the bar that separates the two sides (⌀ changes to ↔).

7 Drag the bar to a new location.

CONTINUED

USING WINDOWS NT EXPLORER

A folder may contain
other folders. You
can easily display or
hide these folders at
any time.

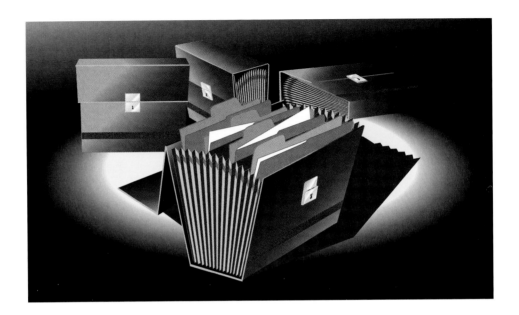

DISPLAY HIDDEN FOLDERS

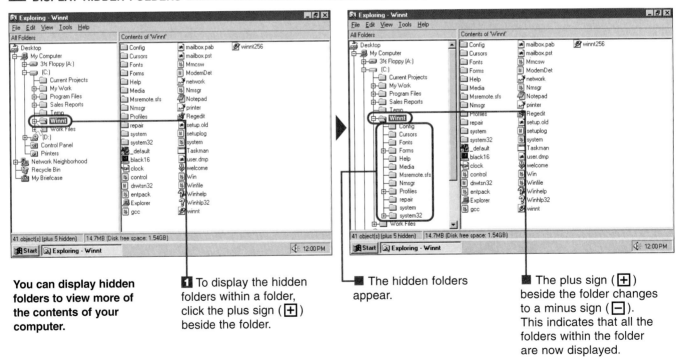

You can display hidden
folders to view more of
the contents of your
computer.

1 To display the hidden
folders within a folder,
click the plus sign (⊞)
beside the folder.

■ The hidden folders
appear.

■ The plus sign (⊞)
beside the folder changes
to a minus sign (⊟).
This indicates that all the
folders within the folder
are now displayed.

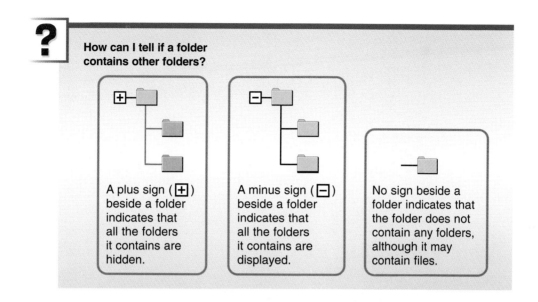

How can I tell if a folder contains other folders?

A plus sign (⊞) beside a folder indicates that all the folders it contains are hidden.

A minus sign (⊟) beside a folder indicates that all the folders it contains are displayed.

No sign beside a folder indicates that the folder does not contain any folders, although it may contain files.

HIDE FOLDERS

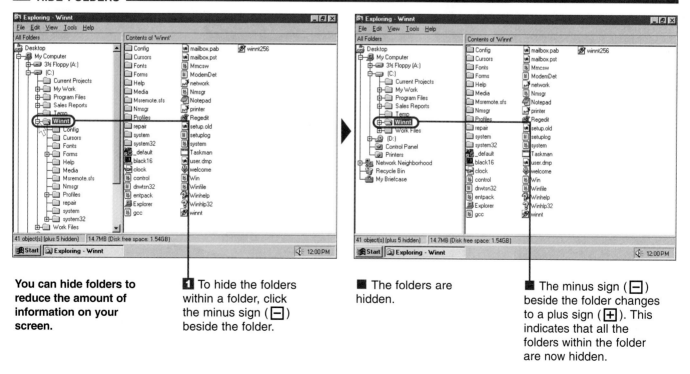

You can hide folders to reduce the amount of information on your screen.

1 To hide the folders within a folder, click the minus sign (⊟) beside the folder.

■ The folders are hidden.

■ The minus sign (⊟) beside the folder changes to a plus sign (⊞). This indicates that all the folders within the folder are now hidden.

CHAPTER 6

Work With Files

There are many ways you can manage the files stored on your computer. This chapter will show you how to open, copy and print a file, plus much more.

OPEN A FILE

You can open a file to display its contents on your screen. This lets you review and make changes to the file.

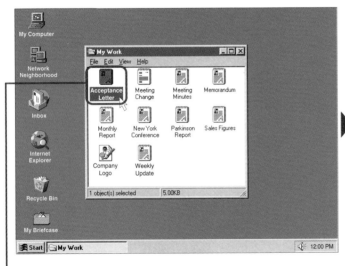

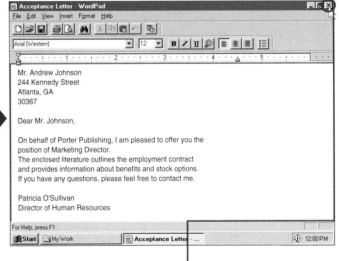

1 Double-click the file you want to open.

■ The file opens. You can review and make changes to the file.

2 When you finish working with the file, click ☒ to close the file.

OPEN A RECENTLY USED FILE

Windows NT remembers the files you most recently used. You can quickly open any of these files.

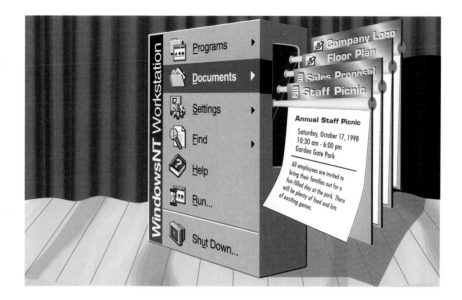

OPEN A RECENTLY USED FILE

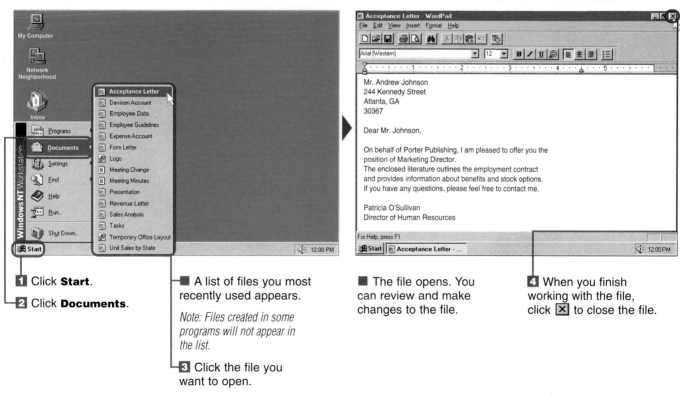

1 Click **Start**.

2 Click **Documents**.

■ A list of files you most recently used appears.

Note: Files created in some programs will not appear in the list.

3 Click the file you want to open.

■ The file opens. You can review and make changes to the file.

4 When you finish working with the file, click ☒ to close the file.

SELECT FILES

Before working with files, you must first select the files you want to work with. Selected files appear highlighted on your screen.

You can select folders the same way you select files. Selecting a folder will select all the files in the folder.

SELECT FILES

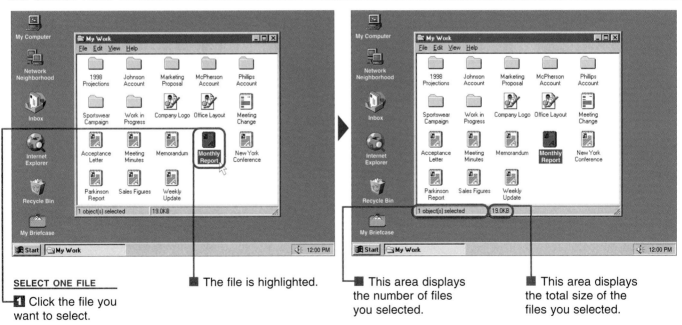

SELECT FILES

SELECT ONE FILE

1 Click the file you want to select.

■ The file is highlighted.

■ This area displays the number of files you selected.

■ This area displays the total size of the files you selected.

How do I deselect files?

To deselect all of the files in a window, click a blank area in the window.

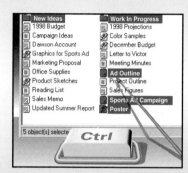

To deselect one or more files from a group of selected files, press and hold down the Ctrl key while you click each file you want to deselect.

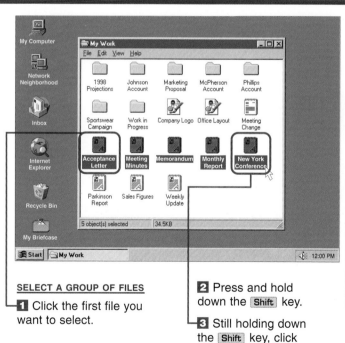

SELECT A GROUP OF FILES

1 Click the first file you want to select.

2 Press and hold down the Shift key.

3 Still holding down the Shift key, click the last file you want to select.

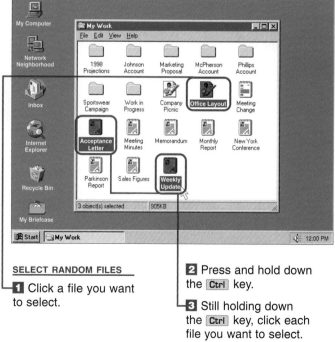

SELECT RANDOM FILES

1 Click a file you want to select.

2 Press and hold down the Ctrl key.

3 Still holding down the Ctrl key, click each file you want to select.

RENAME A FILE

You can give a file a new name to better describe the contents of the file. This can make the file easier to find.

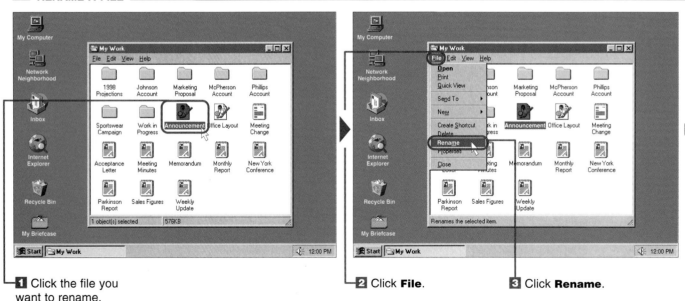

1 Click the file you want to rename.

2 Click **File**.

3 Click **Rename**.

? **Can I rename a folder?**

You should only rename folders that you have created. To rename a folder, perform the steps below, selecting the folder you want to rename in step **1**.

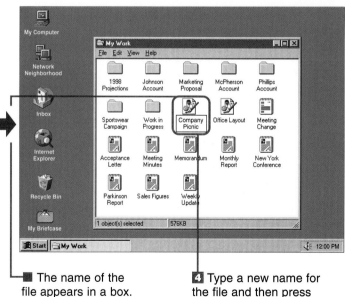

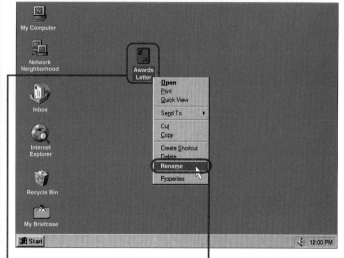

■ The name of the file appears in a box.

4 Type a new name for the file and then press the `Enter` key.

Note: You can use up to 255 characters to name a file. The name cannot contain the \ /:?"< > or I characters.*

You can easily rename a file on your desktop.

1 Right-click the file you want to rename. A menu appears.

2 Click **Rename**.

3 Type a new name and then press the `Enter` key.

CREATE A NEW FOLDER

You can create a new folder to help you better organize the information stored on your computer. Creating a folder is like placing a new folder in a filing cabinet.

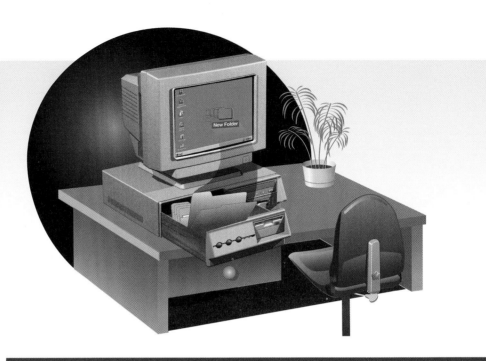

CREATE A NEW FOLDER

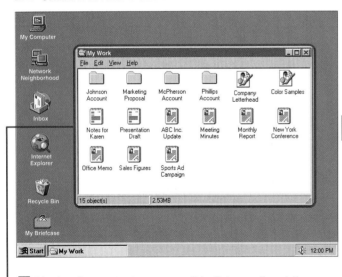

1 Display the contents of the folder where you want to place the new folder.

Note: To browse through the contents of your computer, see page 66.

2 Click **File**.

3 Click **New**.

4 Click **Folder**.

84

How can creating new folders help me organize the information on my computer?

You can create as many new folders as you need to develop a filing system that works for you. You can then organize your files by moving them to the new folders. To move files, see page 88.

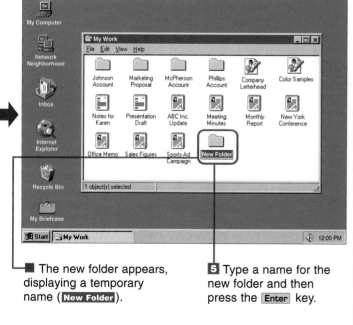

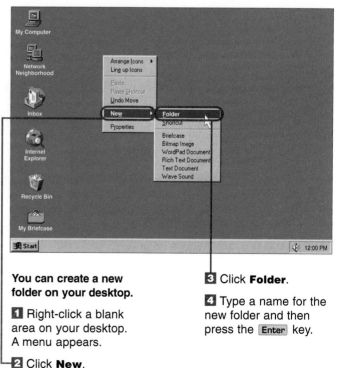

■ The new folder appears, displaying a temporary name (New Folder).

5 Type a name for the new folder and then press the Enter key.

You can create a new folder on your desktop.

1 Right-click a blank area on your desktop. A menu appears.

2 Click **New**.

3 Click **Folder**.

4 Type a name for the new folder and then press the Enter key.

CREATE A NEW FILE

You can instantly create, name and store a new file in the appropriate location without starting any programs.

You can focus on the organization of your files rather than the programs you need to accomplish your tasks.

CREATE A NEW FILE

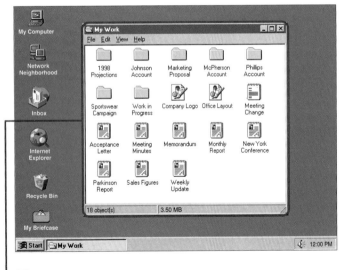

1 Display the contents of the folder where you want to place the new file.

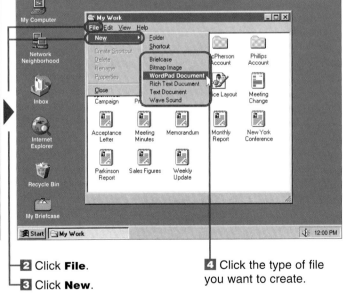

2 Click **File**.

3 Click **New**.

4 Click the type of file you want to create.

What types of files can I create?

The types of files you can create depends on the programs installed on your computer. By default, Windows NT allows you to create the types of files listed to the right.

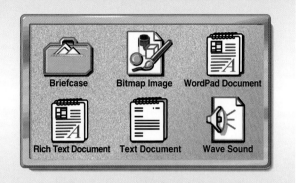

Briefcase · Bitmap Image · WordPad Document
Rich Text Document · Text Document · Wave Sound

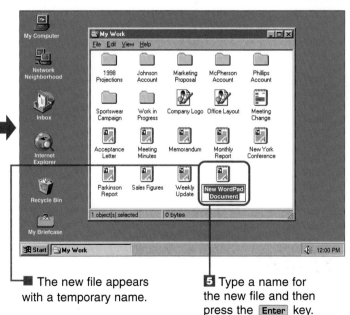

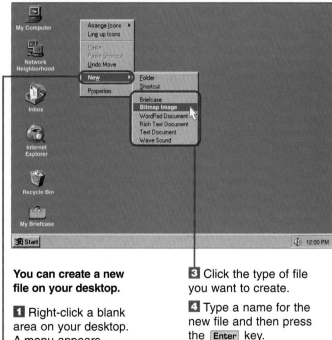

■ The new file appears with a temporary name.

5 Type a name for the new file and then press the **Enter** key.

You can create a new file on your desktop.

1 Right-click a blank area on your desktop. A menu appears.

2 Click **New**.

3 Click the type of file you want to create.

4 Type a name for the new file and then press the **Enter** key.

87

MOVE AND COPY FILES

You can organize the files stored on your computer by moving or copying them to new locations.

Organizing files on your computer is similar to organizing files in a filing cabinet.

MOVE AND COPY FILES

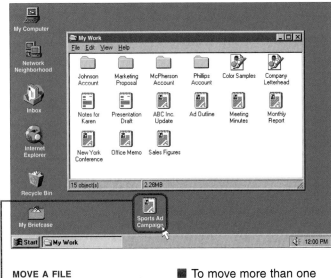

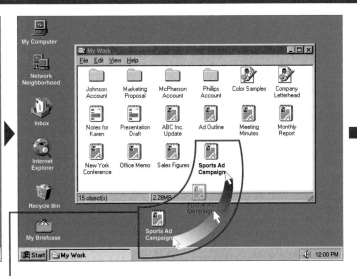

MOVE A FILE

1 Position the mouse ⬚ over the file you want to move.

■ To move more than one file, select all the files you want to move. Then position the mouse ⬚ over one of the files.

Note: To select multiple files, see page 81.

2 Drag the file to a new location on your computer.

What is the difference between moving and copying a file?

Move a File

When you move a file, you place the file in a new location on your computer.

Copy a File

When you copy a file, you make an exact copy of the file and then place the copy in a new location. This lets you store the file in two locations.

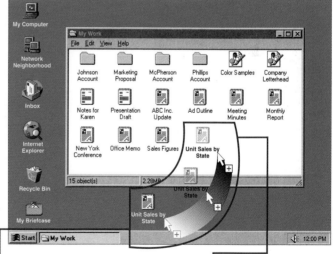

■ The file moves to the new location.

Note: You can move folders the same way you move files. When you move a folder, all the files in the folder also move.

COPY A FILE

1 Position the mouse ↖ over the file you want to copy.

2 Press and hold down the `Ctrl` key.

3 Still holding down the `Ctrl` key, drag the file to a new location.

COPY A FILE TO A FLOPPY DISK

You can make an exact copy of a file and then place the copy on a floppy disk. This is useful if you want to give a colleague a copy of the file.

COPY A FILE TO A FLOPPY DISK

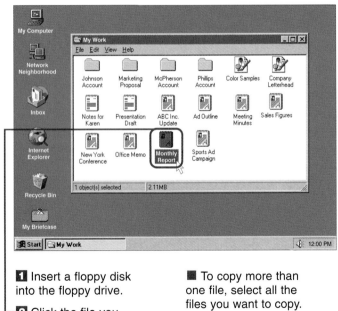

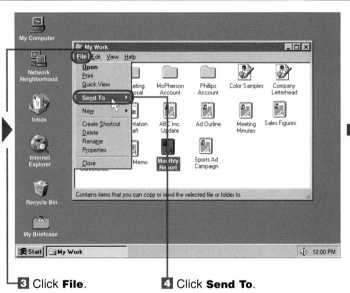

1 Insert a floppy disk into the floppy drive.

2 Click the file you want to copy.

■ To copy more than one file, select all the files you want to copy.

Note: To select multiple files, see page 81.

3 Click **File**.

4 Click **Send To**.

?

How can I protect the information on my floppy disks?

You should keep floppy disks away from magnets, which can damage the information stored on the disks. Also be careful not to spill liquids, such as coffee or soda, on the disks.

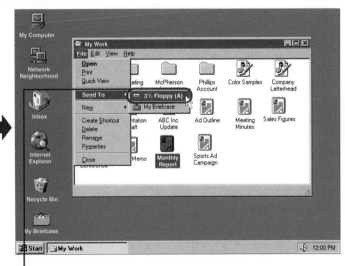

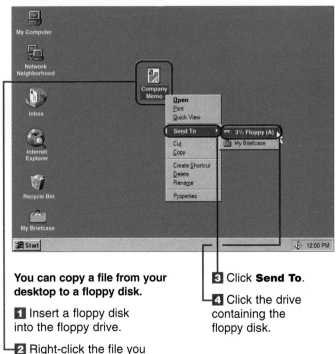

5 Click the drive containing the floppy disk.

■ Windows NT places a copy of the file on the floppy disk.

Note: You can copy a folder the same way you copy a file. When you copy a folder, all the files in the folder are also copied.

You can copy a file from your desktop to a floppy disk.

1 Insert a floppy disk into the floppy drive.

2 Right-click the file you want to copy. A menu appears.

3 Click **Send To**.

4 Click the drive containing the floppy disk.

DELETE A FILE

You can delete a file you no longer need.

Before you delete any files you have created, consider the value of your work. Do not delete a file unless you are certain you no longer need the file.

■ DELETE A FILE

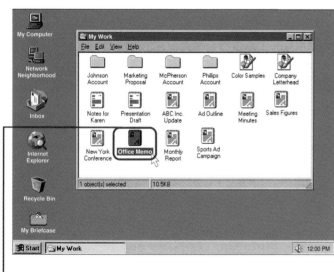

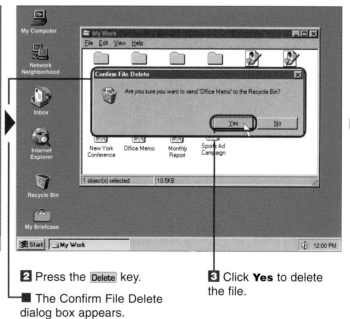

1 Click the file you want to delete.

■ To delete more than one file, select the files.

Note: To select multiple files, see page 81.

2 Press the Delete key.

■ The Confirm File Delete dialog box appears.

3 Click **Yes** to delete the file.

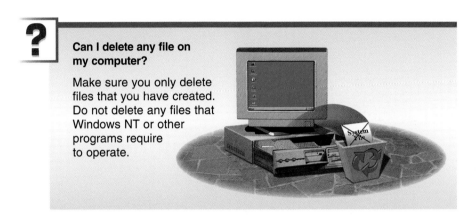

Can I delete any file on my computer?

Make sure you only delete files that you have created. Do not delete any files that Windows NT or other programs require to operate.

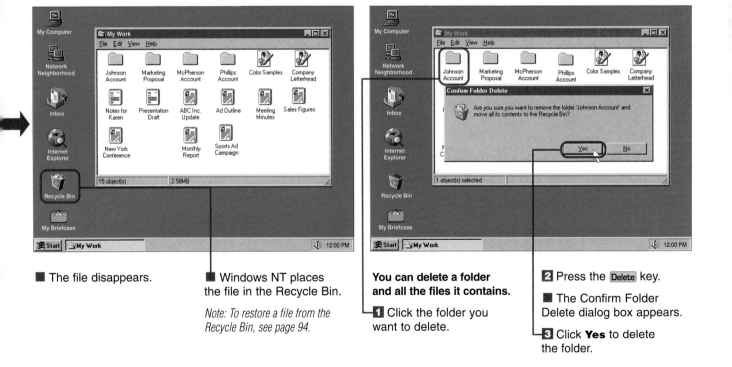

■ The file disappears.

■ Windows NT places the file in the Recycle Bin.

Note: To restore a file from the Recycle Bin, see page 94.

You can delete a folder and all the files it contains.

■1 Click the folder you want to delete.

■2 Press the Delete key.

■ The Confirm Folder Delete dialog box appears.

■3 Click **Yes** to delete the folder.

RESTORE A DELETED FILE

The Recycle Bin stores all
the files you have deleted.
You can easily restore any
of these files.

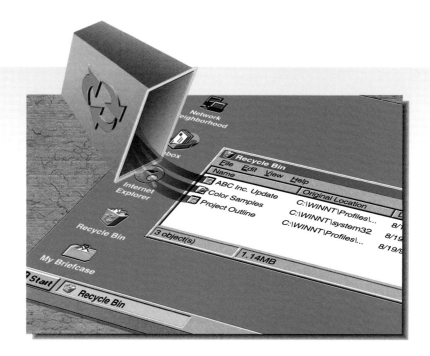

RESTORE A DELETED FILE

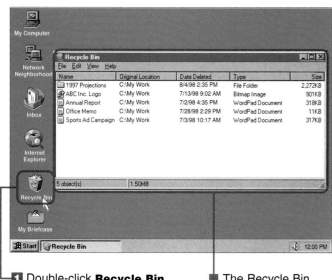

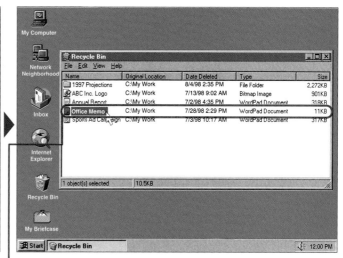

1 Double-click **Recycle Bin** to display all the files you have deleted.

■ The Recycle Bin window appears, displaying all the files you have deleted.

2 Click the file you want to restore.

■ To restore more than one file, select the files.

Note: To select multiple files, see page 81.

How can I tell if the Recycle Bin contains deleted files?

The appearance of the Recycle Bin indicates whether or not the bin contains deleted files.

Contains deleted files **Does not contain deleted files**

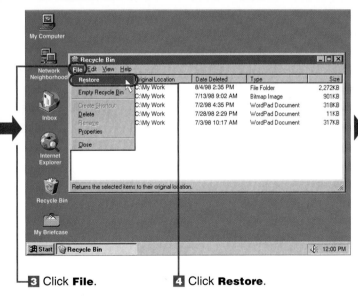

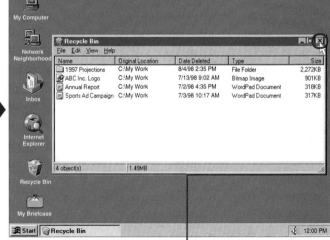

3 Click **File**.

4 Click **Restore**.

■ The file disappears from the Recycle Bin window. Windows NT places the file back in its original location.

5 Click ☒ to close the Recycle Bin window.

Note: You can restore folders the same way you restore files. When you restore a folder, all the files in the folder are also restored.

EMPTY THE RECYCLE BIN

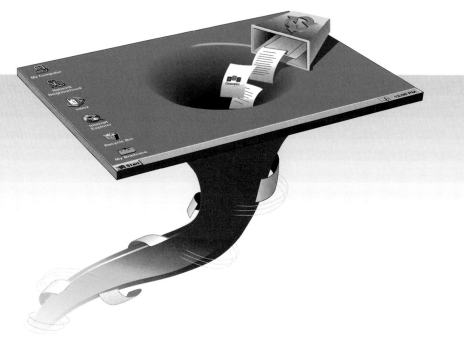

You can create more free space on your computer by permanently removing all the files from the Recycle Bin.

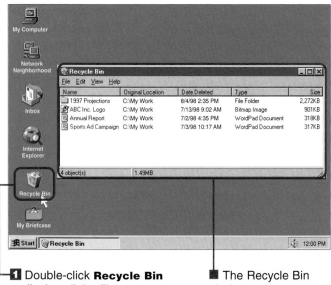

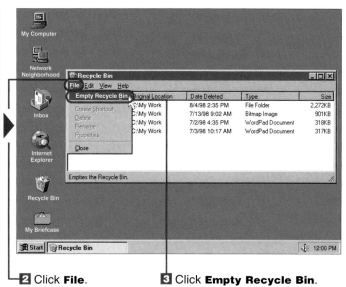

1 Double-click **Recycle Bin** to display all the files you have deleted.

■ The Recycle Bin window appears, displaying all the files you have deleted.

2 Click **File**.

3 Click **Empty Recycle Bin**.

What if the Recycle Bin contains a file I may need?

Before emptying the Recycle Bin, make sure it does not contain files you may need in the future. To restore a file you may need, see page 94. Once you empty the Recycle Bin, the files are permanently removed from your computer and cannot be restored.

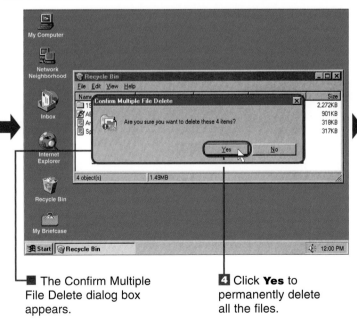

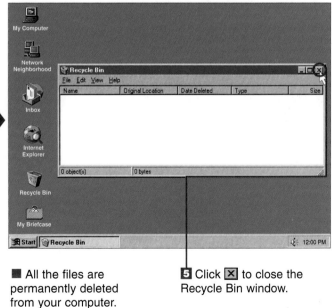

■ The Confirm Multiple File Delete dialog box appears.

4 Click **Yes** to permanently delete all the files.

■ All the files are permanently deleted from your computer.

5 Click ⊠ to close the Recycle Bin window.

PRINT A FILE

You can produce a paper copy of a file stored on your computer. Before printing, make sure your printer is turned on and contains paper.

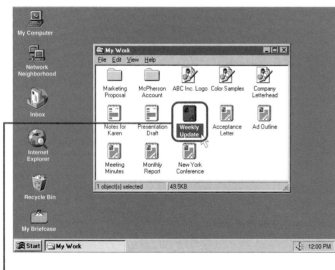

PRINT A FILE

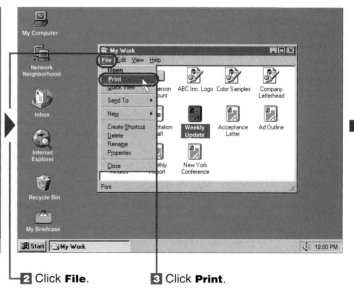

1 Click the file you want to print.

■ To print more than one file, select the files.

Note: To select multiple files, see page 81.

2 Click **File**.

3 Click **Print**.

**What types of printers can
I use to print my files?**

Windows NT works with
many types of printers.
Ink-jet and laser printers
are two common types
of printers.

Ink-jet

An ink-jet printer produces
documents that are suitable
for routine business and
personal use.

Laser

A laser printer is faster and
produces higher-quality
documents than an ink-jet
printer, but is more expensive.

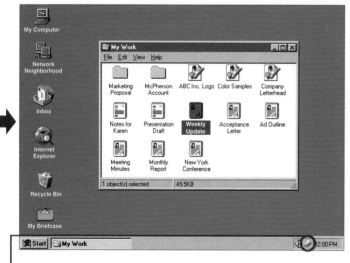

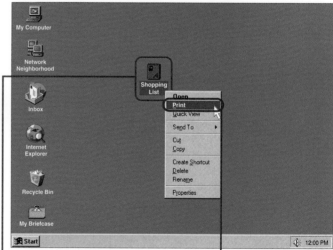

■ When you print a file, the
printer icon ( ) appears in
this area. The icon disappears
when the file has finished
printing.

**You can print a file located
on your desktop.**

◀ Right-click the file you
want to print. A menu
appears.

2 Click **Print**.

VIEW FILES SENT TO THE PRINTER

You can view information about the files you sent to the printer.

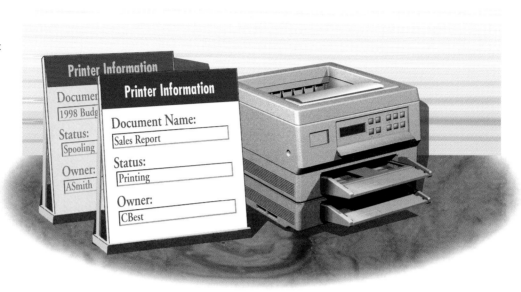

VIEW FILES SENT TO THE PRINTER

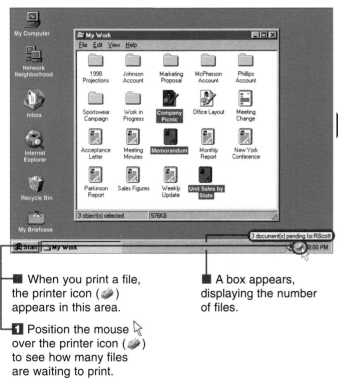

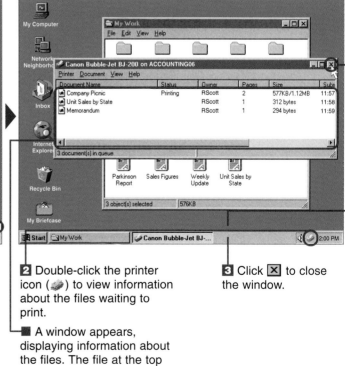

■ When you print a file, the printer icon (🖨) appears in this area.

1 Position the mouse over the printer icon (🖨) to see how many files are waiting to print.

■ A box appears, displaying the number of files.

2 Double-click the printer icon (🖨) to view information about the files waiting to print.

■ A window appears, displaying information about the files. The file at the top of the list will print first.

3 Click ☒ to close the window.

CANCEL PRINTING

You can stop a file
from printing. This
is useful if you want
to make last-minute
changes to the file.

CANCEL PRINTING

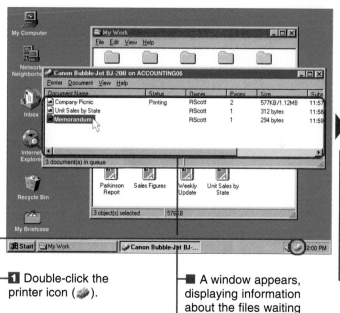

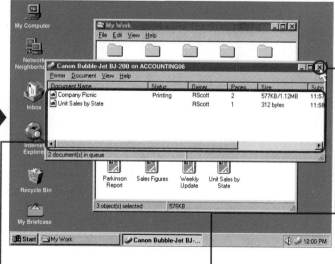

1 Double-click the
printer icon (🖨️).

■ A window appears,
displaying information
about the files waiting
to print.

2 Click the file you no
longer want to print.

3 Press the `Delete` key
and the file disappears
from the list.

4 Click ☒ to close
the window.

FIND A FILE

If you cannot remember the exact name or location of a file you want to work with, you can have Windows NT search for the file.

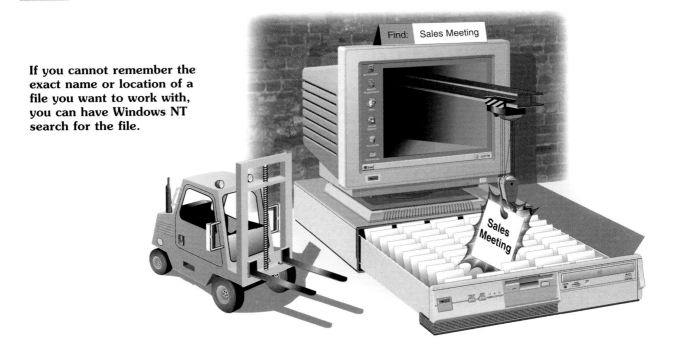

FIND A FILE

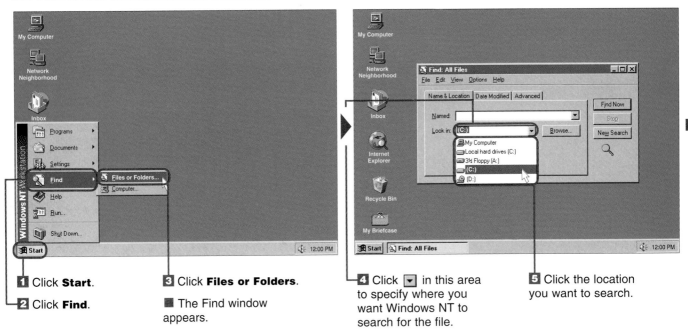

1 Click **Start**.

2 Click **Find**.

3 Click **Files or Folders**.

■ The Find window appears.

4 Click ▼ in this area to specify where you want Windows NT to search for the file.

5 Click the location you want to search.

? Can I search for a file if I know only part of the file name?

If you search for part of a file name, Windows NT will find all the files and folders with names that contain the word you specified. For example, searching for the word "report" will find every file or folder with a name containing the word "report."

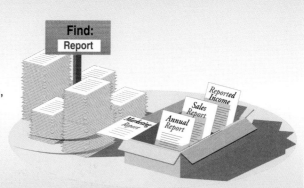

Find:
Report

Reported Income

Sales Report

Annual Report

Marketing Report

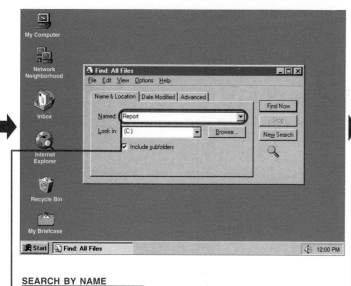

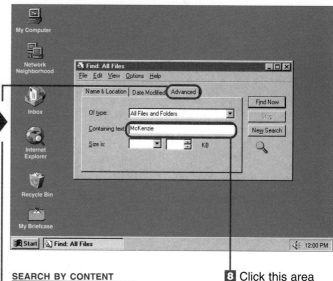

SEARCH BY NAME

◄─ 6 To specify the name of the file you want to find, click this area. Then type all or part of the name.

SEARCH BY CONTENT

◄─ 7 To specify a word or phrase within the file you want to find, click the **Advanced** tab.

8 Click this area and then type the word or phrase.

CONTINUED ▶

FIND A FILE

You can search for a
specific type of file,
such as files created
in WordPad. You can
also search for a file
you worked with during
a specific time period.

Find: Files created in WordPad

WordPad

■■■ FIND A FILE (CONTINUED) ■■■

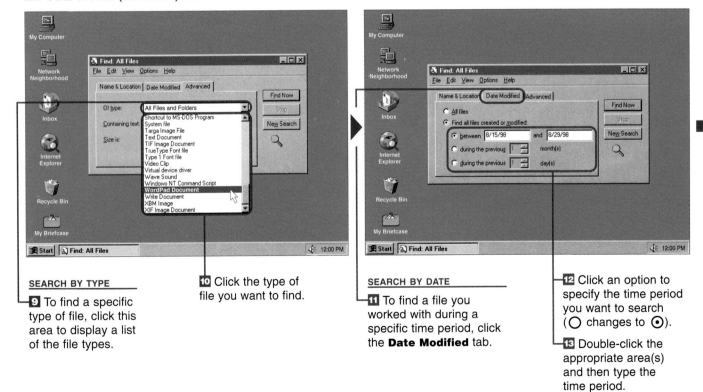

SEARCH BY TYPE

9 To find a specific
type of file, click this
area to display a list
of the file types.

10 Click the type of
file you want to find.

SEARCH BY DATE

11 To find a file you
worked with during a
specific time period, click
the **Date Modified** tab.

12 Click an option to
specify the time period
you want to search
(○ changes to ⊙).

13 Double-click the
appropriate area(s)
and then type the
time period.

How can I find all the programs on my computer?

To find all the programs on your computer, perform steps **1** to **5** on page 102 and then perform steps **7**, **9** and **10**, selecting **Application** in step **10**. Then perform step **14**.

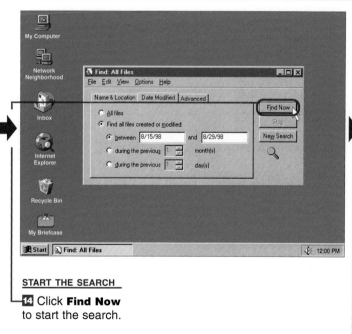

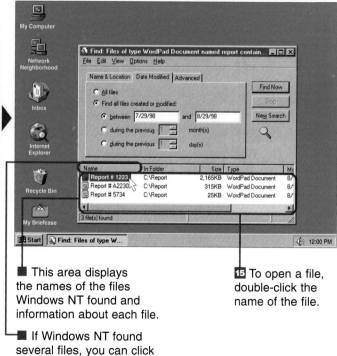

START THE SEARCH

14 Click **Find Now** to start the search.

■ This area displays the names of the files Windows NT found and information about each file.

■ If Windows NT found several files, you can click the **Name** heading to sort the files alphabetically.

15 To open a file, double-click the name of the file.

ADD A SHORTCUT TO THE DESKTOP

You can add a shortcut to
the desktop to provide a
quick way of opening a
file you use regularly.

ADD A SHORTCUT TO THE DESKTOP

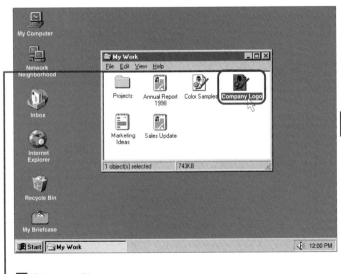

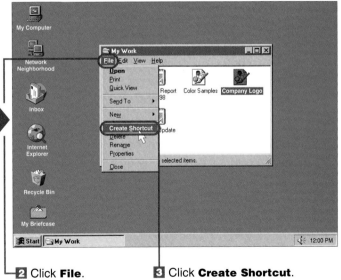

1 Click the file you want
to create a shortcut to.

2 Click **File**.

3 Click **Create Shortcut**.

How do I rename or delete a shortcut?

You can rename or delete a shortcut the same way you would rename or delete any file. Renaming or deleting a shortcut does not affect the original file. For information on renaming a file, see page 82. For information on deleting a file, see page 92.

Rename   **Delete**

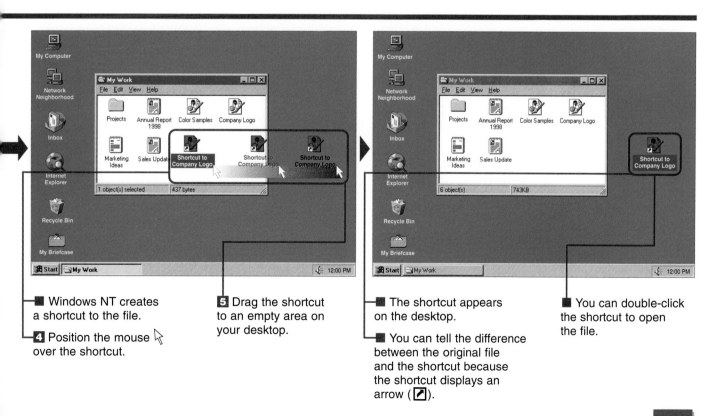

■ Windows NT creates a shortcut to the file.

4 Position the mouse over the shortcut.

5 Drag the shortcut to an empty area on your desktop.

■ The shortcut appears on the desktop.

■ You can tell the difference between the original file and the shortcut because the shortcut displays an arrow (↗).

■ You can double-click the shortcut to open the file.

USE BRIEFCASE

Briefcase lets you work with files while you are away from the office. When you return, Briefcase will update all the files you have changed.

TRANSFER FILES TO BRIEFCASE

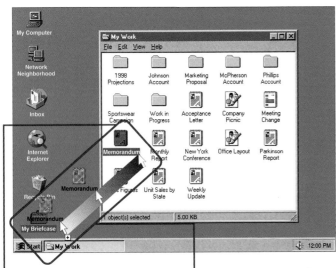

Perform the following steps on your office computer.

1 Locate a file you want to work with while away from the office.

2 Position the mouse over the file and then drag the file to the Briefcase.

Note: If a Briefcase icon does not appear on your desktop, you need to create a new Briefcase. See page 115 to create a new Briefcase.

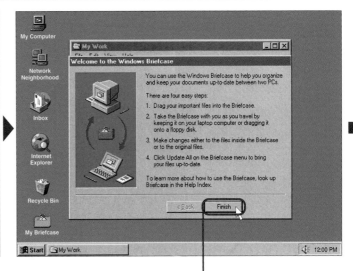

■ The first time you copy a file to a Briefcase, Windows NT displays a welcome message.

3 Click **Finish** to close the message.

4 Repeat steps **1** and **2** for each file you want to work with while away from the office.

When would I use Briefcase?

When traveling, you
can use Briefcase to
work with office files on
a portable computer.

When at home, you
can use Briefcase to
work with office files on
your home computer.

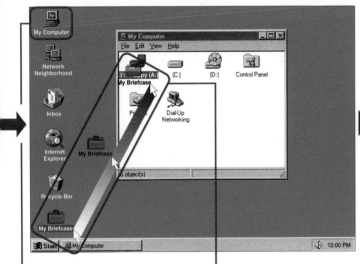

5 Insert a floppy disk
into a drive.

6 Double-click
My Computer.

■ The My Computer
window appears.

7 Position the mouse
over the Briefcase and
then drag the Briefcase
to the drive that contains
the floppy disk.

■ Windows NT moves the
Briefcase to the floppy disk.
The Briefcase disappears
from your screen.

■ You can now remove
the floppy disk from the
drive so you can transfer
the Briefcase to your home
or portable computer.

CONTINUED

USE BRIEFCASE

When traveling or at home, you can work with Briefcase files as you would work with any files on your computer.

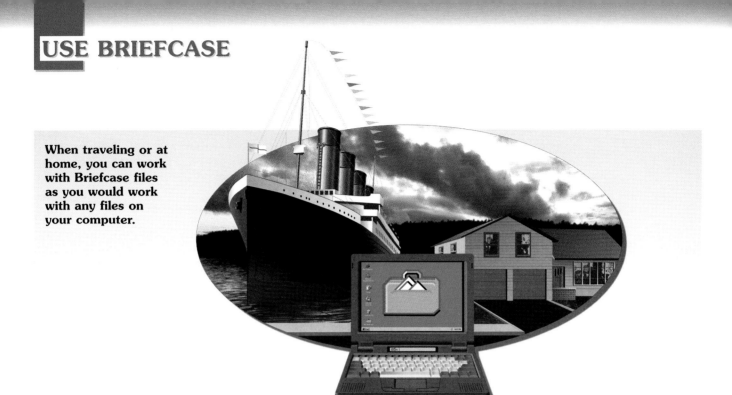

WORK WITH BRIEFCASE FILES

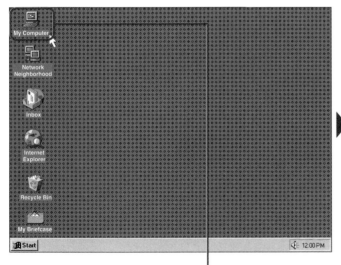

Perform the following steps on your home or portable computer.

1 Insert the floppy disk containing the Briefcase into a drive.

2 Double-click **My Computer**.

■ The My Computer window appears.

3 Double-click the drive that contains the floppy disk.

Can I rename the files in a Briefcase?

Do not rename the files in a Briefcase or the original files on your office computer. If you rename the files, Briefcase will not be able to update the files.

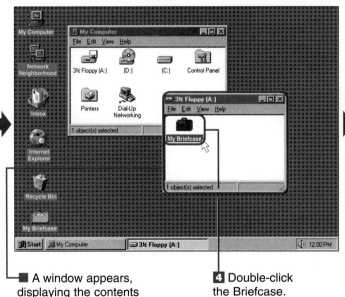

■ A window appears, displaying the contents of the floppy disk.

4 Double-click the Briefcase.

■ A window appears, displaying the contents of the Briefcase. You can open and edit the files in the Briefcase as you would open and edit any files.

5 When you finish working with the files, save and close the files.

6 Remove the floppy disk from the drive and return the disk to your office computer.

CONTINUED ▶

USE BRIEFCASE

When you return to
the office, you can
update the files you
have changed.

UPDATE BRIEFCASE FILES

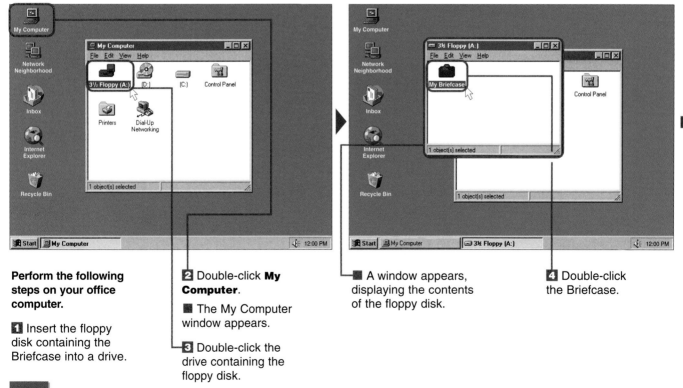

**Perform the following
steps on your office
computer.**

1 Insert the floppy
disk containing the
Briefcase into a drive.

2 Double-click **My
Computer**.

■ The My Computer
window appears.

3 Double-click the
drive containing the
floppy disk.

■ A window appears,
displaying the contents
of the floppy disk.

4 Double-click
the Briefcase.

How does Windows NT know which files need to be updated?

Windows NT compares the files in the Briefcase to the files on your office computer to decide which files need to be updated.

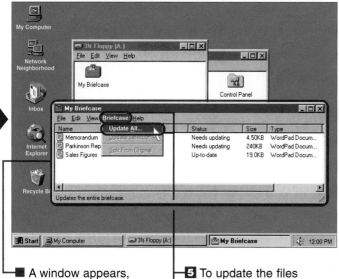

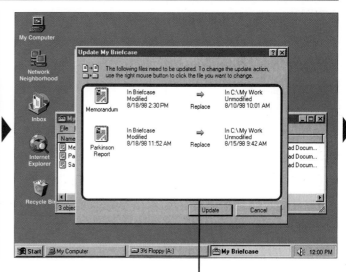

■ A window appears, displaying the contents of the Briefcase.

5 To update the files on your office computer, click **Briefcase**.

6 Click **Update All**.

■ The Update dialog box appears.

■ This area displays the name of each file that needs to be updated and the way Windows NT will update each file.

CONTINUED ▶

USE BRIEFCASE

When using Briefcase, you can change the way Windows NT updates a file.

Replace office file with Briefcase file (➡).

Do not update the file (↘).

Replace Briefcase file with office file (⬅).

UPDATE BRIEFCASE FILES (CONTINUED)

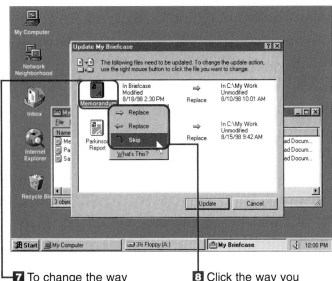

7 To change the way Windows NT updates a file, right-click the file. A menu appears.

8 Click the way you want to update the file.

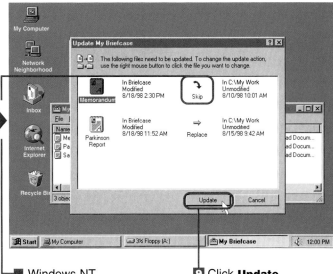

■ Windows NT changes the way it will update the file.

9 Click **Update**.

■ Windows NT updates the files.

?

Can I delete a Briefcase I no longer need?

You can delete an old Briefcase as you would delete any file. To delete a file, see page 92. Deleting a Briefcase does not remove the original files from your computer.

CREATE A NEW BRIEFCASE

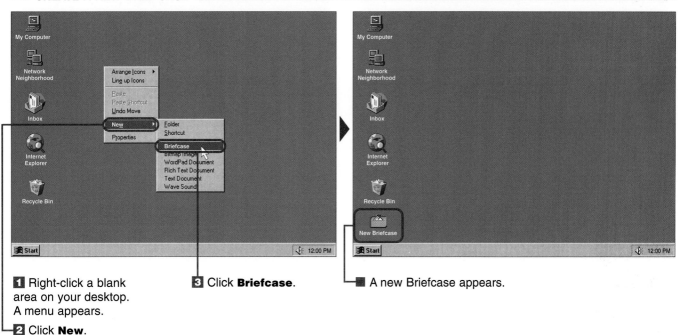

1 Right-click a blank area on your desktop. A menu appears.

2 Click **New**.

3 Click **Briefcase**.

■ A new Briefcase appears.

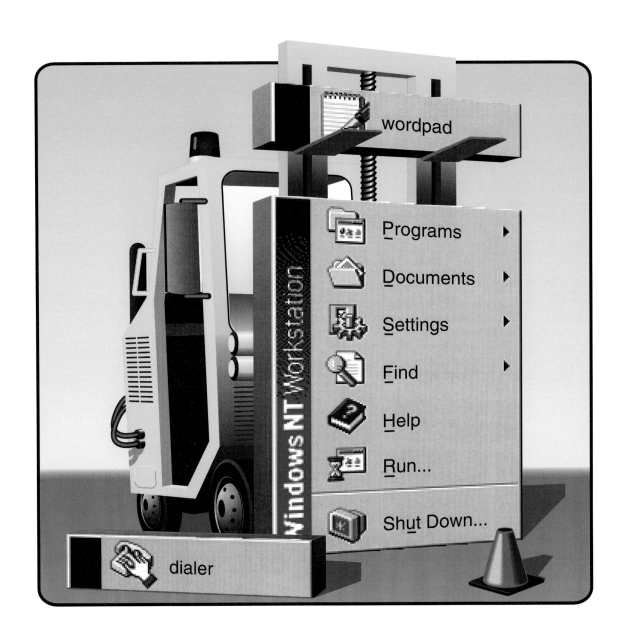

CHAPTER 7

Customize Windows NT

Windows NT includes a number of features that allow you to personalize your computer. In this chapter you will learn how to change desktop icons, add wallpaper, set up a screen saver and more.

MOVE THE TASKBAR

You can move the
taskbar to a more
convenient location
on your screen.

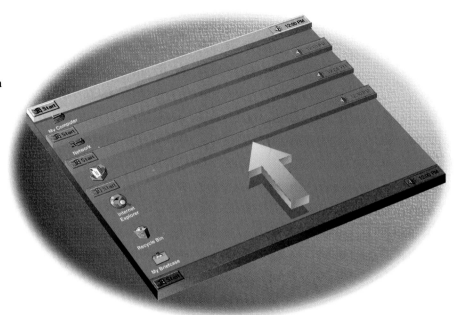

MOVE THE TASKBAR

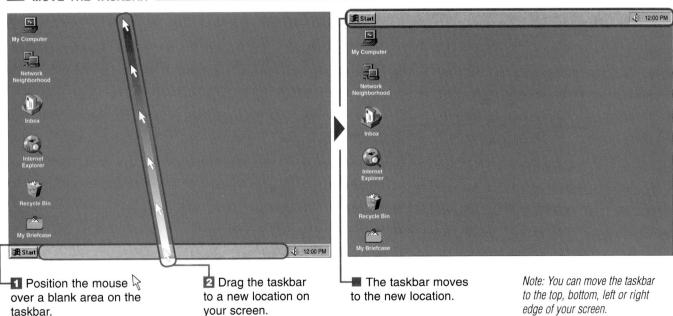

1 Position the mouse ⌖
over a blank area on the
taskbar.

2 Drag the taskbar
to a new location on
your screen.

■ The taskbar moves
to the new location.

*Note: You can move the taskbar
to the top, bottom, left or right
edge of your screen.*

SIZE THE TASKBAR

You can change the size
of the taskbar so it can
display more information.

SIZE THE TASKBAR

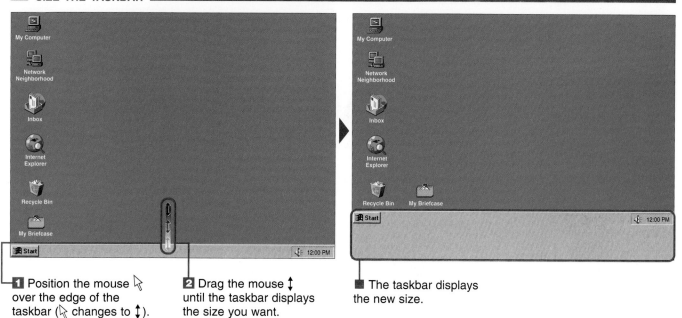

1 Position the mouse ▹
over the edge of the
taskbar (▹ changes to ↕).

2 Drag the mouse ↕
until the taskbar displays
the size you want.

■ The taskbar displays
the new size.

HIDE THE TASKBAR

You can hide the taskbar to give you more room on the screen to accomplish tasks.

HIDE THE TASKBAR

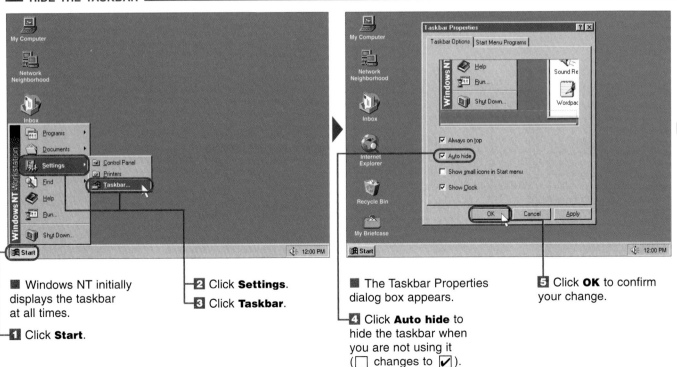

■ Windows NT initially displays the taskbar at all times.

1 Click **Start**.

2 Click **Settings**.

3 Click **Taskbar**.

■ The Taskbar Properties dialog box appears.

4 Click **Auto hide** to hide the taskbar when you are not using it (☐ changes to ☑).

5 Click **OK** to confirm your change.

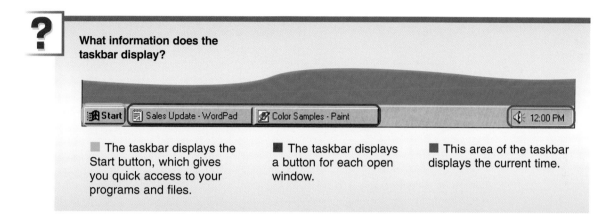

What information does the taskbar display?

■ The taskbar displays the Start button, which gives you quick access to your programs and files.

■ The taskbar displays a button for each open window.

■ This area of the taskbar displays the current time.

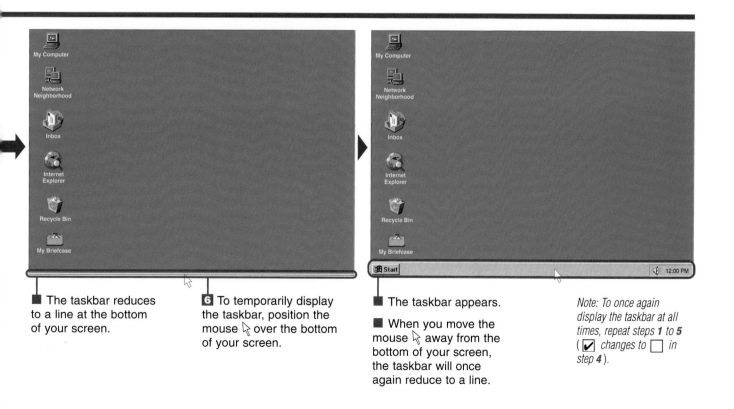

■ The taskbar reduces to a line at the bottom of your screen.

6 To temporarily display the taskbar, position the mouse over the bottom of your screen.

■ The taskbar appears.

■ When you move the mouse away from the bottom of your screen, the taskbar will once again reduce to a line.

Note: To once again display the taskbar at all times, repeat steps 1 to 5 (☑ changes to ☐ in step 4).

You should make sure the correct date and time are set in your computer. Windows NT uses this information to determine when you create and update your documents.

If you are unable to change the date and time, the network administrator did not grant you the necessary privileges. Contact your network administrator for information.

■■ CHANGE THE DATE AND TIME ■■

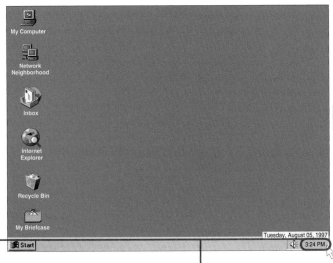

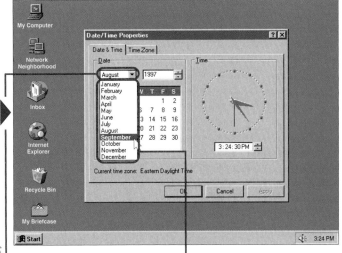

■ This area displays the time set in your computer.

1 To display the date set in your computer, position the mouse ⌖ over this area. A box appears, displaying the date.

2 To change the date or time set in your computer, double-click this area.

■ The Date/Time Properties dialog box appears.

■ This area displays the month set in your computer.

3 To change the month, click this area.

4 Click the correct month.

Will Windows NT keep track of the date and time even when I turn off my computer?

Yes. Your computer has a built-in clock that keeps track of the date and time even when you turn off the computer.

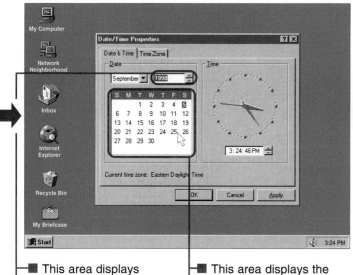

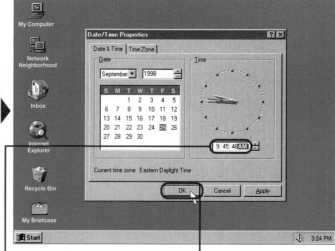

■ This area displays the year set in your computer.

5 To change the year, click ▲ or ▼ in this area until the correct year appears.

■ This area displays the days in the month. The current day is highlighted.

6 To change the day, click the correct day.

■ This area displays the time set in your computer.

7 To change the time, double-click the part of the time you want to change. Then type the correct information.

8 Click **OK** to confirm your changes.

CHANGE DESKTOP ICONS

You can change the appearance of icons on your desktop to customize your computer.

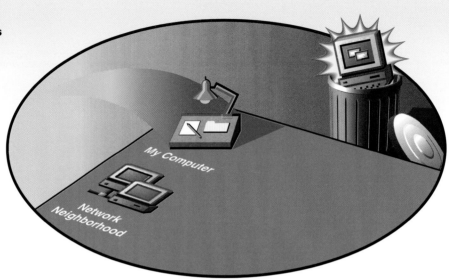

CHANGE DESKTOP ICONS

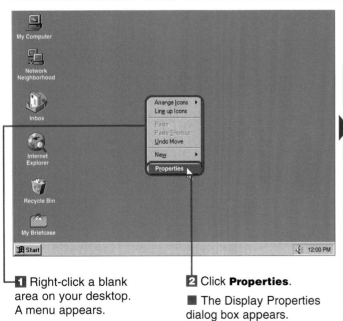

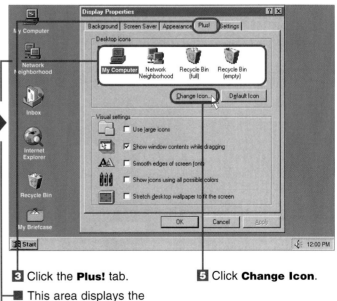

1 Right-click a blank area on your desktop. A menu appears.

2 Click **Properties**.

■ The Display Properties dialog box appears.

3 Click the **Plus!** tab.

■ This area displays the icons on your desktop.

4 To change the appearance of a desktop icon, click the icon.

5 Click **Change Icon**.

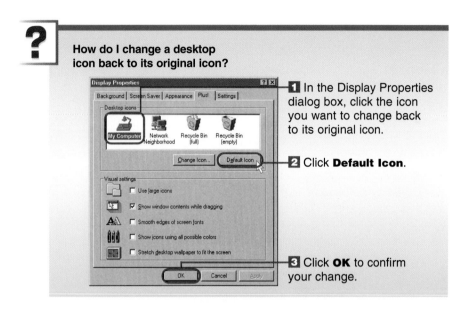

? **How do I change a desktop icon back to its original icon?**

1 In the Display Properties dialog box, click the icon you want to change back to its original icon.

2 Click **Default Icon**.

3 Click **OK** to confirm your change.

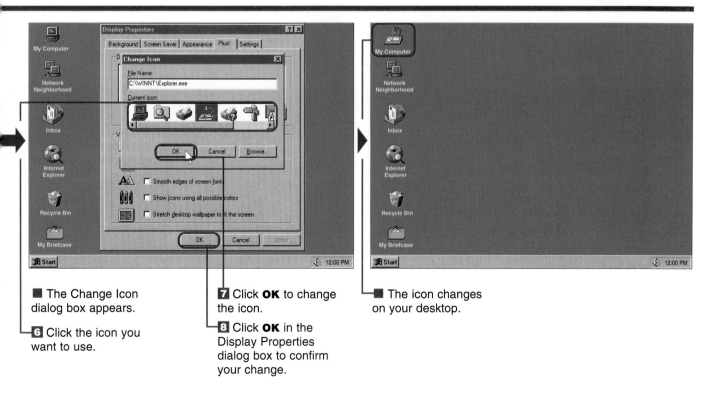

■ The Change Icon dialog box appears.

6 Click the icon you want to use.

7 Click **OK** to change the icon.

8 Click **OK** in the Display Properties dialog box to confirm your change.

■ The icon changes on your desktop.

ADD WALLPAPER

You can decorate
your screen by
adding wallpaper.

ADD WALLPAPER

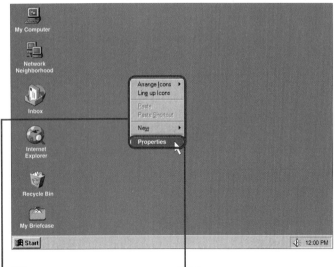

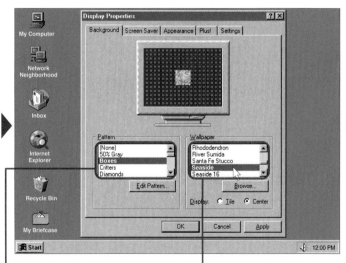

1 Right-click a blank
area on your desktop.
A menu appears.

2 Click **Properties**.

■ The Display Properties
dialog box appears.

3 To select a pattern,
click the pattern you
want to display.

4 To select a wallpaper
image, click the wallpaper
you want to display.

*Note: For more wallpaper images,
add the Desktop Wallpaper
component from the Accessories
category. To add Windows NT
components, see page 166.*

How can I display wallpaper on my screen?

Tile

Repeats the wallpaper until it fills your screen.

Center

Places the wallpaper in the middle of your screen.

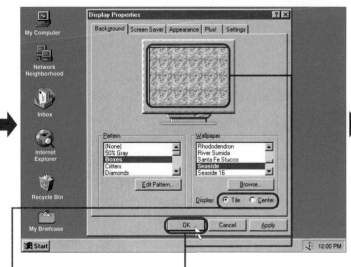

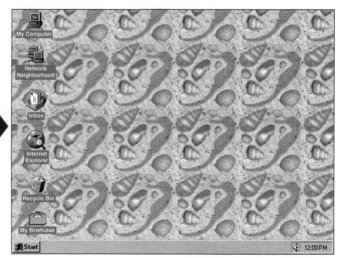

5 If you selected a wallpaper image, click the way you want to display the image (○ changes to ⊙). For more information, see the top of this page.

Note: If you choose the Tile option, the wallpaper will cover any pattern you selected in step 3.

■ This area displays how your screen will appear.

6 Click **OK**.

■ The appearance of your screen changes.

■ To remove a pattern or wallpaper image from your screen, repeat steps **1** to **4**, selecting **(None)** in step **3** or **4**. Then perform step **6**.

CHANGE SCREEN COLORS

You can change
the colors displayed
on your screen
to personalize and
enhance Windows NT.

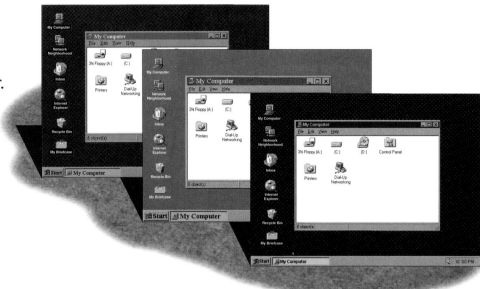

■■■ **CHANGE SCREEN COLORS** ■■■

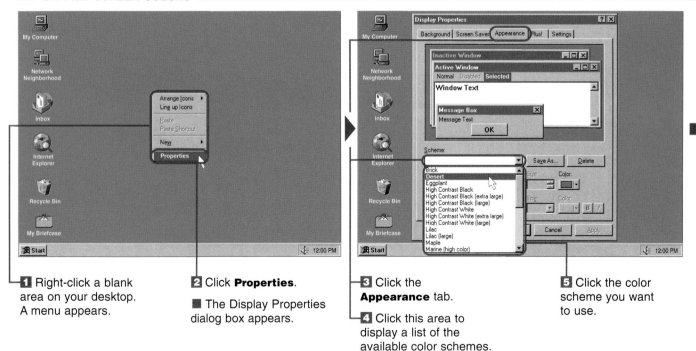

1 Right-click a blank
area on your desktop.
A menu appears.

2 Click **Properties**.

■ The Display Properties
dialog box appears.

3 Click the
Appearance tab.

4 Click this area to
display a list of the
available color schemes.

5 Click the color
scheme you want
to use.

? **What is the difference between the High Contrast, high color and VGA color schemes?**

Note: For information on changing the number of colors your computer displays, see page 130.

High Contrast schemes are designed for people with vision impairments.

High color schemes are designed for computers displaying more than 256 colors.

VGA schemes are designed for computers limited to 16 colors.

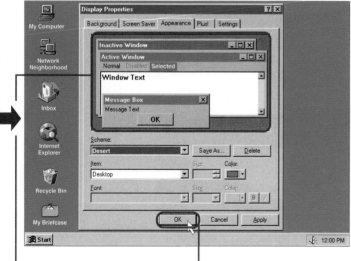

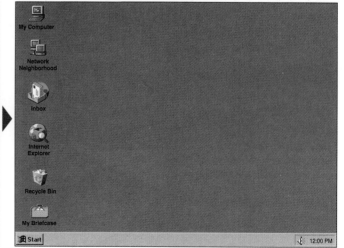

■ This area displays how your screen will look with the color scheme you selected.

6 Click **OK** to add the color scheme.

■ Your screen displays the color scheme you selected.

■ To return to the original color scheme, perform steps **1** to **6**, selecting **Windows Standard** in step **5**.

CHANGE SCREEN RESOLUTION OR COLOR DEPTH

CHANGE SCREEN RESOLUTION

You can change the amount of information that can fit on your screen.

Lower resolutions display larger images on the screen. This lets you see information more clearly.

Higher resolutions display smaller images on the screen. This lets you display more information at once.

CHANGE SCREEN RESOLUTION OR COLOR DEPTH

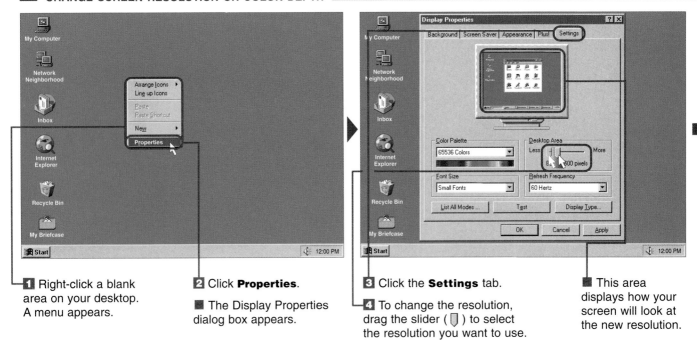

1 Right-click a blank area on your desktop. A menu appears.

2 Click **Properties**.

■ The Display Properties dialog box appears.

3 Click the **Settings** tab.

4 To change the resolution, drag the slider ( ) to select the resolution you want to use.

■ This area displays how your screen will look at the new resolution.

CHANGE COLOR DEPTH

You can change the number of colors displayed on your screen. More colors result in more realistic images.

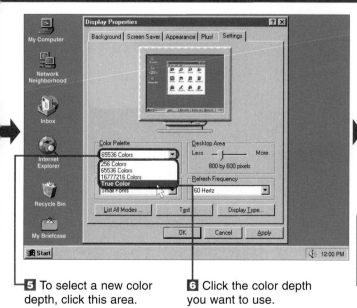

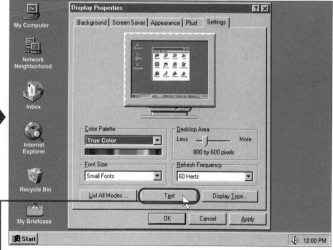

5 To select a new color depth, click this area.

6 Click the color depth you want to use.

7 Click **Test** to test the new settings.

CONTINUED

Windows NT will check to make sure your computer can support the screen resolution and color depth you select.

Your monitor and video card determine if you can change the screen resolution and color depth.

CHANGE SCREEN RESOLUTION OR COLOR DEPTH (CONTINUED)

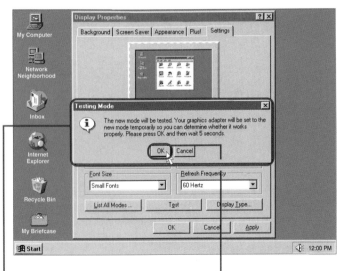

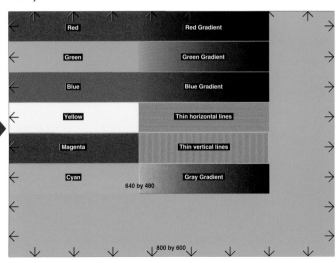

■ The Testing Mode dialog box appears, stating that your video card will be changed to the new settings temporarily. This will allow you to determine if your computer can support the new settings.

8 Click **OK** to test the settings.

■ Windows NT tests the settings by showing colored boxes and text.

? **When would I change the number of colors displayed on my screen?**

You may want to display more colors on your screen when viewing photographs, playing videos or playing games on your computer.

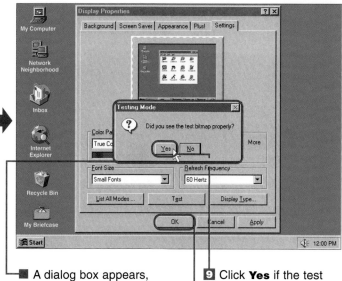

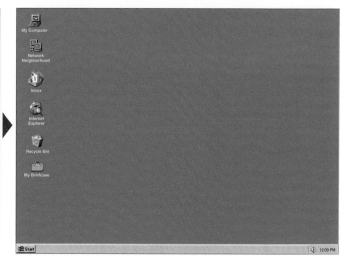

■ A dialog box appears, asking if the test appeared properly on your screen.

9 Click **Yes** if the test appeared properly.

10 Click **OK** to change the settings.

■ Windows NT changes the appearance of your screen.

SET UP A SCREEN SAVER

A screen saver is a moving picture or pattern that appears on the screen when you do not use your computer for a period of time.

SET UP A SCREEN SAVER

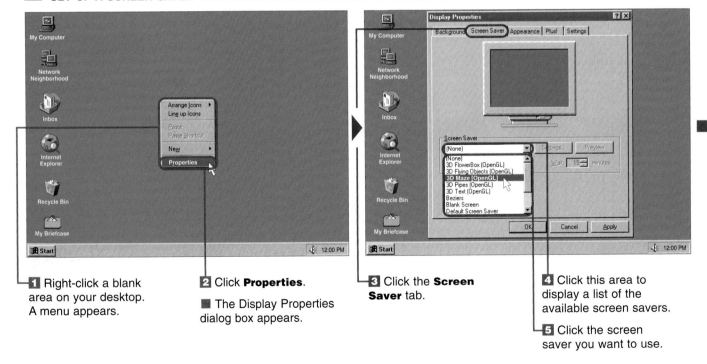

1 Right-click a blank area on your desktop. A menu appears.

2 Click **Properties**.

■ The Display Properties dialog box appears.

3 Click the **Screen Saver** tab.

4 Click this area to display a list of the available screen savers.

5 Click the screen saver you want to use.

Do I need to use a screen saver?

Screen savers were originally designed to prevent screen burn, which occurs when an image appears in a fixed position on the screen for a period of time. Today's monitors are better designed to prevent screen burn, but people still use screen savers for their entertainment value.

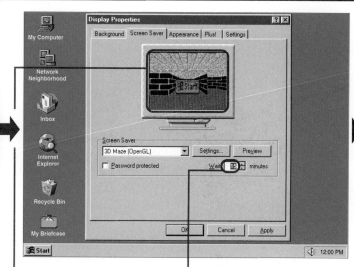

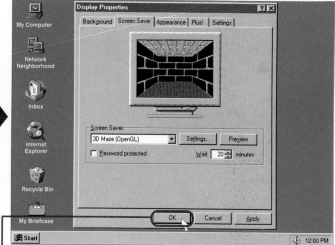

■ This area displays how the screen saver will look on your screen.

■ The screen saver will appear when you do not use your computer for the number of minutes shown in this area.

6 To change the number of minutes, double-click this area. Then type a new number.

7 Click **OK** to turn the screen saver on.

■ When the screen saver appears on your screen, you can move the mouse or press a key on your keyboard to remove the screen saver.

■ To turn the screen saver off, perform steps **1** to **5**, selecting **(None)** in step **5**. Then perform step **7**.

CHANGE MOUSE SETTINGS

You can change the
way your mouse works
to suit your needs.

CHANGE MOUSE SETTINGS

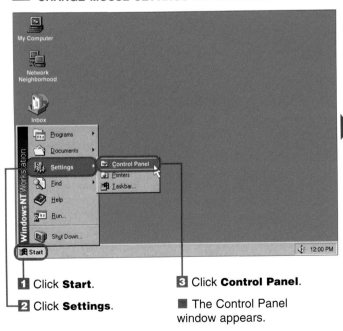

1 Click **Start**.

2 Click **Settings**.

3 Click **Control Panel**.

■ The Control Panel
window appears.

4 Double-click **Mouse**
to change the mouse
settings.

■ The Mouse Properties
dialog box appears.

?

What mouse settings can I change?

Switch Buttons

If you are left-handed, you can switch the functions of the left and right mouse buttons to make the mouse easier to use.

Double-click Speed

You can change the amount of time that can pass between two clicks of the mouse button for Windows NT to recognize a double-click. If you are an inexperienced mouse user, you may find a slower speed easier to use.

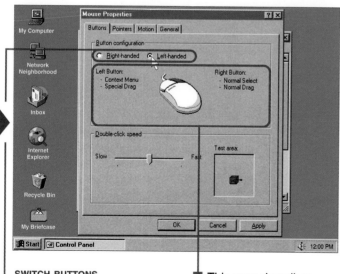

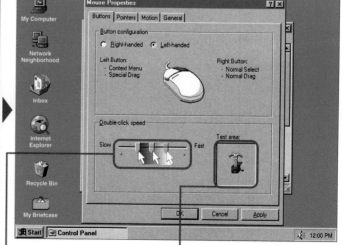

SWITCH BUTTONS

5 To switch the functions of the left and right mouse buttons, click an option to specify if you are right-handed or left-handed (○ changes to ◉).

■ This area describes the functions of the left and right mouse buttons.

DOUBLE-CLICK SPEED

6 To change the double-click speed, drag the slider (▯) to a new position.

7 Double-click this area to test the double-click speed.

■ The jack-in-the-box appears if you clicked at the correct speed.

CONTINUED ▶

CHANGE MOUSE SETTINGS

You can change the appearance of the mouse pointers Windows NT displays.

The mouse pointer assumes different shapes, depending on its location on your screen and the task you are performing.

CHANGE MOUSE SETTINGS (CONTINUED)

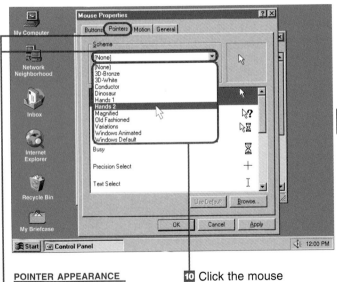

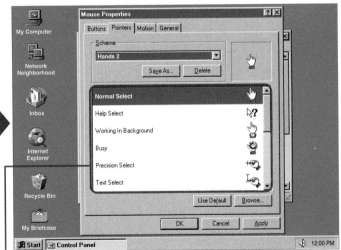

POINTER APPEARANCE

8 To change the appearance of the mouse pointers, click the **Pointers** tab.

9 Click this area to display a list of the mouse pointer sets.

10 Click the mouse pointer set you want to use.

■ This area displays the mouse pointers that make up the set you selected.

Note: If there are no mouse pointer sets available, you need to add the Mouse Pointers component from the Accessories category. To add Windows NT components, see page 166.

?

Should I use a mouse pad?

A mouse pad provides a smooth surface for moving the mouse on your desk. A mouse pad reduces the amount of dirt that enters the mouse and protects your desk from scratches. Hard plastic mouse pads attract less dirt and provide a smoother surface than fabric mouse pads.

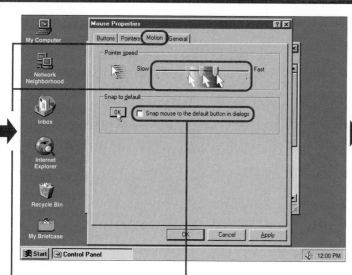

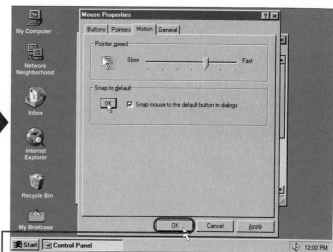

POINTER SPEED

11 To make the mouse pointer on your screen move faster or slower, click the **Motion** tab.

12 Drag the slider (⬛) to a new position to change the pointer speed.

SNAP TO DEFAULT

13 To make the mouse pointer automatically appear over the default button when you open a dialog box, click this option (☐ changes to ☑).

CONFIRM CHANGES

14 Click **OK** when you finish selecting all the mouse settings you want to change.

ADD A PROGRAM TO THE START MENU

You can add your favorite programs to the Start menu so you can quickly open them.

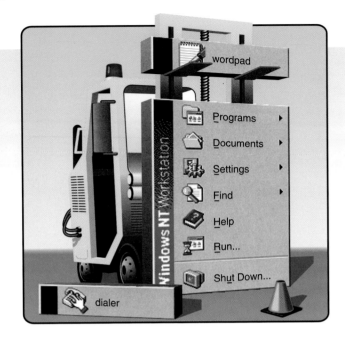

ADD A PROGRAM TO THE START MENU

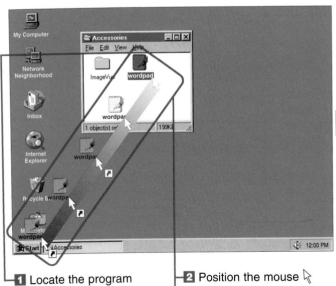

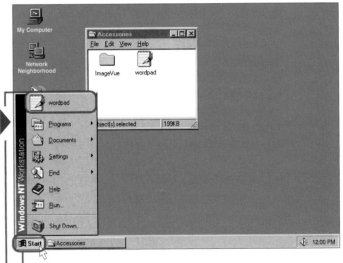

1 Locate the program you want to add to the Start menu.

Note: To find a program on your computer, see the top of page 105.

2 Position the mouse over the program.

3 Drag the program to the **Start** button.

4 Click **Start** to display the Start menu. The Start menu appears.

■ The Start menu displays the program. You can click the program to start the program.

■ To close the Start menu without selecting an item, click outside the menu area or press the **Alt** key.

140

? **Can I add files and folders to the Start menu?**

You can perform the steps on page 140 to add a file or folder to the Start menu. Adding files and folders you frequently use to the Start menu gives you instant access to the items.

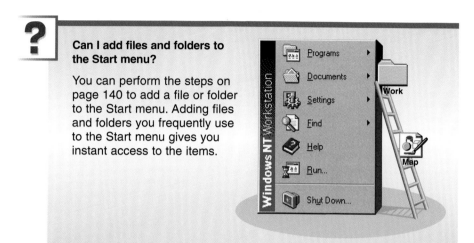

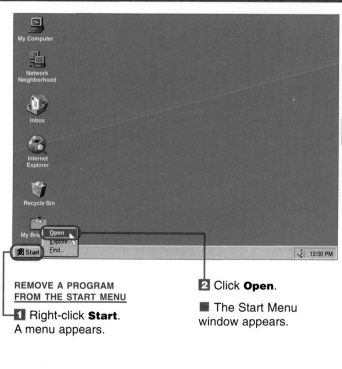

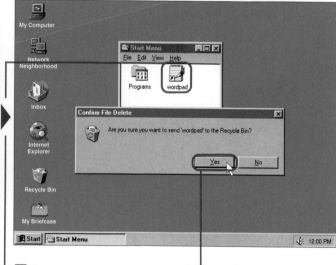

REMOVE A PROGRAM FROM THE START MENU

1 Right-click **Start**. A menu appears.

2 Click **Open**.

■ The Start Menu window appears.

3 Click the program you no longer want to appear on the Start menu.

4 Press the `Delete` key.

■ A confirmation dialog box appears.

5 Click **Yes** to remove the program from the Start menu.

Note: Removing a program from the Start menu does not delete the program from your computer.

START A PROGRAM AUTOMATICALLY

If you use the same program every day, you can have the program start automatically every time you turn on your computer.

Click

START A PROGRAM AUTOMATICALLY

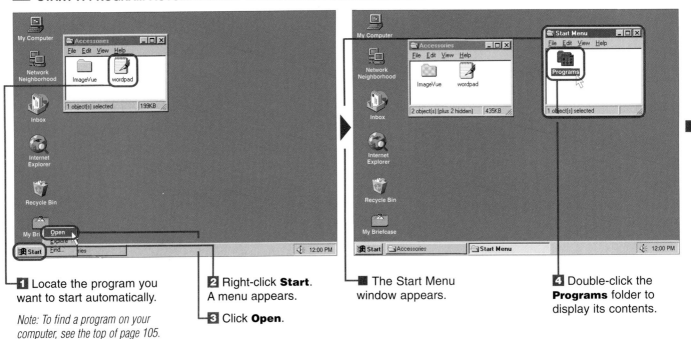

1 Locate the program you want to start automatically.

Note: To find a program on your computer, see the top of page 105.

2 Right-click **Start**. A menu appears.

3 Click **Open**.

■ The Start Menu window appears.

4 Double-click the **Programs** folder to display its contents.

?

How do I stop a program from starting automatically?

If you no longer want a program to start automatically, delete the shortcut for the program from the Startup folder. You can delete a shortcut the same way you would delete a file. For information on deleting a file, see page 92. Deleting a shortcut from the Startup folder will not remove the program from your computer.

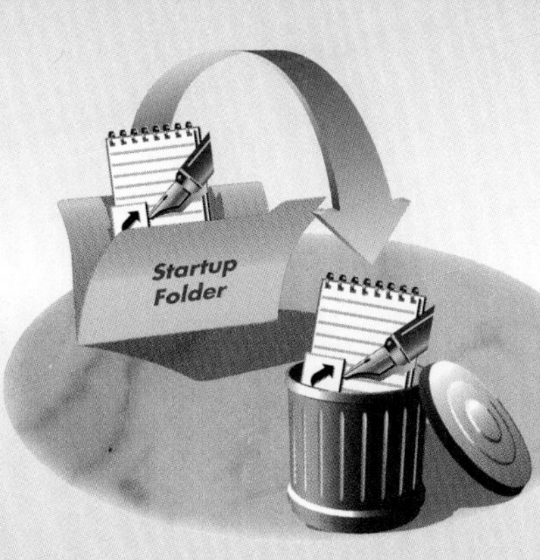

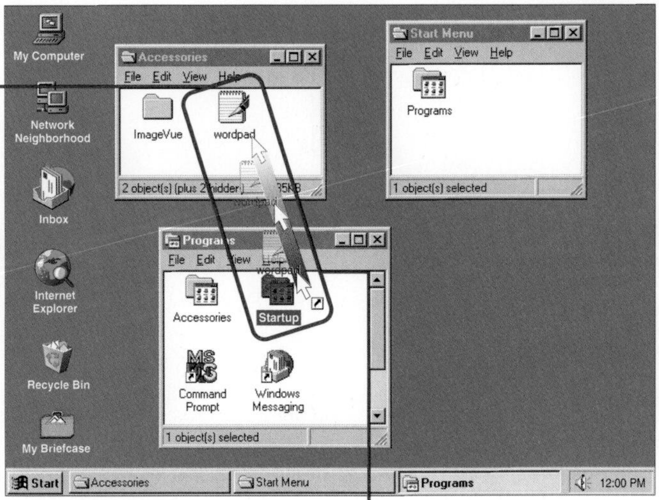

■ The Programs window appears.

5 Position the mouse over the program you want to start automatically.

6 Drag the program to the Startup folder.

7 Double-click the **Startup** folder to display its contents.

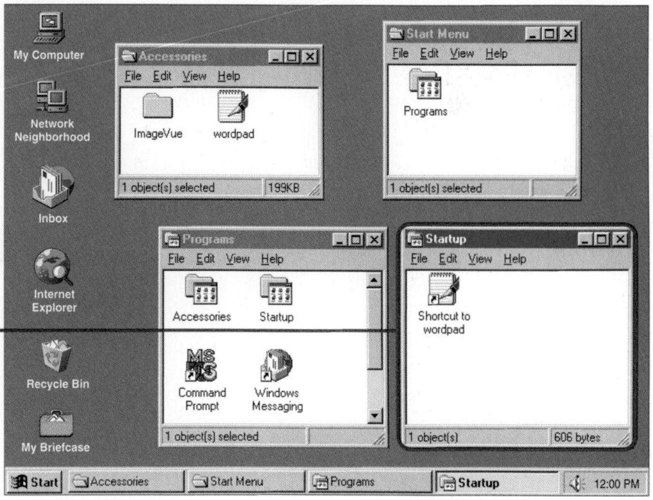

■ The Startup window appears.

■ Windows NT placed a shortcut to the program in the folder.

Note: For information on shortcuts, see page 106.

■ The programs in the Startup folder start automatically every time you turn on your computer.

CHAPTER 8

Have Fun With Windows NT

Windows NT offers many fun features. In this chapter you will learn how to listen to music CDs, play games and watch videos.

PLAY A MUSIC CD

You can use your computer to play music CDs while you work.

You need a CD-ROM drive, a sound card and speakers to play music CDs.

PLAY A MUSIC CD

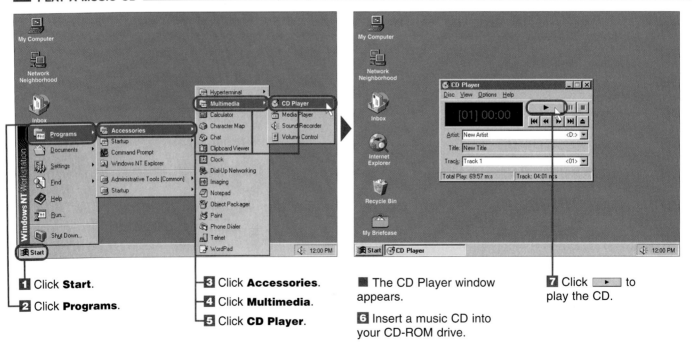

1 Click **Start**.

2 Click **Programs**.

3 Click **Accessories**.

4 Click **Multimedia**.

5 Click **CD Player**.

■ The CD Player window appears.

6 Insert a music CD into your CD-ROM drive.

7 Click [►] to play the CD.

? **Can I listen to music privately?**

You can listen to music privately by plugging a headset into your CD-ROM drive.

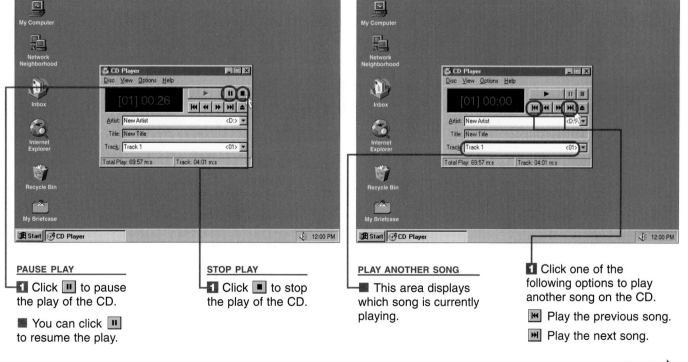

PAUSE PLAY

1 Click [ll] to pause the play of the CD.

■ You can click [ll] to resume the play.

STOP PLAY

1 Click [■] to stop the play of the CD.

PLAY ANOTHER SONG

■ This area displays which song is currently playing.

1 Click one of the following options to play another song on the CD.

[◄◄] Play the previous song.

[►►] Play the next song.

CONTINUED ►

PLAY A MUSIC CD

You can have Windows NT
play the songs on a CD
in random order.

PLAY A MUSIC CD (CONTINUED)

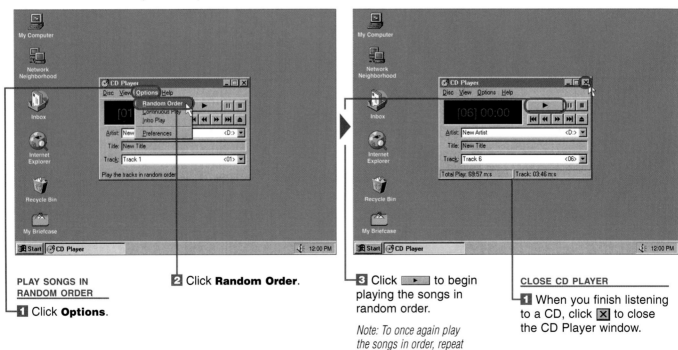

**PLAY SONGS IN
RANDOM ORDER**

1 Click **Options**.

2 Click **Random Order**.

3 Click ▶ to begin
playing the songs in
random order.

*Note: To once again play
the songs in order, repeat
steps 1 and 2.*

CLOSE CD PLAYER

1 When you finish listening
to a CD, click ⊠ to close
the CD Player window.

ADJUST THE VOLUME

You can easily adjust
the volume of sound
coming from your
speakers.

ADJUST THE VOLUME

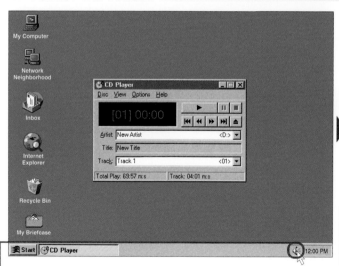

1 Click 🔊 to display
the Volume control.

2 Drag the slider (▭)
up or down to increase
or decrease the volume.

■ To hide the Volume
control, click outside
the box.

PLAY GAMES

Windows NT includes several games you can play on your computer. Games are a fun way to improve your mouse skills and hand-eye coordination.

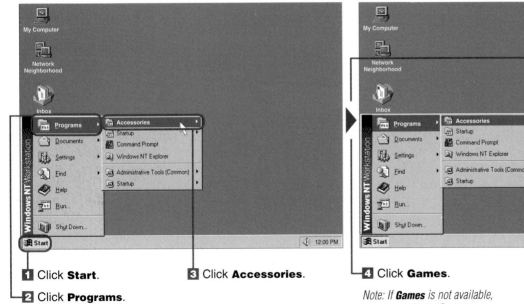

1 Click **Start**.

2 Click **Programs**.

3 Click **Accessories**.

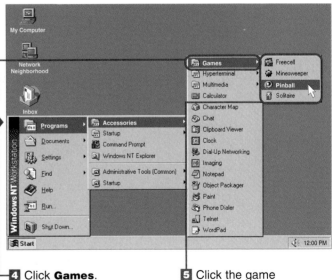

4 Click **Games**.

*Note: If **Games** is not available, you must add the Games component to your computer. To add a Windows NT component, see page 166.*

5 Click the game you want to play.

What other games are included with Windows NT?

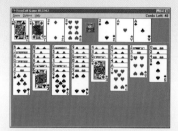

Freecell

Freecell is a single-player card game.

Minesweeper

Minesweeper is a strategy game in which you try to avoid being blown up by mines.

PINBALL

Pinball is similar to a pinball game you would find at an arcade. You launch a ball and then try to score as many points as possible.

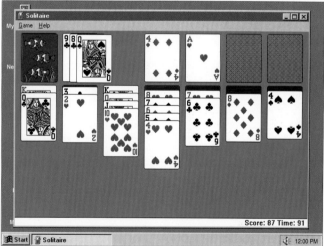

SOLITAIRE

Solitaire is a classic card game that you play on your own. You try to put all the cards in order from ace to king in four stacks, one stack for each suit.

PLAY VIDEOS

You can play videos on your computer.

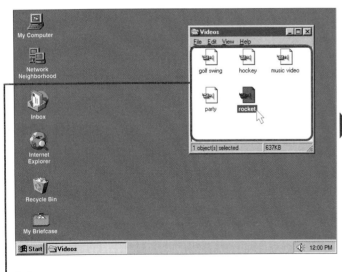

1 Double-click the video you want to play.

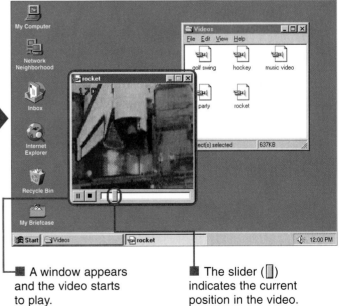

■ A window appears and the video starts to play.

■ The slider (▯) indicates the current position in the video.

152

Where can I get videos?

You can get videos on the Internet or purchase videos at computer stores. Windows NT can play videos with the .avi extension (example: film.avi).

2 Click one of these options to pause (▌▌) or stop (■) the play of the video.

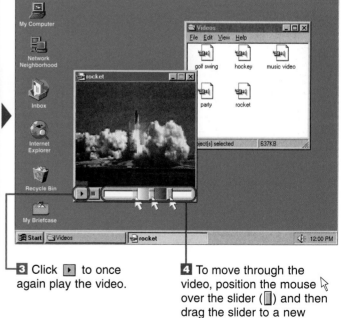

3 Click ▶ to once again play the video.

4 To move through the video, position the mouse ⬉ over the slider (▌) and then drag the slider to a new location.

ASSIGN SOUNDS TO PROGRAM EVENTS

You can have Windows NT play sound effects when you perform certain tasks on your computer.

You need a sound card and speakers to hear sounds on your computer.

For example, you can hear thunder when you exit Windows NT.

◼◼ ASSIGN SOUNDS TO PROGRAM EVENTS ◼◼◼◼◼◼◼◼◼◼◼◼◼◼◼◼◼◼◼◼

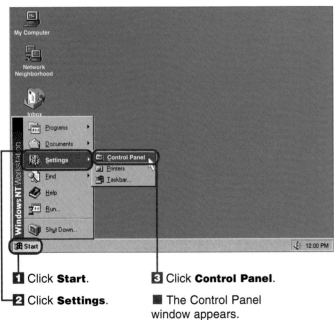

1 Click **Start**.

2 Click **Settings**.

3 Click **Control Panel**.

◼ The Control Panel window appears.

4 Double-click **Sounds**.

◼ The Sounds Properties dialog box appears.

?

How can I get more sound schemes?

Windows NT includes other sound schemes you can use by adding the Sound Scheme components found in the Multimedia category. To add a Windows NT component, see page 166.

Jungle   Musica   Robotz   Utopia

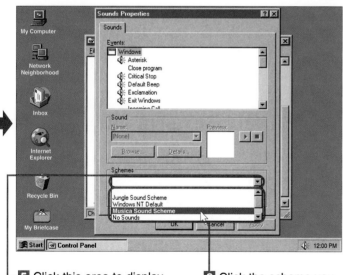

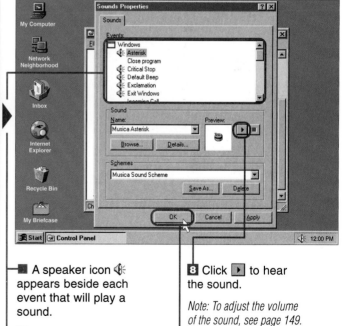

5 Click this area to display a list of the available sound schemes. Each scheme will change the sounds for many events at once.

6 Click the scheme you want to use.

*Note: A dialog box may appear, asking if you want to save the previous scheme. Click **No** to continue without saving.*

■ A speaker icon 🔊 appears beside each event that will play a sound.

7 To hear the sound an event will play, click the event.

8 Click ▶ to hear the sound.

Note: To adjust the volume of the sound, see page 149.

9 Click **OK** to confirm your selection.

RECORD SOUNDS

You can use Sound
Recorder to record
your own sounds.

You need a sound
card and speakers
to record and play
sounds.

RECORD SOUNDS

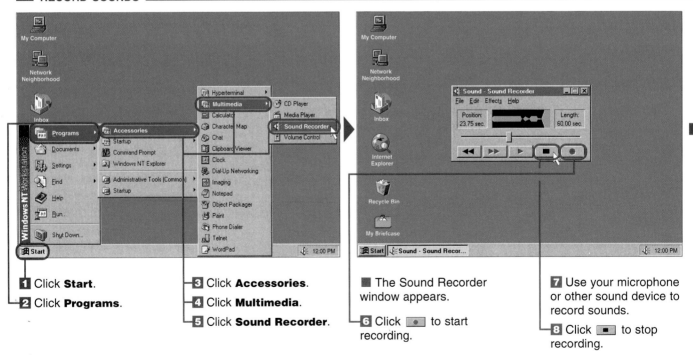

1 Click **Start**.

2 Click **Programs**.

3 Click **Accessories**.

4 Click **Multimedia**.

5 Click **Sound Recorder**.

■ The Sound Recorder
window appears.

6 Click ▣ to start
recording.

7 Use your microphone
or other sound device to
record sounds.

8 Click ▣ to stop
recording.

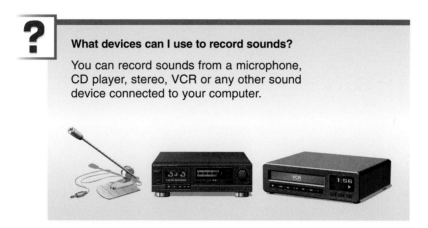

What devices can I use to record sounds?

You can record sounds from a microphone, CD player, stereo, VCR or any other sound device connected to your computer.

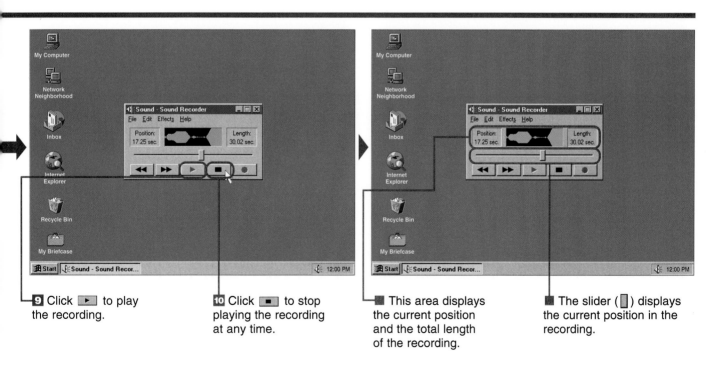

9 Click ▶ to play the recording.

10 Click ■ to stop playing the recording at any time.

■ This area displays the current position and the total length of the recording.

■ The slider ( ) displays the current position in the recording.

CONTINUED ▶

RECORD SOUNDS

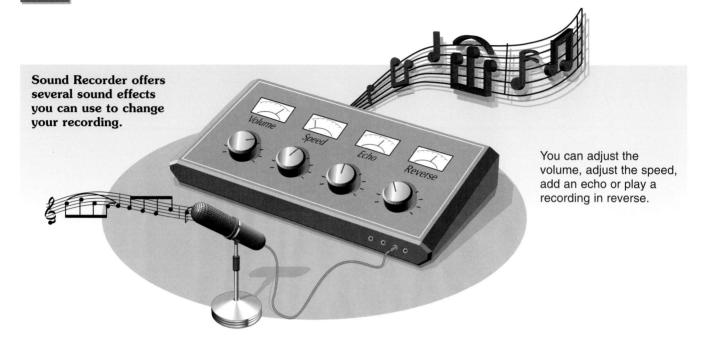

Sound Recorder offers several sound effects you can use to change your recording.

You can adjust the volume, adjust the speed, add an echo or play a recording in reverse.

RECORD SOUNDS (CONTINUED)

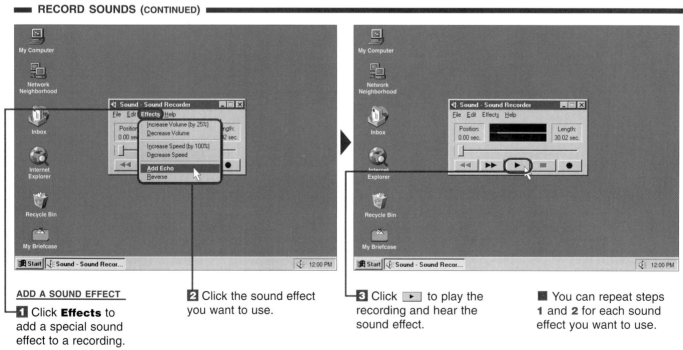

ADD A SOUND EFFECT

1 Click **Effects** to add a special sound effect to a recording.

2 Click the sound effect you want to use.

3 Click ► to play the recording and hear the sound effect.

■ You can repeat steps **1** and **2** for each sound effect you want to use.

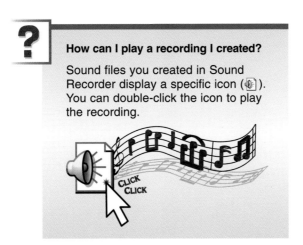

?

How can I play a recording I created?

Sound files you created in Sound Recorder display a specific icon (⛭). You can double-click the icon to play the recording.

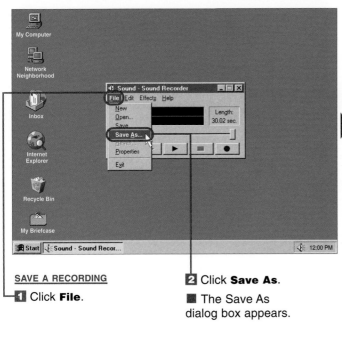

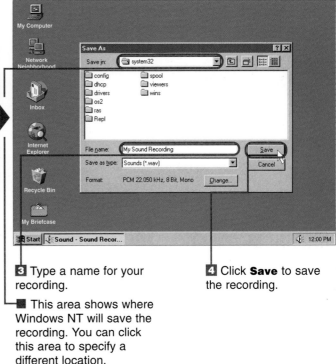

SAVE A RECORDING

1 Click **File**.

2 Click **Save As**.

■ The Save As dialog box appears.

3 Type a name for your recording.

■ This area shows where Windows NT will save the recording. You can click this area to specify a different location.

4 Click **Save** to save the recording.

CHAPTER 9

Work With Software and Hardware

In this chapter you will learn how to add Windows NT components, install a program, format a floppy disk and much more.

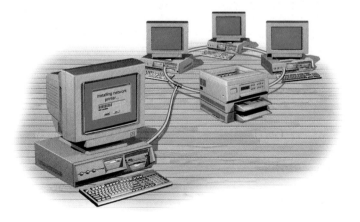

ADD FONTS TO YOUR COMPUTER

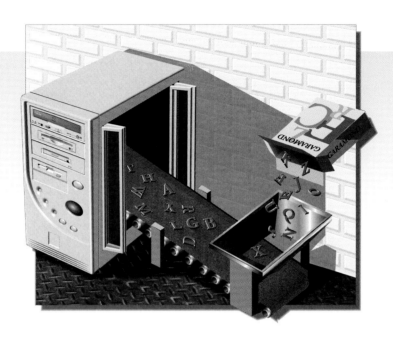

You can add fonts to
your computer to give
you more choices when
creating documents.

ADD FONTS TO YOUR COMPUTER

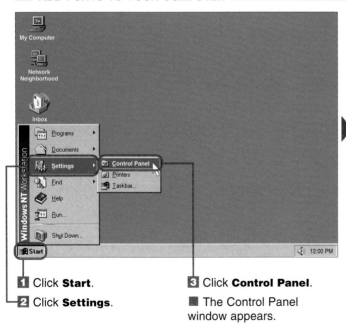

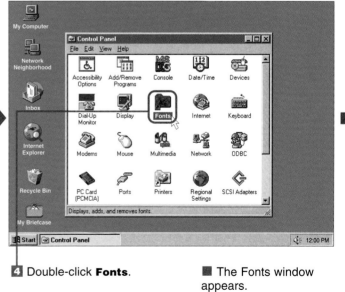

1 Click **Start**.

2 Click **Settings**.

3 Click **Control Panel**.

■ The Control Panel
window appears.

4 Double-click **Fonts**.

■ The Fonts window
appears.

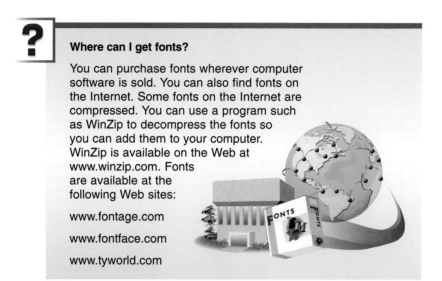

? **Where can I get fonts?**

You can purchase fonts wherever computer software is sold. You can also find fonts on the Internet. Some fonts on the Internet are compressed. You can use a program such as WinZip to decompress the fonts so you can add them to your computer. WinZip is available on the Web at www.winzip.com. Fonts are available at the following Web sites:

www.fontage.com

www.fontface.com

www.tyworld.com

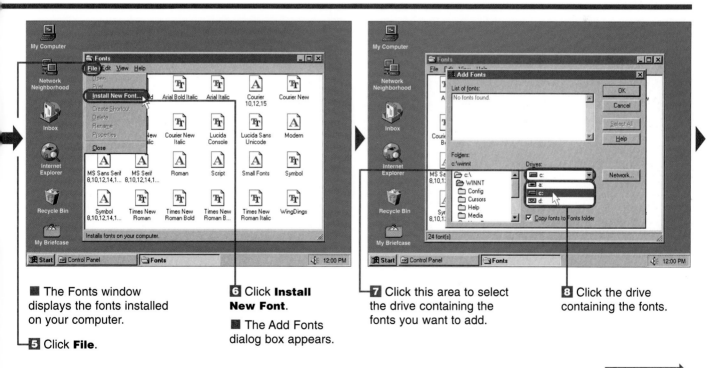

■ The Fonts window displays the fonts installed on your computer.

5 Click **File**.

6 Click **Install New Font**.

■ The Add Fonts dialog box appears.

7 Click this area to select the drive containing the fonts you want to add.

8 Click the drive containing the fonts.

CONTINUED ▶

ADD FONTS TO YOUR COMPUTER

When you add fonts to your computer, you will be able to use the fonts in all of your programs.

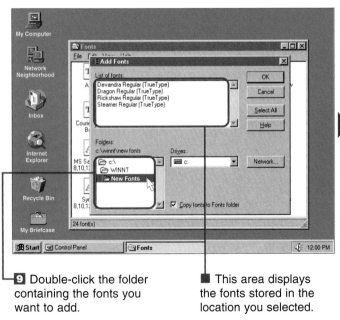

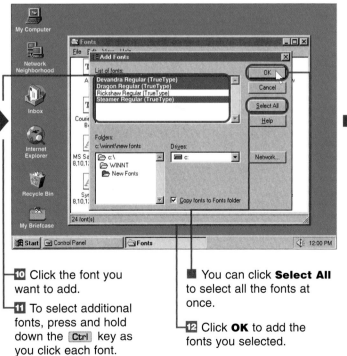

9 Double-click the folder containing the fonts you want to add.

■ This area displays the fonts stored in the location you selected.

10 Click the font you want to add.

11 To select additional fonts, press and hold down the `Ctrl` key as you click each font.

■ You can click **Select All** to select all the fonts at once.

12 Click **OK** to add the fonts you selected.

? **What types of fonts are available on my computer?**

TrueType Fonts

Most of the fonts included with Windows NT are TrueType fonts. A TrueType font will print exactly as it appears on your screen.

System Fonts

Windows NT uses system fonts to display text in menus and dialog boxes.

Printer Fonts

Most printers include built-in fonts which are stored in the printer's memory. A printer font may not print as it appears on your screen. Printer fonts do not appear in the Fonts window.

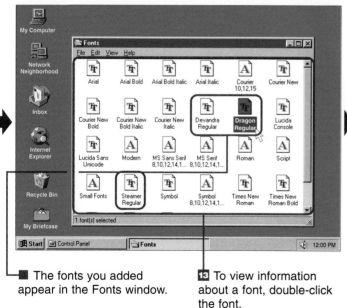

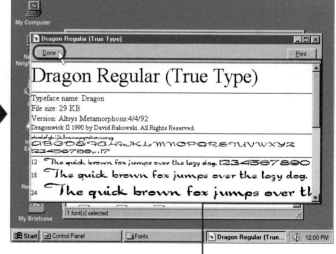

■ The fonts you added appear in the Fonts window.

13 To view information about a font, double-click the font.

■ A window appears, displaying information about the font you selected and samples of the font in various sizes.

14 When you finish reviewing the information, click **Done** to close the window.

ADD WINDOWS NT COMPONENTS

You can add components to your computer that were not added when you first set up Windows NT.

If you are unable to add Windows NT components, the network administrator did not grant you the necessary privileges. Contact your network administrator for information.

■■■ ADD WINDOWS NT COMPONENTS ■■■■■■■■■■■■■■■■■■■■■■■■■■■■■■■■■■■■■■

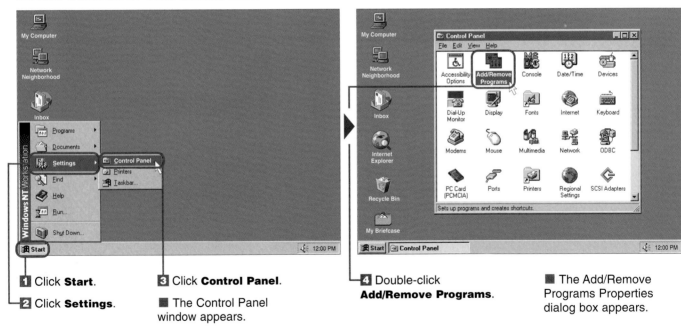

1 Click **Start**.

2 Click **Settings**.

3 Click **Control Panel**.

■ The Control Panel window appears.

4 Double-click **Add/Remove Programs**.

■ The Add/Remove Programs Properties dialog box appears.

9 WORK WITH SOFTWARE AND HARDWARE

Which Windows NT components can I add to my computer?

Some Windows NT components you can add to your computer include:

Games
Provides entertaining games such as Pinball and Solitaire.

Desktop Wallpaper
Provides images you can use to decorate your screen.

Sound Schemes
Provides sound effects Windows NT can play when you perform certain tasks on your computer.

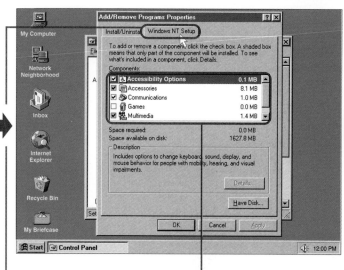

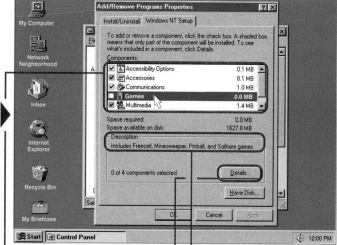

■5 Click the **Windows NT Setup** tab.

Note: Windows NT may take a moment to display the information.

■ This area displays the categories of components you can add to your computer.

■ The box beside each category indicates if all (☑), some (☑) or none (☐) of the components in the category are installed on your computer.

■6 Click a category to display a description of the components in the category.

■ This area displays a description of the components in the category.

■7 Click **Details** to display the components in the category.

CONTINUED ▶

ADD WINDOWS NT COMPONENTS

When adding Windows NT components, you will be asked to insert the CD-ROM disc you used to install Windows NT.

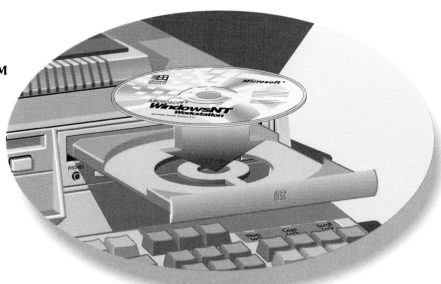

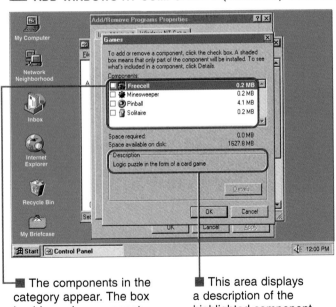

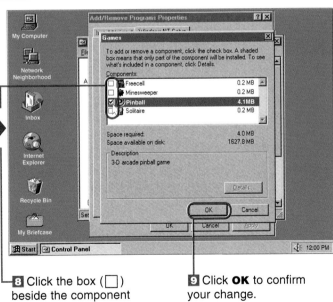

■ The components in the category appear. The box beside each component indicates if the component is installed ([✔]) or is not installed ([ ]) on your computer.

■ This area displays a description of the highlighted component.

8 Click the box ([ ]) beside the component you want to add to your computer ([ ] changes to [✔]).

9 Click **OK** to confirm your change.

168

How do I remove a component I do not use?

You can remove a component you do not use by performing steps **1** to **10** starting on page 166. When you select a component you want to remove, ☑ changes to ☐ in step **8**.

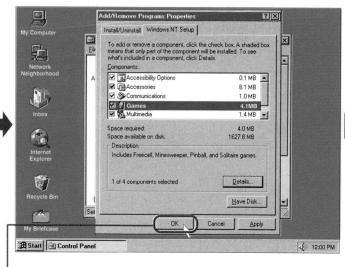

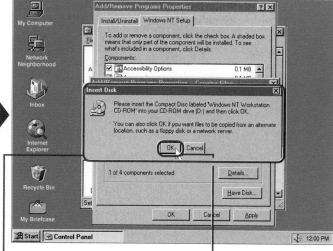

10 Click **OK** to close the Add/Remove Programs Properties dialog box.

■ The Insert Disk dialog box appears, asking you to insert the Windows NT CD-ROM disc.

11 Insert the CD-ROM disc.

Note: If the Windows NT CD-ROM window appears after you insert the CD-ROM disc, click ☒ to close the window.

12 Click **OK** to continue.

■ Windows NT copies the necessary files to your computer.

INSTALL A PROGRAM

You can add a new program to your computer. Programs come on a CD-ROM disc or floppy disks.

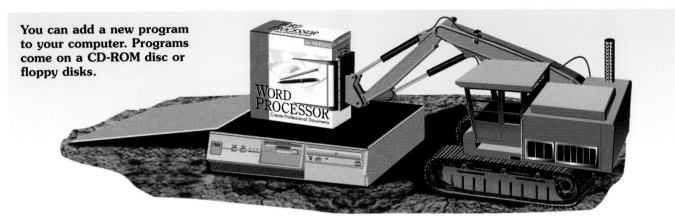

If you are unable to install a program, the network administrator did not grant you the necessary privileges. Contact your network administrator for information.

INSTALL A PROGRAM

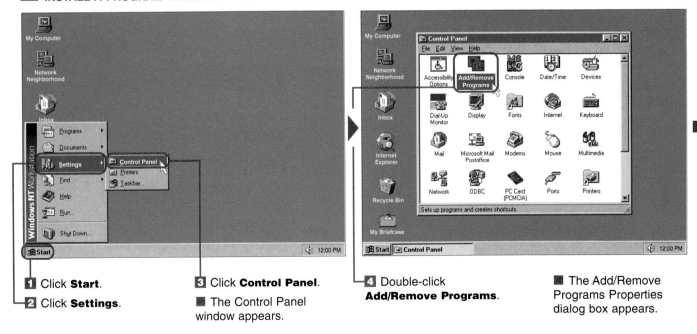

1 Click **Start**.

2 Click **Settings**.

3 Click **Control Panel**.

■ The Control Panel window appears.

4 Double-click **Add/Remove Programs**.

■ The Add/Remove Programs Properties dialog box appears.

9 WORK WITH SOFTWARE AND HARDWARE

Why did an installation program automatically start?

Most Windows programs available on a CD-ROM disc will automatically start an installation program when you insert the CD-ROM disc into the drive. Follow the instructions on your screen to install the program.

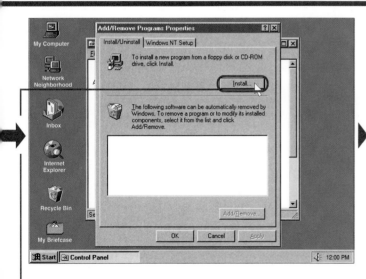

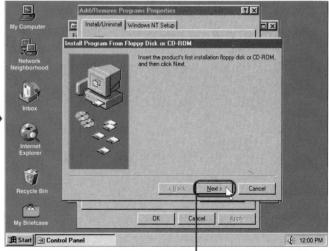

5 Click **Install** to install a new program.

■ The Install Program From Floppy Disk or CD-ROM wizard appears.

6 Insert the program's first installation floppy disk or CD-ROM disc into a drive.

7 Click **Next** to continue.

CONTINUED

171

INSTALL A PROGRAM

There are three common ways to install a program.

Typical

Sets up the program with the most common components.

Custom

Lets you customize the program to suit your specific needs.

Minimum

Sets up the program with a minimum number of components. This is ideal for computers with limited disk space.

INSTALL A PROGRAM (CONTINUED)

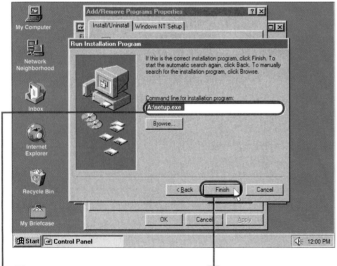

■ Windows NT locates the file needed to install the program.

8 Click **Finish** to install the program.

9 Follow the instructions on your screen. Every program will ask you a different set of questions.

■ After you install a program, make sure you keep the program's CD-ROM disc or floppy disks in a safe place. If your computer fails or you accidentally erase the program files, you may need to install the program again.

REMOVE A PROGRAM

You can remove a program from your computer that you no longer use. Removing a program will free up space on your hard drive.

REMOVE A PROGRAM

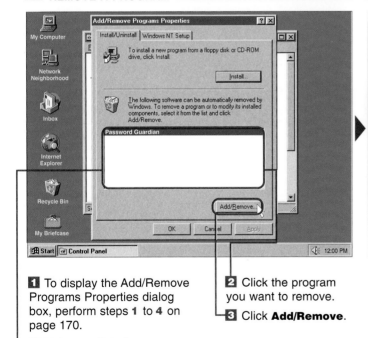

1 To display the Add/Remove Programs Properties dialog box, perform steps **1** to **4** on page 170.

◾ This area lists the programs Windows NT can automatically remove.

2 Click the program you want to remove.

3 Click **Add/Remove**.

4 Follow the instructions on your screen. Every program will take you through different steps to remove the program.

INSTALL A LOCAL PRINTER

Before you can use a new printer, you need to install the printer on your computer.

You will need the Windows NT CD-ROM disc to install a new printer.

If you are unable to install a local printer, the network administrator did not grant you the necessary privileges. Contact your network administrator for information.

■■ INSTALL A LOCAL PRINTER ■■

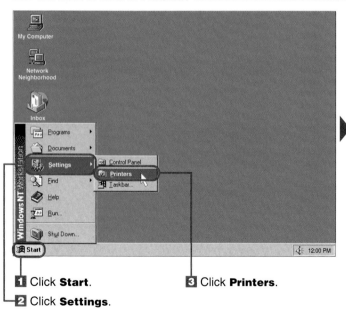

1 Click **Start**.

2 Click **Settings**.

3 Click **Printers**.

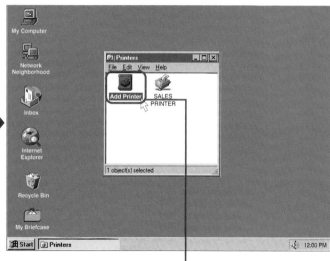

■ The Printers window appears, displaying an icon for each printer installed on your computer.

4 Double-click **Add Printer** to install a new printer.

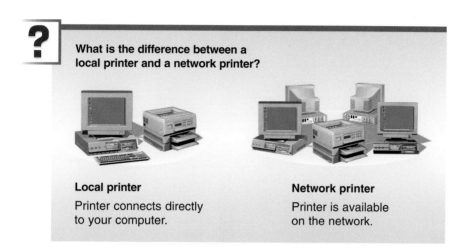

? What is the difference between a local printer and a network printer?

Local printer
Printer connects directly to your computer.

Network printer
Printer is available on the network.

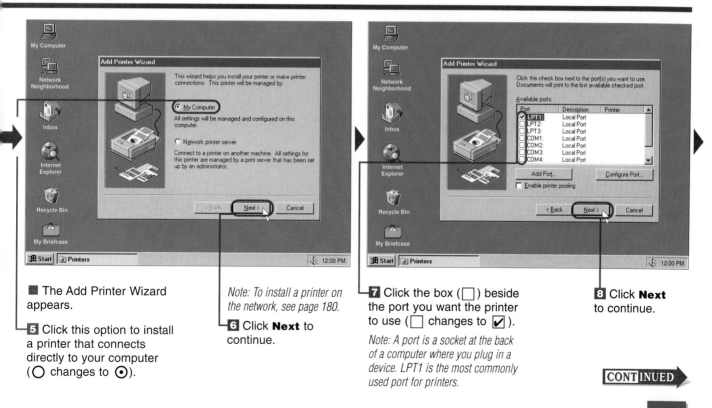

■ The Add Printer Wizard appears.

5 Click this option to install a printer that connects directly to your computer (○ changes to ⊙).

Note: To install a printer on the network, see page 180.

6 Click **Next** to continue.

7 Click the box (□) beside the port you want the printer to use (□ changes to ☑).

Note: A port is a socket at the back of a computer where you plug in a device. LPT1 is the most commonly used port for printers.

8 Click **Next** to continue.

CONTINUED

When installing a printer, you must specify the manufacturer and model of the printer.

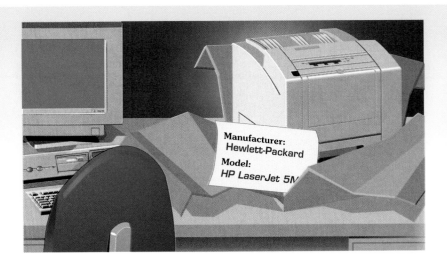

Manufacturer:
Hewlett-Packard

Model:
HP LaserJet 5M

INSTALL A LOCAL PRINTER (CONTINUED)

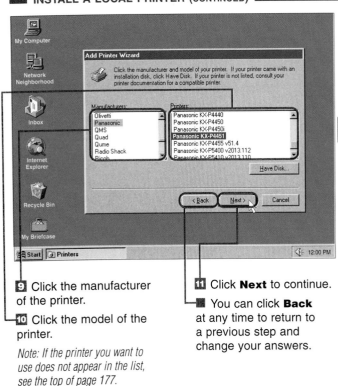

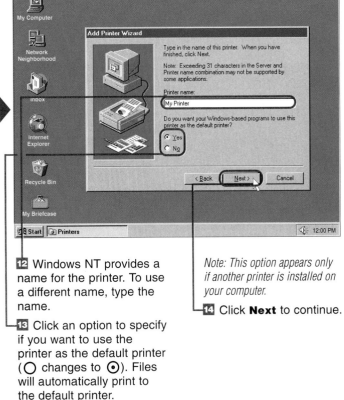

9 Click the manufacturer of the printer.

10 Click the model of the printer.

Note: If the printer you want to use does not appear in the list, see the top of page 177.

11 Click **Next** to continue.

■ You can click **Back** at any time to return to a previous step and change your answers.

12 Windows NT provides a name for the printer. To use a different name, type the name.

13 Click an option to specify if you want to use the printer as the default printer (○ changes to ◉). Files will automatically print to the default printer.

Note: This option appears only if another printer is installed on your computer.

14 Click **Next** to continue.

What if Windows NT does not list the printer I want to install?

If Windows NT does not list the printer you want to install, you can use the installation disk(s) that came with the printer.

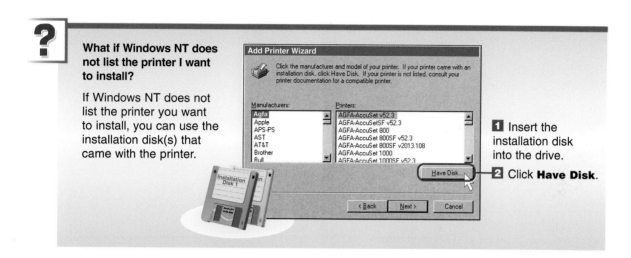

1 Insert the installation disk into the drive.

2 Click **Have Disk**.

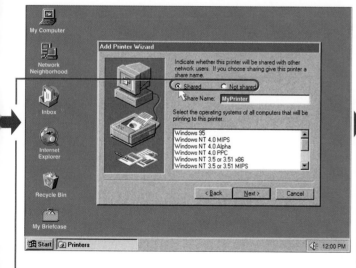

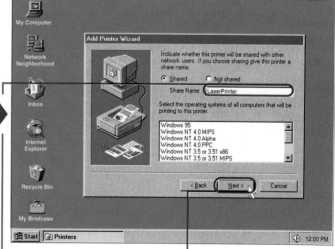

15 Click an option to specify if you want to share the printer with others on the network (○ changes to ⊙).

Note: For information on sharing a printer, see page 200.

16 This area displays the name of the printer people will see on the network. To change the name, type a new name.

17 Click **Next** to continue.

*Note: A warning message appears if you typed a printer name in step **16** that contains spaces or more than 12 characters. Click **Yes** to use the printer name.*

CONTINUED

INSTALL A LOCAL PRINTER

Windows NT allows you to print a test page to confirm that your printer is properly installed.

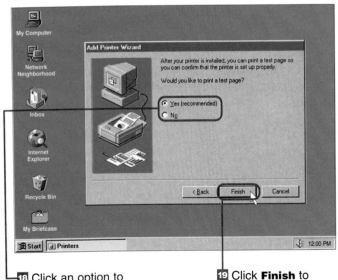

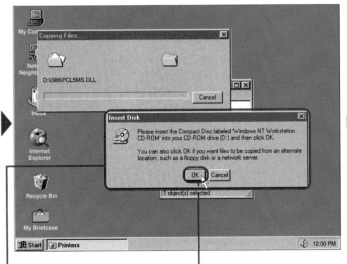

■ Click an option to specify if you want to print a test page (○ changes to ⊙).

■ Click **Finish** to install the printer.

■ The Insert Disk dialog box appears, asking you to insert the Windows NT CD-ROM disc.

■ Insert the CD-ROM disc into the drive.

Note: If the Windows NT CD-ROM window appears after you insert the CD-ROM disc, click ☒ to close the window.

■ Click **OK** to copy the files to your computer.

Why do I need the Windows NT CD-ROM disc to install a printer?

Your computer needs special software, called a driver, to be able to use a new printer. A driver is a program that allows your computer to communicate with the printer. The Windows NT CD-ROM disc includes the most popular drivers.

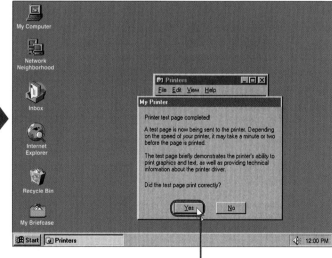

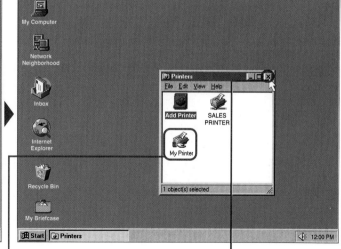

■ A dialog box appears, asking if the test page printed correctly.

*Note: This dialog box does not appear if you selected **No** in step 18.*

22 Click **Yes** if the page printed correctly.

■ An icon for the printer appears in the Printers window.

■ A hand (✋) appears under the printer if you chose to share the printer in step 15.

11 Click ✕ to close the Printers window.

INSTALL A NETWORK PRINTER

Before you can use a printer available on the network, you need to install the printer on your computer.

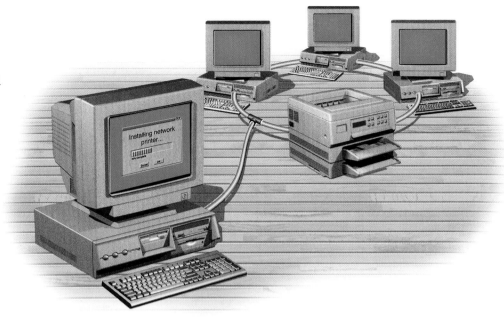

INSTALL A NETWORK PRINTER

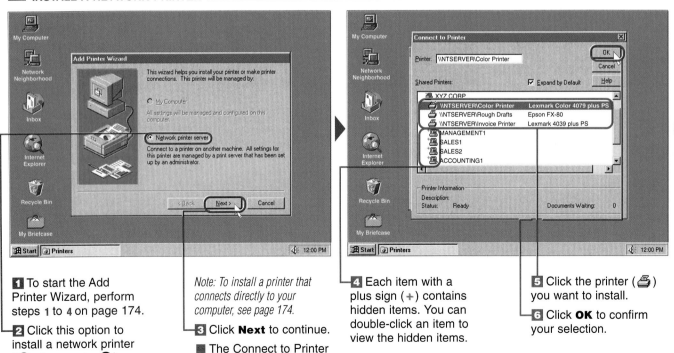

1 To start the Add Printer Wizard, perform steps 1 to 4 on page 174.

2 Click this option to install a network printer (○ changes to ⊙).

Note: To install a printer that connects directly to your computer, see page 174.

3 Click **Next** to continue.

■ The Connect to Printer dialog box appears.

4 Each item with a plus sign (+) contains hidden items. You can double-click an item to view the hidden items.

5 Click the printer (🖨) you want to install.

6 Click **OK** to confirm your selection.

9 WORK WITH SOFTWARE AND HARDWARE

?

Can I install more than one network printer?

Yes. You may want to install a lower quality printer to print the rough drafts of documents and a higher quality printer to print the finished copies. When you print documents, you will need to select which network printer you want to use.

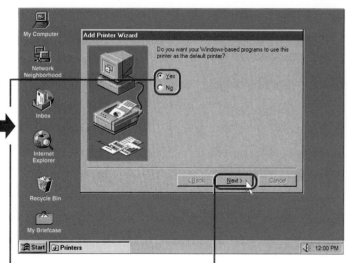

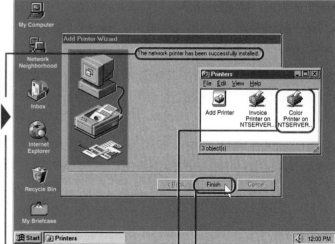

7 Click an option to specify if you want to use the printer as the default printer (○ changes to ⊙). Files will automatically print to the default printer.

Note: This option only appears if another printer is installed on your computer.

8 Click **Next** to continue.

■ A message appears, stating that the printer was successfully installed.

9 Click **Finish** to close the wizard.

■ An icon for the printer appears in the Printers window.

FORMAT A FLOPPY DISK

You must format a
floppy disk before
you can use the disk
to store information.

Floppy disks you buy
at computer stores are
usually formatted. You
may want to later format
a disk to erase the
information it contains
and prepare the disk for
storing new information.

▬ FORMAT A FLOPPY DISK ▬

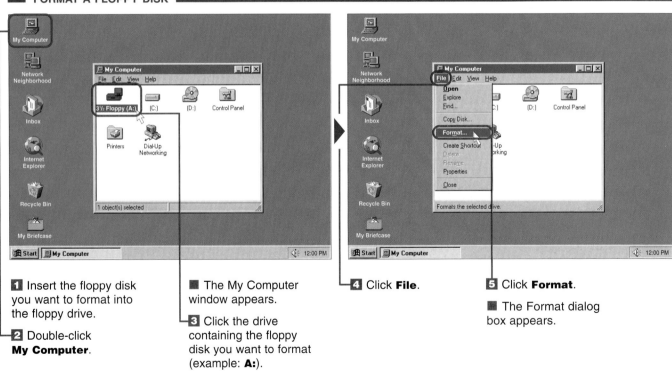

1 Insert the floppy disk
you want to format into
the floppy drive.

2 Double-click
My Computer.

■ The My Computer
window appears.

3 Click the drive
containing the floppy
disk you want to format
(example: **A:**).

4 Click **File**.

5 Click **Format**.

■ The Format dialog
box appears.

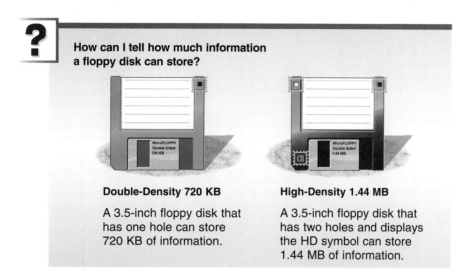

?

How can I tell how much information a floppy disk can store?

Double-Density 720 KB

A 3.5-inch floppy disk that has one hole can store 720 KB of information.

High-Density 1.44 MB

A 3.5-inch floppy disk that has two holes and displays the HD symbol can store 1.44 MB of information.

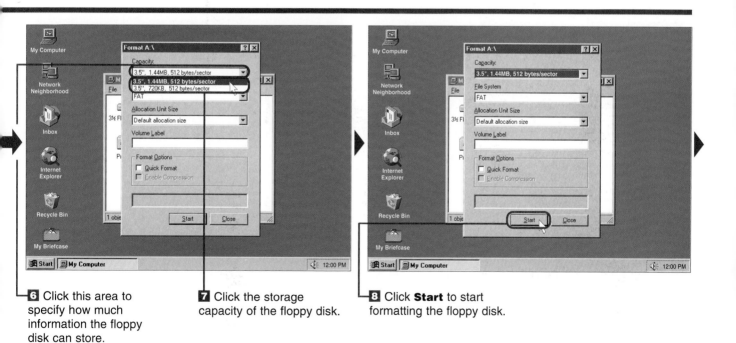

6 Click this area to specify how much information the floppy disk can store.

7 Click the storage capacity of the floppy disk.

8 Click **Start** to start formatting the floppy disk.

CONTINUED

FORMAT A FLOPPY DISK

Before formatting a floppy disk, make sure the disk does not contain information you may need. Formatting a floppy disk will permanently remove all the information on the disk.

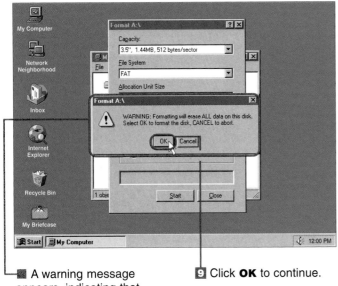

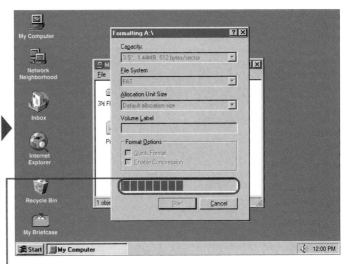

◪ A warning message appears, indicating that formatting the floppy disk will erase all the data on the disk.

9 Click **OK** to continue.

◪ This area displays the progress of the format.

184

?

How can I tell if a floppy disk is formatted?

Windows NT will display an error message when you try to view the contents of a disk that is not formatted. You cannot tell if a floppy disk is formatted just by looking at the disk.

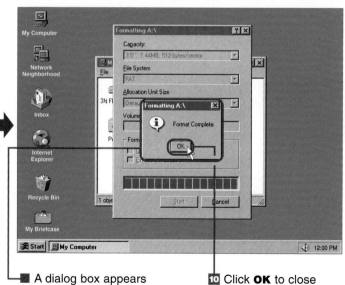

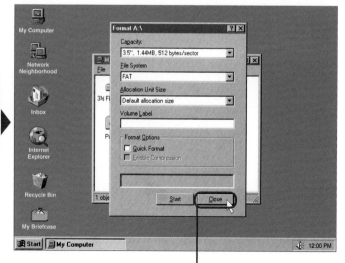

■ A dialog box appears when the format is complete.

10 Click **OK** to close the dialog box.

■ To format another floppy disk, insert the disk and then repeat steps **6** to **10** starting on page 183.

11 Click **Close** to close the Format dialog box.

CHAPTER 10

Work on a Network

A network is a group of connected computers. This chapter teaches you how to share information and equipment on a network.

INTRODUCTION TO NETWORKS

A network is a group of connected computers that allow people to share information and equipment.

Networks let people share information such as documents and programs. Computers connected to a network can share equipment such as a printer.

LAN and WAN

A Local Area Network (LAN) connects computers and devices located close to each other, such as in a building. A Wide Area Network (WAN) connects local area networks which can be located across a city or country.

Domain and Workgroup

A network can consist of domains and workgroups. A domain is a collection of computers that are administered together. A workgroup is a collection of computers that frequently share resources.

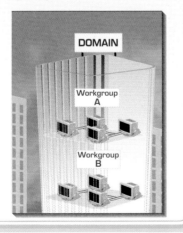

Network Administrator

A network administrator manages the network and makes sure the network runs smoothly.

Peer-to-Peer Network

A peer-to-peer network provides a simple and inexpensive way to connect fewer than ten computers.

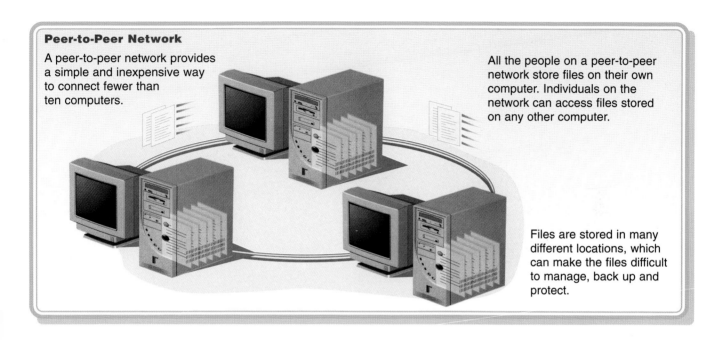

All the people on a peer-to-peer network store files on their own computer. Individuals on the network can access files stored on any other computer.

Files are stored in many different locations, which can make the files difficult to manage, back up and protect.

Client/Server Network

A client/server network provides an efficient way to connect ten or more computers or computers exchanging large amounts of information.

All the people on a client/server network store files on a central computer, called a server. Everyone connected to the network can access the files stored on the server. Windows NT server is one of the most popular types of servers.

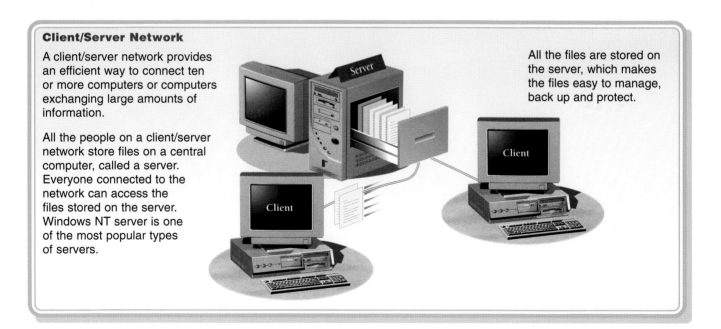

All the files are stored on the server, which makes the files easy to manage, back up and protect.

BROWSE THROUGH A NETWORK

You can browse through the information available on your network.

A network can consist of domains and workgroups. A domain is a collection of computers that are administered together. A workgroup is a collection of computers that frequently share resources.

BROWSE THROUGH A NETWORK

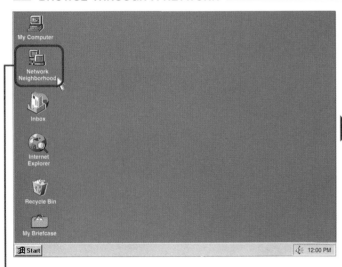

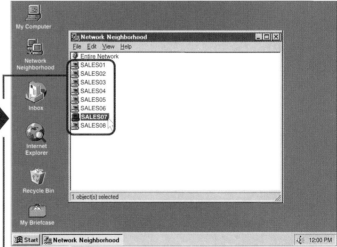

1 Double-click **Network Neighborhood**.

■ The Network Neighborhood window appears. The window displays all the computers in your domain or workgroup.

2 Double-click the computer containing the files you want to work with.

*Note: You can double-click **Entire Network** to view all the domains and workgroups on your network.*

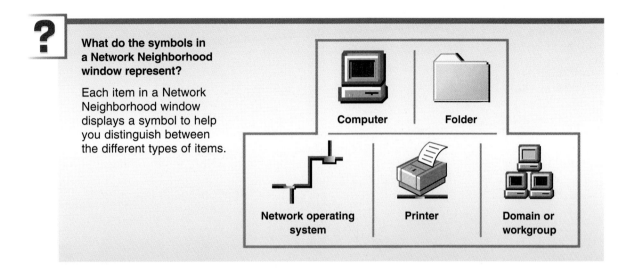

?

What do the symbols in a Network Neighborhood window represent?

Each item in a Network Neighborhood window displays a symbol to help you distinguish between the different types of items.

Computer

Folder

Network operating system

Printer

Domain or workgroup

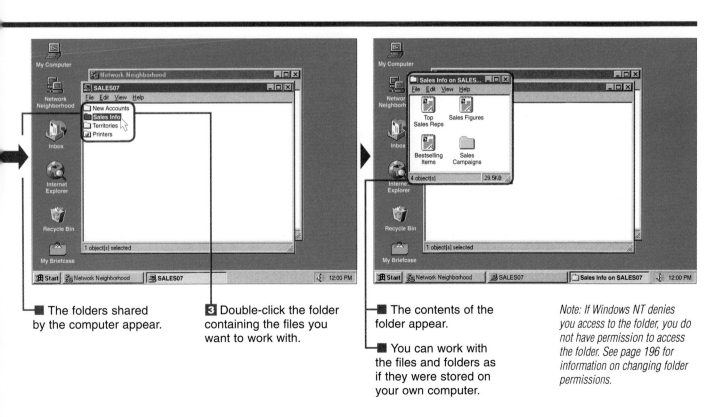

■ The folders shared by the computer appear.

3 Double-click the folder containing the files you want to work with.

■ The contents of the folder appear.

■ You can work with the files and folders as if they were stored on your own computer.

Note: If Windows NT denies you access to the folder, you do not have permission to access the folder. See page 196 for information on changing folder permissions.

FIND A COMPUTER

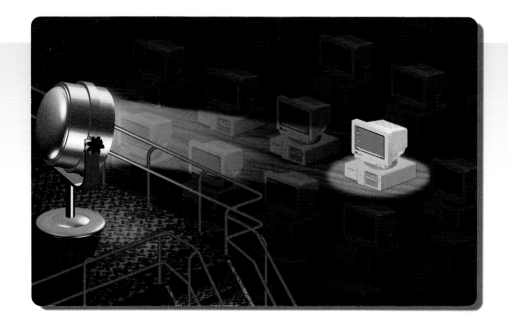

You can search for a computer on the network that stores files you want to work with. This is especially useful on large networks.

FIND A COMPUTER

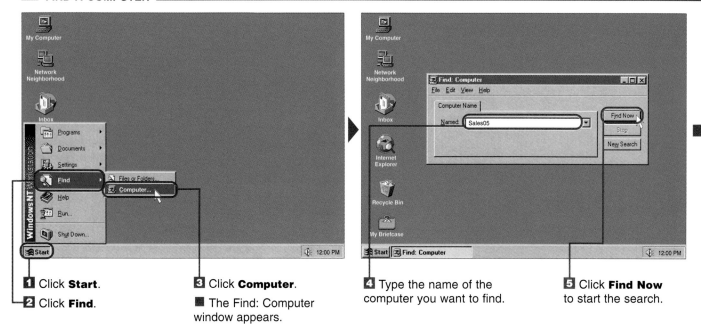

1 Click **Start**.

2 Click **Find**.

3 Click **Computer**.

■ The Find: Computer window appears.

4 Type the name of the computer you want to find.

5 Click **Find Now** to start the search.

Why doesn't the computer I found display the information I want to work with?

The information you want to work with must be shared. Ask your network administrator or the owner of the computer to share the information you require. See page 194 for information on sharing a folder.

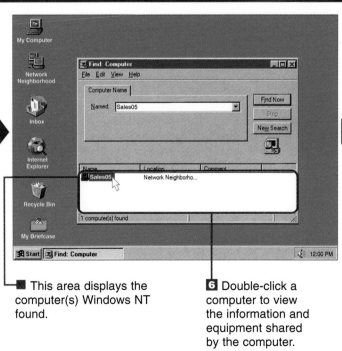

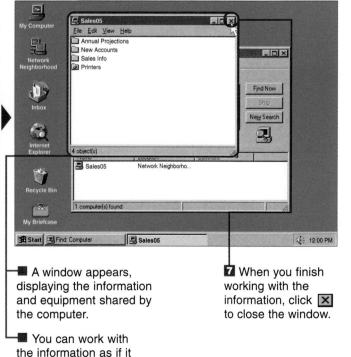

■ This area displays the computer(s) Windows NT found.

6 Double-click a computer to view the information and equipment shared by the computer.

■ A window appears, displaying the information and equipment shared by the computer.

■ You can work with the information as if it were stored on your own computer.

7 When you finish working with the information, click ☒ to close the window.

SHARE A FOLDER

You can specify what information on your computer you want to share with individuals on a network.

Sharing information is useful if you and your colleagues are working together on a project and need to access the same files.

If you are unable to share a folder, the network administrator did not grant you the necessary privileges. Contact your network administrator for information.

SHARE A FOLDER

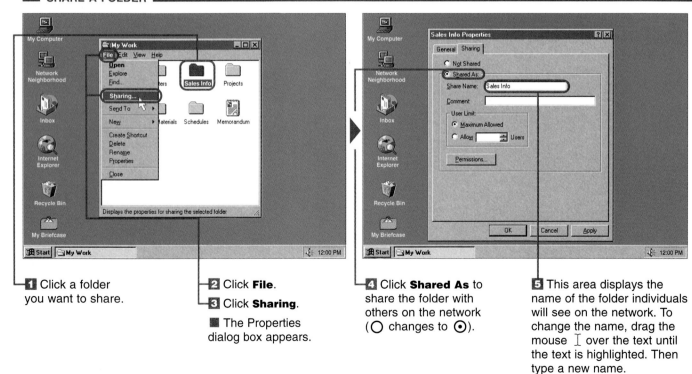

1 Click a folder you want to share.

2 Click **File**.

3 Click **Sharing**.

■ The Properties dialog box appears.

4 Click **Shared As** to share the folder with others on the network (○ changes to ◉).

5 This area displays the name of the folder individuals will see on the network. To change the name, drag the mouse I over the text until the text is highlighted. Then type a new name.

?

How can I tell which folders on my computer are shared?

A hand () appears under the icon for each shared folder on your computer. You can use Network Neighborhood to see a list of the folders shared by your computer and other computers on the network. See page 190 to use Network Neighborhood.

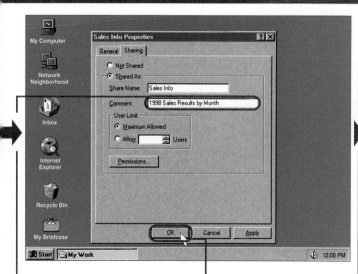

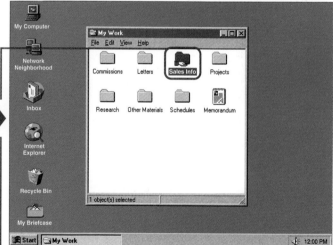

6 To enter a comment about the folder that individuals can see on the network, click this area and then type a comment.

7 Click **OK** to confirm your changes.

*Note: A warning message appears if you typed a folder name in step **5** that contains more than 8 characters. Click **Yes** to use the folder name.*

■ A hand ( ) appears under the icon for the shared folder. Individuals on the network will have access to all the folders and files within the shared folder.

Note: To specify who you want to have access to the folder, see page 196.

■ To stop sharing a folder, repeat steps **1** to **4**, selecting **Not Shared** in step **4**. Then click **OK**.

CHANGE FOLDER PERMISSIONS

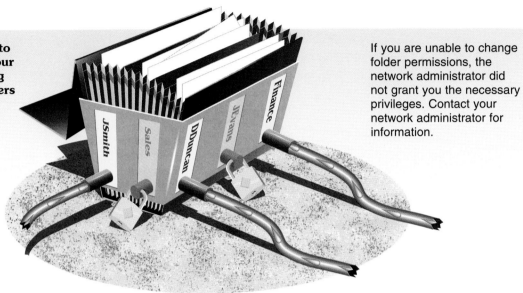

You can limit access to a shared folder on your computer by selecting which groups and users on the network you want to have access to the folder.

If you are unable to change folder permissions, the network administrator did not grant you the necessary privileges. Contact your network administrator for information.

■ CHANGE FOLDER PERMISSIONS ■

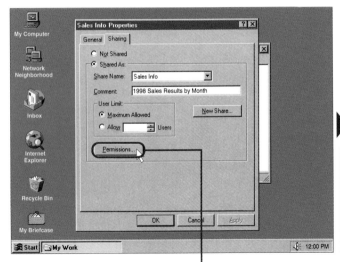

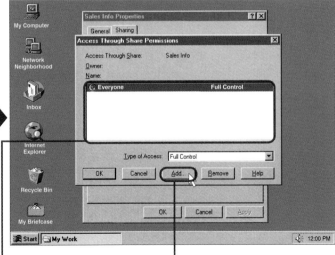

1 Before you can change the permissions for a folder, you must share the folder. To share a folder, see page 194.

2 To display the Properties dialog box, perform steps **1** to **3** on page 194.

3 Click **Permissions** to specify who you want to have access to the folder.

■ The Access Through Share Permissions dialog box appears.

■ This area lists each group that has access to the folder and the type of access.

ADD A GROUP OR USER

4 To add a group or user to the list, click **Add**.

■ The Add Users and Groups dialog box appears.

What groups can I grant access to a shared folder?

Here are some groups available on the network.

Domain Guests

Users granted limited access.

Everyone

Every user is a member of this group.

Domain Users

Users can perform common tasks.

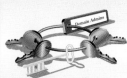

Domain Admins

Users can perform administrative tasks.

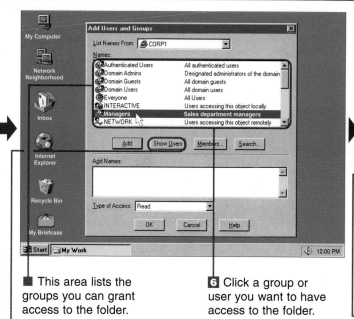

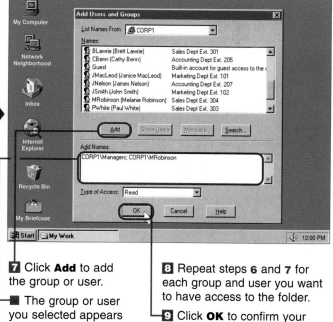

■ This area lists the groups you can grant access to the folder.

5 To view users in the list, click **Show Users**.

6 Click a group or user you want to have access to the folder.

7 Click **Add** to add the group or user.

■ The group or user you selected appears in this area.

8 Repeat steps **6** and **7** for each group and user you want to have access to the folder.

9 Click **OK** to confirm your selections.

CONTINUED ➡

CHANGE FOLDER PERMISSIONS

You can grant groups and users on the network different types of access to a shared folder on your computer.

By default, everyone on the network has Full Control access to a shared folder on your computer. To grant groups and users different types of access, you must remove the "Everyone" group.

CHANGE FOLDER PERMISSIONS (CONTINUED)

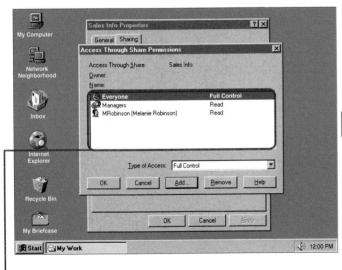

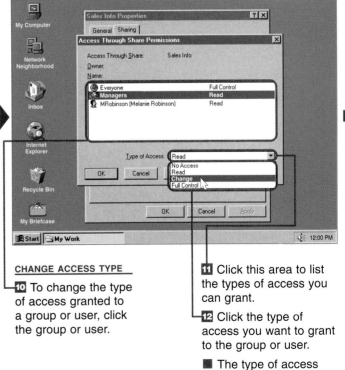

■ This area lists the groups and users you added and the type of access granted to each.

CHANGE ACCESS TYPE

10 To change the type of access granted to a group or user, click the group or user.

11 Click this area to list the types of access you can grant.

12 Click the type of access you want to grant to the group or user.

■ The type of access changes.

What types of access can I grant to a shared folder on my computer?

No Access

Users cannot access the folder.

Read

Users can open but not change files in the folder.

Change

Users can open, change, create, move and delete files in the folder.

Full Control

Users can open, change, create, move, delete and administer files in the folder.

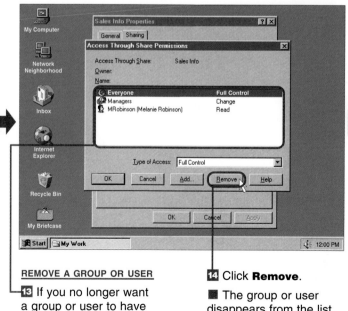

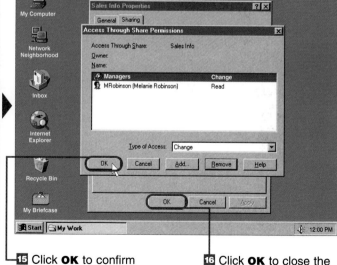

REMOVE A GROUP OR USER

13 If you no longer want a group or user to have access to the folder, click the group or user.

14 Click **Remove**.

■ The group or user disappears from the list.

15 Click **OK** to confirm your changes.

16 Click **OK** to close the Properties dialog box.

SHARE A PRINTER

You can share your printer on the network. This allows others to use your printer to print documents.

You can only share a printer that is directly connected to your computer.

If you are unable to share a printer, the network administrator did not grant you the necessary privileges. Contact your network administrator for information.

■ SHARE A PRINTER ■

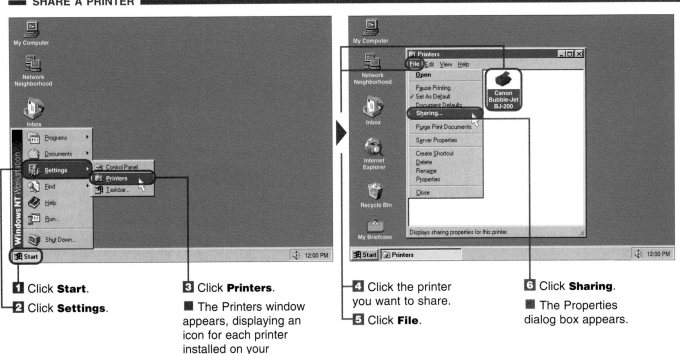

1 Click **Start**.

2 Click **Settings**.

3 Click **Printers**.

■ The Printers window appears, displaying an icon for each printer installed on your computer.

4 Click the printer you want to share.

5 Click **File**.

6 Click **Sharing**.

■ The Properties dialog box appears.

? Will sharing a printer affect my computer's performance?

When individuals on the network send files to your shared printer, your computer temporarily stores the files before sending them to the printer. As a result, your computer will operate more slowly while other people use your printer.

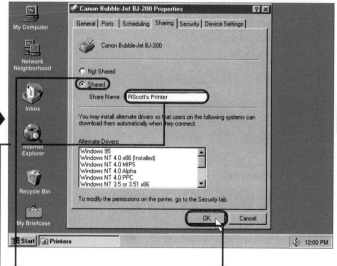

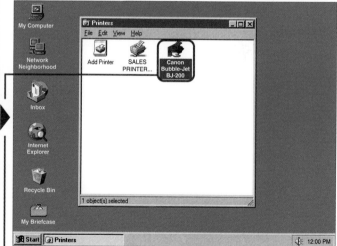

7 Click **Shared** to share the printer with others on the network (○ changes to ⊙).

8 This area displays the name of the printer individuals will see on the network. To change the name, type a new name.

9 Click **OK**.

Note: A warning message appears if you typed a printer name in step 8 that contains spaces or more than 12 characters. Click Yes to use the printer name.

■ A hand (✋) appears under the icon for the shared printer, indicating that the printer is available to others on the network.

Note: To specify who you want to have access to the printer, see page 202.

■ To stop sharing a printer, repeat steps **1** to **7**, selecting **Not Shared** in step **7**. Then click **OK**.

CHANGE PRINTER PERMISSIONS

You can select which groups and users on the network you want to have access to your shared printer.

By default, everyone on the network can use your shared printer to print documents.

If you are unable to change printer permissions, the network administrator did not grant you the necessary privileges. Contact your network administrator for information.

CHANGE PRINTER PERMISSIONS

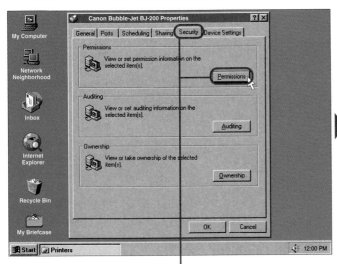

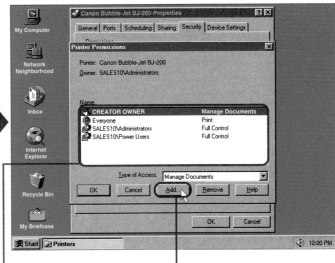

1 Before you can change the permissions for a printer, you must share the printer. To share a printer, see page 200.

2 To display the Properties dialog box, perform steps **1** to **6** on page 200.

3 Click the **Security** tab.

4 Click **Permissions** to specify who you want to have access to the printer.

■ The Printer Permissions dialog box appears.

■ This area lists each group that has access to the printer and the type of access.

ADD A GROUP OR USER

5 To add a group or user to the list, click **Add**.

■ The Add Users and Groups dialog box appears.

?

Why would I change the permissions for a shared printer?

You may want to change the permissions for a shared printer to limit access to the printer. If too many people have access to your printer, you may have to wait a long time for your documents to print.

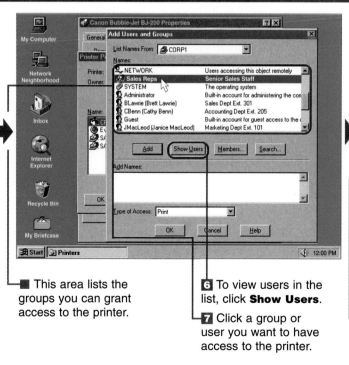

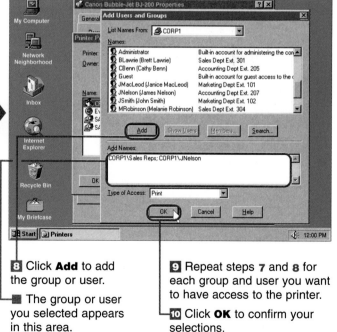

■ This area lists the groups you can grant access to the printer.

6 To view users in the list, click **Show Users**.

7 Click a group or user you want to have access to the printer.

8 Click **Add** to add the group or user.

■ The group or user you selected appears in this area.

9 Repeat steps **7** and **8** for each group and user you want to have access to the printer.

10 Click **OK** to confirm your selections.

CONTINUED ▶

CHANGE PRINTER PERMISSIONS

You can grant groups and users on the network different types of access to your shared printer.

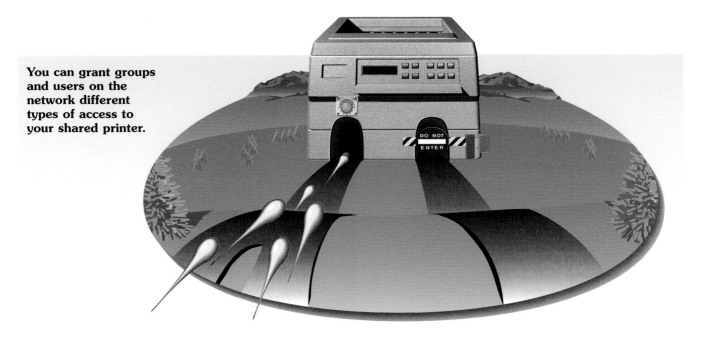

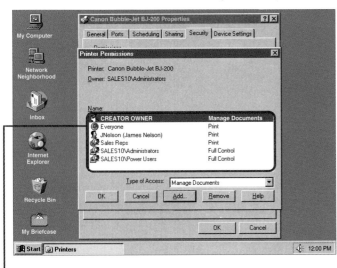

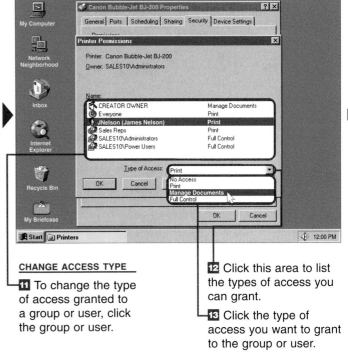

■ This area lists the groups and users you added and the type of access granted to each.

CHANGE ACCESS TYPE

11 To change the type of access granted to a group or user, click the group or user.

12 Click this area to list the types of access you can grant.

13 Click the type of access you want to grant to the group or user.

■ The type of access changes.

? What types of access can I grant to a shared printer?

No Access

Users cannot access the printer.

Print

Users can print and manage their own documents.

Manage Documents

Users can manage all documents waiting to print.

Full Control

Users have full control over the printer.

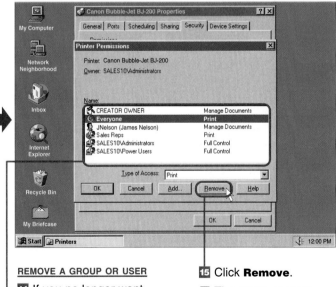

REMOVE A GROUP OR USER

■14 If you no longer want a group or user to have access to your printer, click the group or user.

■15 Click **Remove**.

■ The group or user disappears from the list.

■16 Click **OK** to confirm your changes.

■17 Click **OK** to close the Properties dialog box.

CHANGE THE DEFAULT PRINTER

If you have access to more than one printer, you can choose which printer you want to automatically print your documents.

CHANGE THE DEFAULT PRINTER

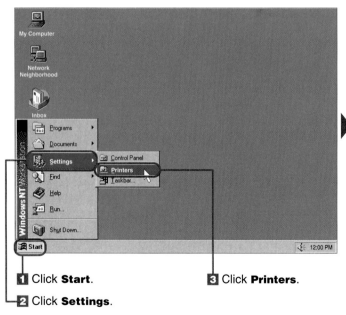

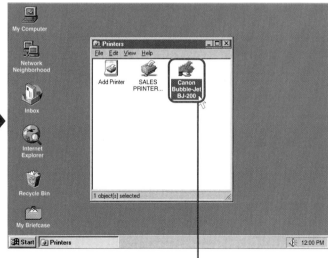

1 Click **Start**.

2 Click **Settings**.

3 Click **Printers**.

■ The Printers window appears, displaying the printers you can use to print your documents.

4 Click the printer you want to set as your new default printer.

206

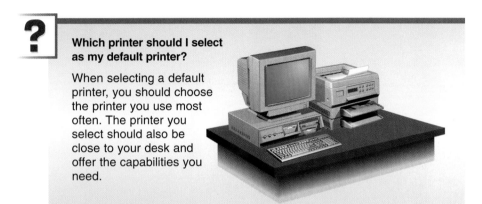

? **Which printer should I select as my default printer?**

When selecting a default printer, you should choose the printer you use most often. The printer you select should also be close to your desk and offer the capabilities you need.

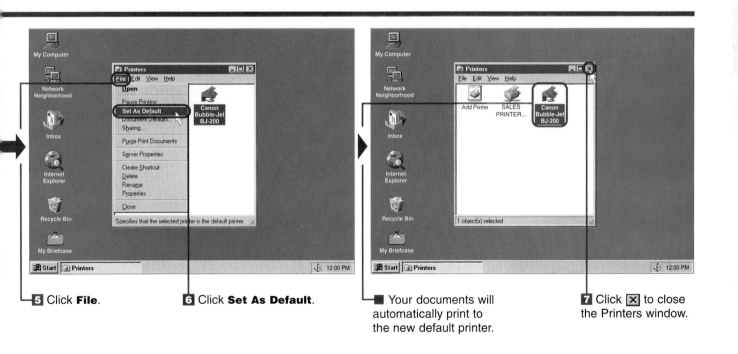

5 Click **File**.

6 Click **Set As Default**.

■ Your documents will automatically print to the new default printer.

7 Click ☒ to close the Printers window.

USE DIAL-UP NETWORKING

When at home or traveling, you can use Dial-Up Networking to access information on the network at work.

You need a modem to connect to the network at work.

USE DIAL-UP NETWORKING

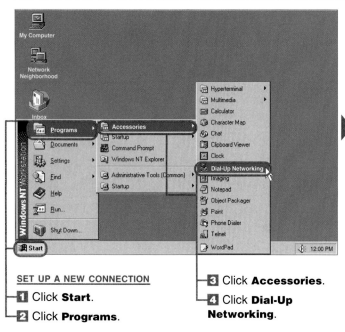

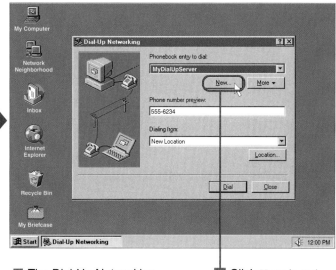

SET UP A NEW CONNECTION

1 Click **Start**.

2 Click **Programs**.

3 Click **Accessories**.

4 Click **Dial-Up Networking**.

■ The Dial-Up Networking dialog box appears.

*Note: If a dialog box appears stating that the phonebook is empty, click **OK** to close the dialog box. Then skip to step **6**.*

5 Click **New** to set up a new connection.

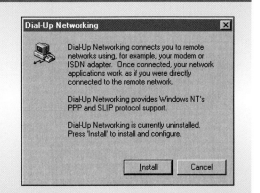

Why does this dialog box appear when I start Dial-Up Networking?

You need to install Dial-Up Networking on your computer. Follow the instructions on your screen to install the program.

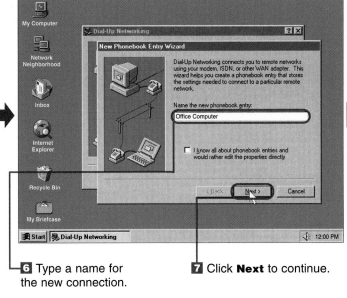

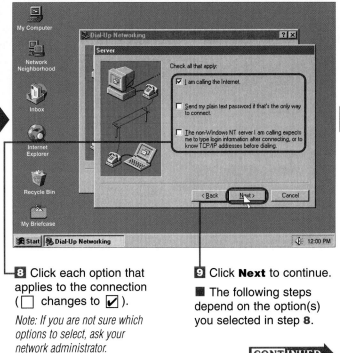

6 Type a name for the new connection.

7 Click **Next** to continue.

8 Click each option that applies to the connection (☐ changes to ☑).

Note: If you are not sure which options to select, ask your network administrator.

9 Click **Next** to continue.

■ The following steps depend on the option(s) you selected in step **8**.

CONTINUED

USE DIAL-UP NETWORKING

You only need to set up a connection to the network at work once. After you set up a connection, you can dial in to the network at any time.

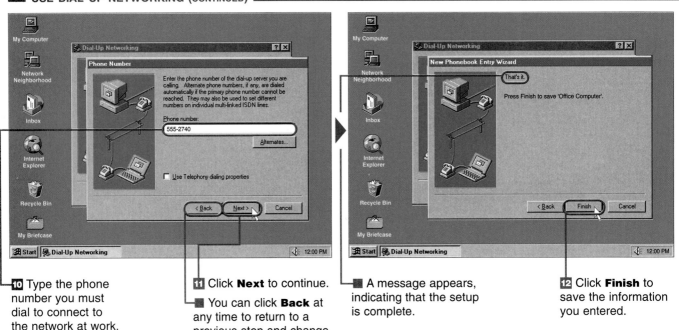

10 Type the phone number you must dial to connect to the network at work.

11 Click **Next** to continue.

You can click **Back** at any time to return to a previous step and change your selections.

A message appears, indicating that the setup is complete.

12 Click **Finish** to save the information you entered.

?

Once I connect to the network at work, what information can I access?

When you connect to the network at work, you can work with the shared information on the network as if the information were stored on your own computer. You can also print documents and exchange electronic mail.

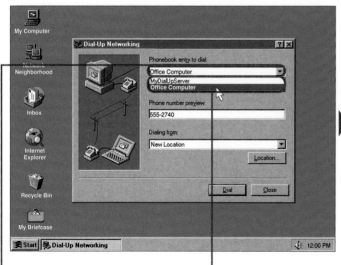

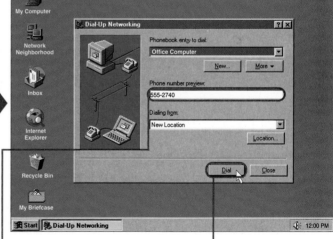

DIAL THE CONNECTION

■ This area displays the name of the connection you set up.

1 If you have created more than one connection, click this area to select the connection you want to dial.

2 Click the connection you want to dial.

■ This area shows the phone number that Windows NT will dial.

3 Click **Dial** to dial the number.

■ The Connect to dialog box appears.

CONTINUED

USE DIAL-UP NETWORKING

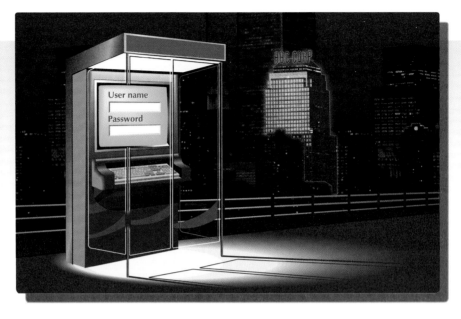

You will need to enter
your user name and
password to access
the network at work.

■■■ USE DIAL-UP NETWORKING (CONTINUED) ■■■

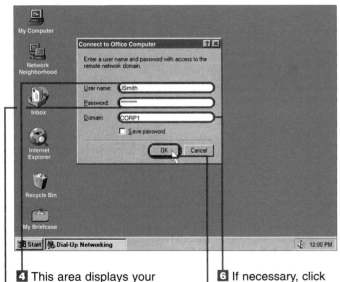

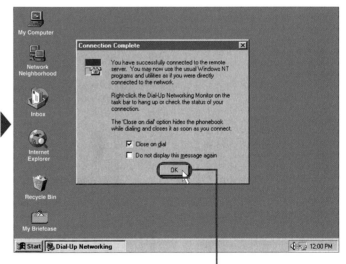

4 This area displays your
user name. To enter a different
user name, drag the mouse I
over the current name until the
text is highlighted. Then type a
new name.

5 Click this area and type
your password.

6 If necessary, click
this area and type the
name of the domain
on the network that
you belong to.

7 Click **OK**.

■ The Connection
Complete dialog box
appears when you are
successfully connected.

8 Click **OK** to close
the dialog box.

■ You can now
access information on
the network at work.

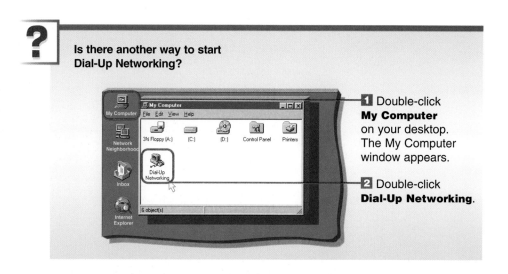

Is there another way to start Dial-Up Networking?

1 Double-click **My Computer** on your desktop. The My Computer window appears.

2 Double-click **Dial-Up Networking**.

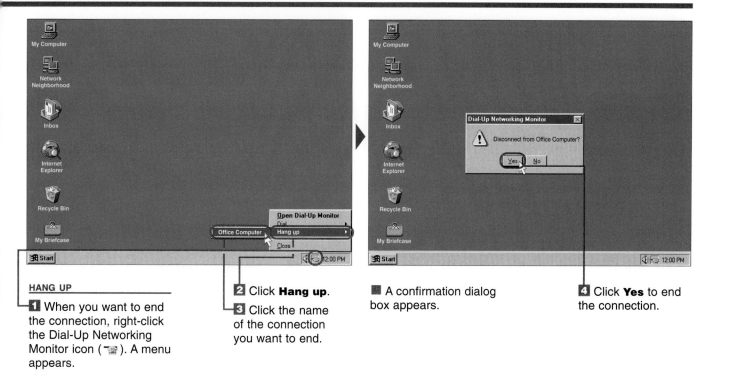

HANG UP

1 When you want to end the connection, right-click the Dial-Up Networking Monitor icon ( ). A menu appears.

2 Click **Hang up**.

3 Click the name of the connection you want to end.

A confirmation dialog box appears.

4 Click **Yes** to end the connection.

CHAPTER 11

Exchange Electronic Mail

You can exchange electronic mail with friends and colleagues over the Internet or a network. In this chapter, you will learn how to compose messages, use the address book and manage your messages.

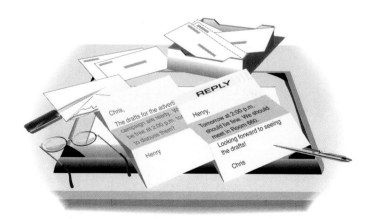

READ MESSAGES

You can easily open
your messages to
read their contents.

Chris,

The drafts for the advertising
campaign are ready. Will you
be free at 2:00 p.m. tomorrow
to discuss them?

Henry

READ MESSAGES

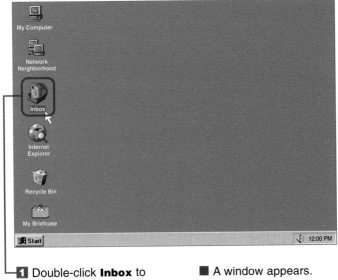

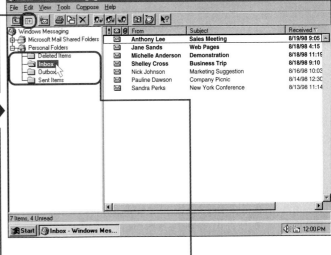

1 Double-click **Inbox** to
start Windows Messaging.

■ A window appears.

2 Click 🖼 to display
the folders that contain
your messages.

*Note: You can click 🖼 to hide
the folders.*

3 Click the folder
containing the messages
you want to read. The
folder is highlighted.

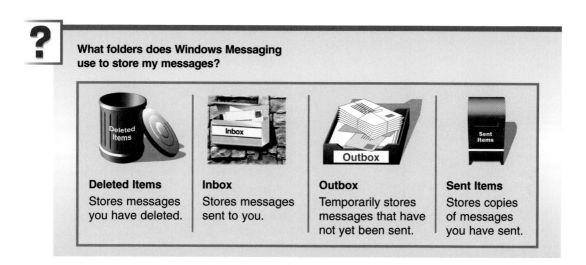

What folders does Windows Messaging use to store my messages?

Deleted Items
Stores messages you have deleted.

Inbox
Stores messages sent to you.

Outbox
Temporarily stores messages that have not yet been sent.

Sent Items
Stores copies of messages you have sent.

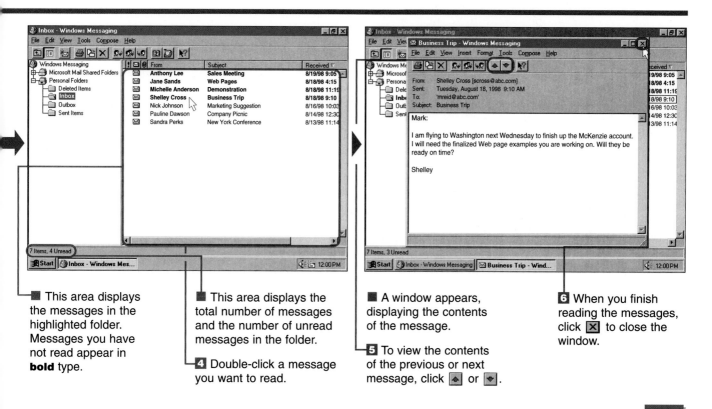

■ This area displays the messages in the highlighted folder. Messages you have not read appear in **bold** type.

■ This area displays the total number of messages and the number of unread messages in the folder.

4 Double-click a message you want to read.

■ A window appears, displaying the contents of the message.

5 To view the contents of the previous or next message, click ▲ or ▼.

6 When you finish reading the messages, click ✕ to close the window.

COMPOSE A MESSAGE

You can send a message over the Internet or a network to exchange ideas or request information.

COMPOSE A MESSAGE

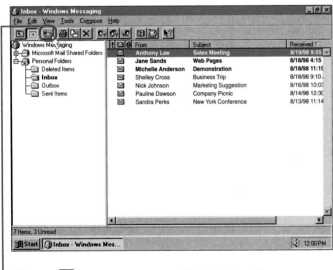

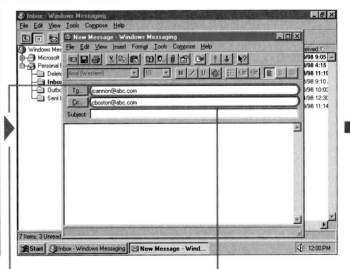

1 Click 📧 to compose a new message.

■ The New Message window appears.

2 Type the e-mail address of the person you want to receive the message.

Note: To select a name from the address book, see page 222. Then skip to step 4.

3 To send a carbon copy of the message to another person, click this area and then type the e-mail address.

Note: For information on sending a carbon copy, see the top of page 223.

218

How can I express emotions in e-mail messages?

You can use special characters, called smileys or emoticons, to express emotions in e-mail messages. These characters resemble human faces if you turn them sideways.

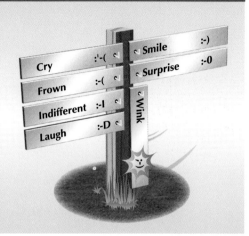

Cry :'-(	Smile :-)
Frown :-(	Surprise :-0
Indifferent :-I	Wink
Laugh :-D	

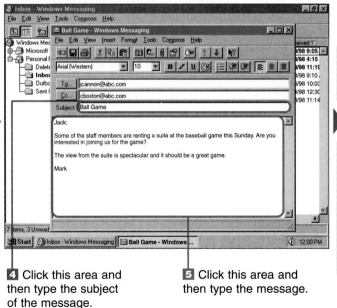

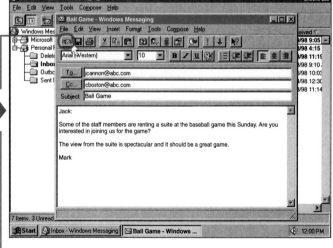

4 Click this area and then type the subject of the message.

5 Click this area and then type the message.

6 Click ☒ to send the message.

■ Windows Messaging stores a copy of each message you send in the Sent Items folder.

ADD A NAME TO THE ADDRESS BOOK

You can use the address book to store the e-mail addresses of people you frequently send messages to.

ADD A NAME TO THE ADDRESS BOOK

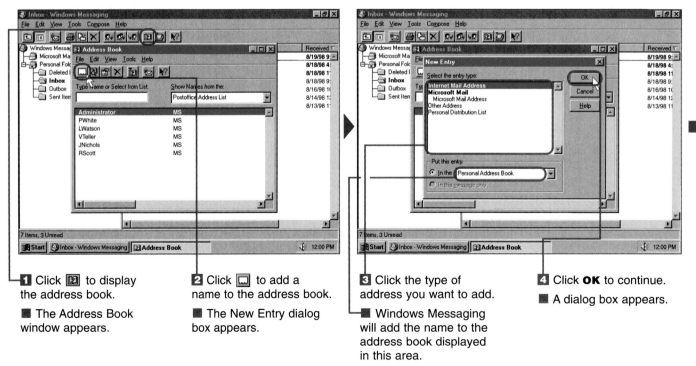

1 Click 🖼 to display the address book.

■ The Address Book window appears.

2 Click 🔲 to add a name to the address book.

■ The New Entry dialog box appears.

3 Click the type of address you want to add.

■ Windows Messaging will add the name to the address book displayed in this area.

4 Click **OK** to continue.

■ A dialog box appears.

Which address books are available?

Postoffice Address List

Lists the address of each person
on your network. This list is set
up by your network administrator.

Personal Address Book

Lists the address of each person
you add to the address book.

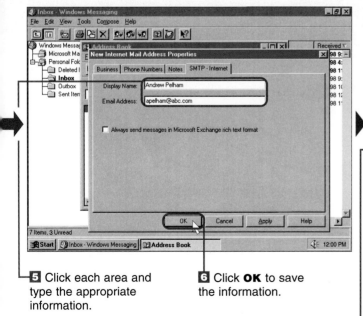

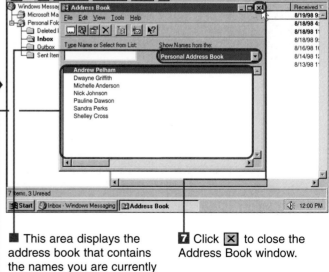

5 Click each area and
type the appropriate
information.

*Note: The information you need
to enter depends on the type of
address you selected in step 3.*

6 Click **OK** to save
the information.

■ This area displays the
address book that contains
the names you are currently
viewing. You can click this
area to view a different
address book.

■ The name appears in
the address book.

7 Click ⊠ to close the
Address Book window.

SELECT A NAME FROM THE ADDRESS BOOK

When sending a message, you can select the name of the person you want to receive the message from the address book.

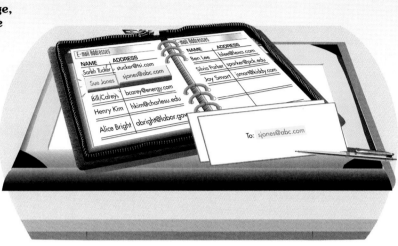

Selecting names from the address book saves you from having to remember e-mail addresses you often use.

SELECT A NAME FROM THE ADDRESS BOOK

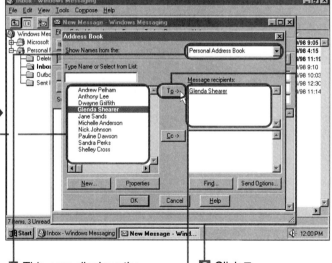

■1 In the New Message window, click 📖 to select a name from the address book.

Note: To display the New Message window, perform step 1 on page 218.

■ The Address Book dialog box appears.

■ This area displays the address book that contains the names you are currently viewing. You can click this area to view a different address book.

■2 Click the name of the person you want to receive the message.

■3 Click **To**.

■ This area displays the name of the person you selected.

■ You can repeat steps **2** and **3** for each person you want to receive the message.

? How can I address a message
I want to send?

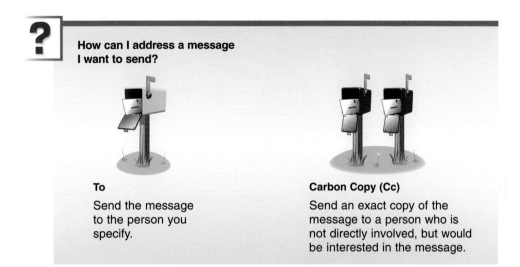

To

Send the message
to the person you
specify.

Carbon Copy (Cc)

Send an exact copy of the
message to a person who is
not directly involved, but would
be interested in the message.

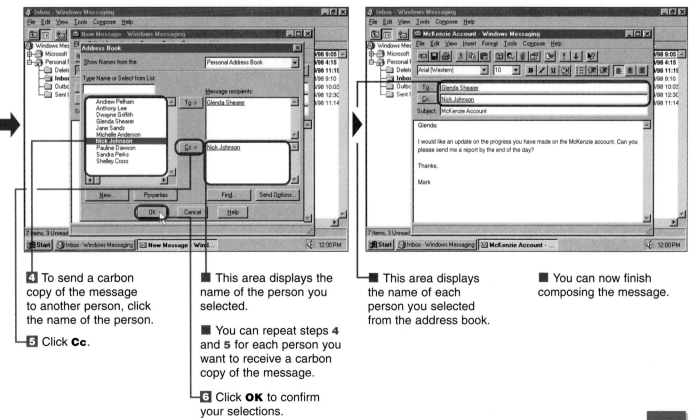

4 To send a carbon
copy of the message
to another person, click
the name of the person.

5 Click **Cc**.

■ This area displays the
name of the person you
selected.

■ You can repeat steps **4**
and **5** for each person you
want to receive a carbon
copy of the message.

6 Click **OK** to confirm
your selections.

■ This area displays
the name of each
person you selected
from the address book.

■ You can now finish
composing the message.

ATTACH A FILE TO A MESSAGE

You can attach a file to a message you are sending. Attaching a file is useful when you want to include additional information with a message.

ATTACH A FILE TO A MESSAGE

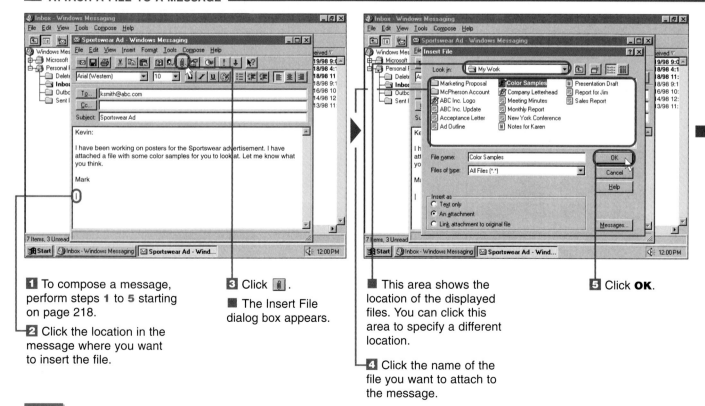

1 To compose a message, perform steps **1** to **5** starting on page 218.

2 Click the location in the message where you want to insert the file.

3 Click 📎.

■ The Insert File dialog box appears.

■ This area shows the location of the displayed files. You can click this area to specify a different location.

4 Click the name of the file you want to attach to the message.

5 Click **OK**.

?

What types of files can I attach to a message?

You can attach files such as documents, pictures, programs, sounds and videos to a message. The computer receiving the message must have the necessary hardware and software to display or play the file.

Attachments

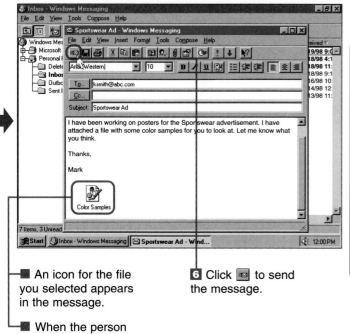

■ An icon for the file you selected appears in the message.

■ When the person receives the message, they can double-click the icon to display the contents of the file.

6 Click ⊠ to send the message.

■ When you receive a message with a file, a paper clip (📎) appears beside the message.

REPLY TO A MESSAGE

You can reply to a
message to answer a
question or comment
on the message.

REPLY TO A MESSAGE

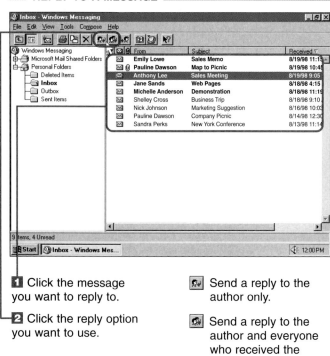

1 Click the message
you want to reply to.

2 Click the reply option
you want to use.

Send a reply to the
author only.

Send a reply to the
author and everyone
who received the
original message.

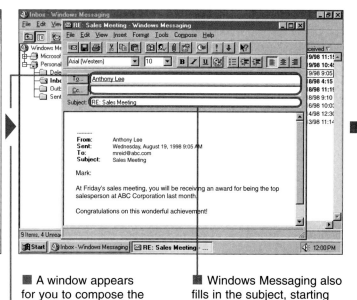

■ A window appears
for you to compose the
message.

■ Windows Messaging
fills in the e-mail
address(es) for you.

■ Windows Messaging also
fills in the subject, starting
the subject with **RE:**.

226

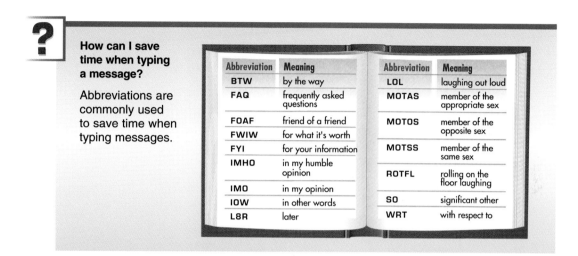

How can I save time when typing a message?

Abbreviations are commonly used to save time when typing messages.

Abbreviation	Meaning
BTW	by the way
FAQ	frequently asked questions
FOAF	friend of a friend
FWIW	for what it's worth
FYI	for your information
IMHO	in my humble opinion
IMO	in my opinion
IOW	in other words
L8R	later

Abbreviation	Meaning
LOL	laughing out loud
MOTAS	member of the appropriate sex
MOTOS	member of the opposite sex
MOTSS	member of the same sex
ROTFL	rolling on the floor laughing
SO	significant other
WRT	with respect to

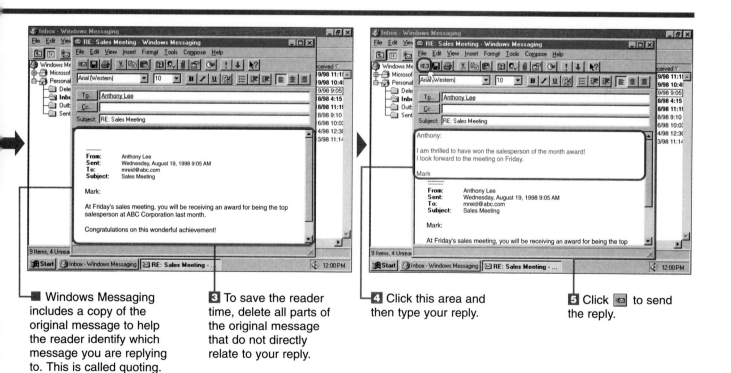

■ Windows Messaging includes a copy of the original message to help the reader identify which message you are replying to. This is called quoting.

3 To save the reader time, delete all parts of the original message that do not directly relate to your reply.

4 Click this area and then type your reply.

5 Click 🖾 to send the reply.

FORWARD A MESSAGE

After reading a message, you can add comments and then forward the message to a friend or colleague.

FORWARD A MESSAGE

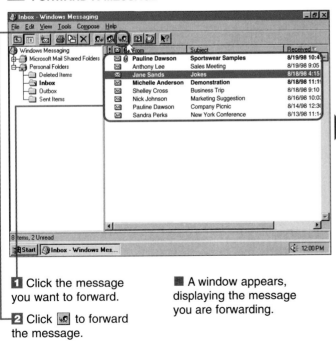

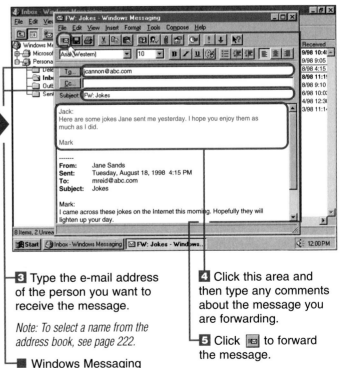

1 Click the message you want to forward.

2 Click ⬛ to forward the message.

■ A window appears, displaying the message you are forwarding.

3 Type the e-mail address of the person you want to receive the message.

Note: To select a name from the address book, see page 222.

■ Windows Messaging fills in the subject for you, starting the subject with **FW:**.

4 Click this area and then type any comments about the message you are forwarding.

5 Click ⬛ to forward the message.

DELETE A MESSAGE

You can delete a message you no longer need. Deleting messages prevents your folders from becoming cluttered with messages.

DELETE A MESSAGE

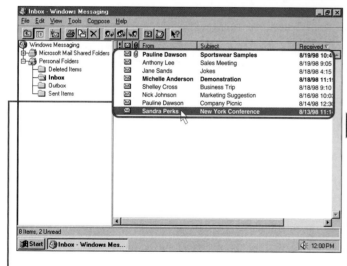

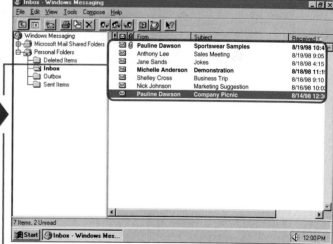

1 Click the message you want to delete.

2 Press the Delete key.

■ Windows Messaging removes the message from the current folder and places the message in the Deleted Items folder.

■ Windows Messaging empties the Deleted Items folder when you exit the program.

SORT MESSAGES

You can sort your
messages to quickly
find the messages
you want to view.

SORT MESSAGES

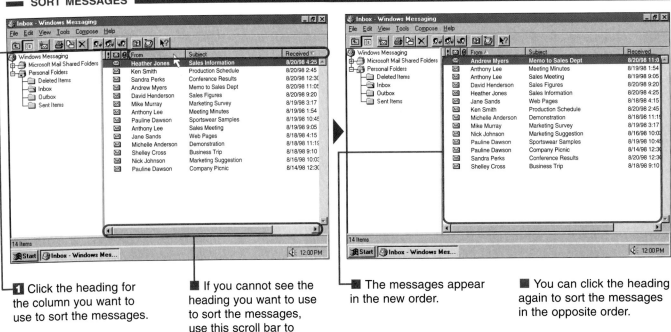

1 Click the heading for the column you want to use to sort the messages.

■ If you cannot see the heading you want to use to sort the messages, use this scroll bar to display the heading.

■ The messages appear in the new order.

■ You can click the heading again to sort the messages in the opposite order.

PRINT MESSAGES

You can produce
a paper copy of
a message you
received.

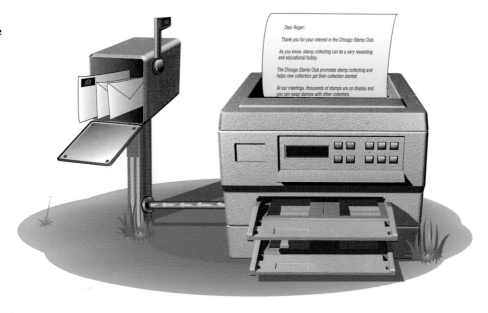

PRINT MESSAGES

1 Click the message
you want to print.

2 Click 🖨 to print
the message.

CHAPTER 12

Browse the Web

In this chapter you will learn how to display Web pages, change your home page, search the Web and more.

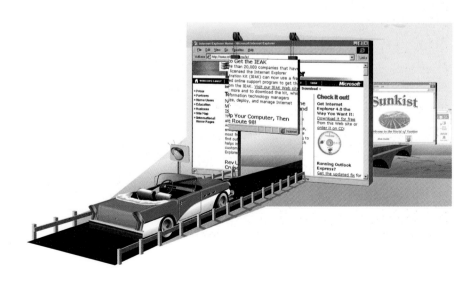

START INTERNET EXPLORER

You can start Internet Explorer to browse through the information on the Web.

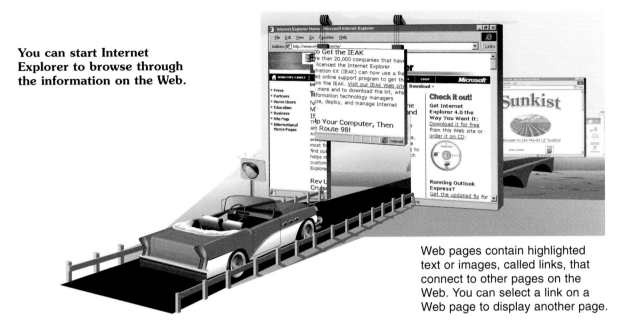

Web pages contain highlighted text or images, called links, that connect to other pages on the Web. You can select a link on a Web page to display another page.

START INTERNET EXPLORER

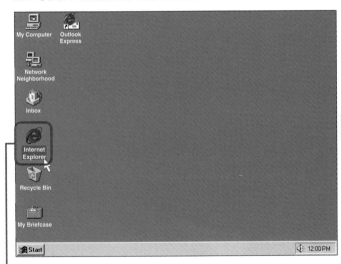

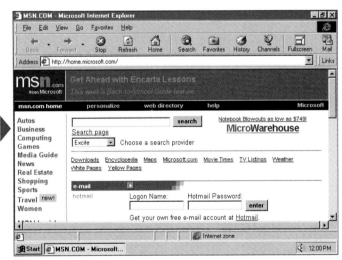

1 Double-click **Internet Explorer** to begin browsing the Web.

Note: If you are not connected to the Internet, a dialog box appears that allows you to connect.

■ The Microsoft Internet Explorer window appears, displaying your home page.

Note: A different Web page may appear on your screen.

Why does my Internet Explorer screen look different than the screen shown below?

Windows NT comes with Internet Explorer version 2.0. You can visit the Microsoft Web site at www.microsoft.com to obtain the latest version of Internet Explorer. This book shows you how to use Internet Explorer version 4.0.

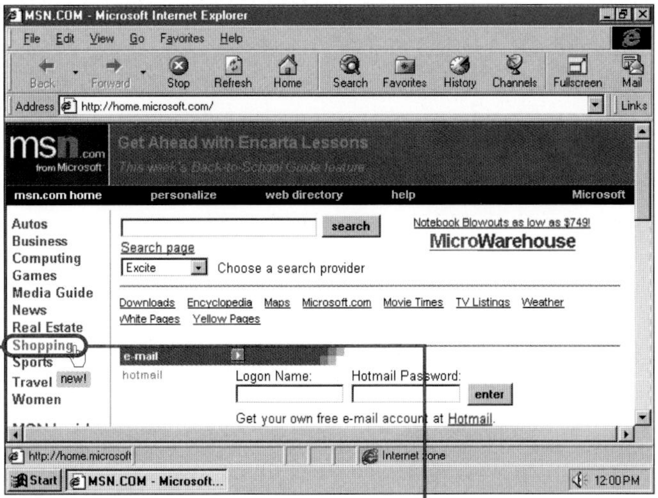

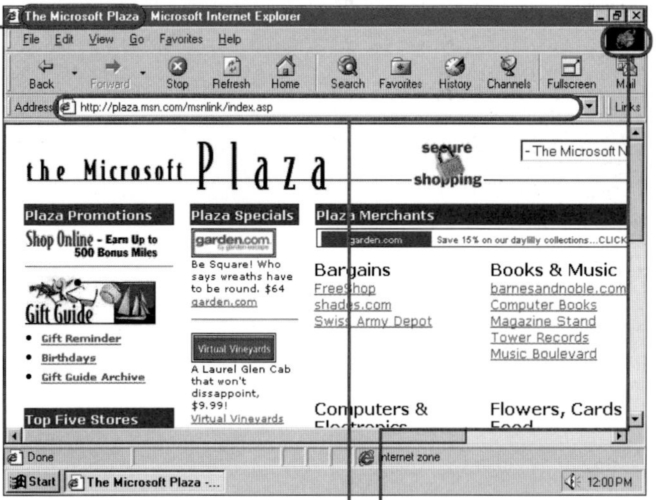

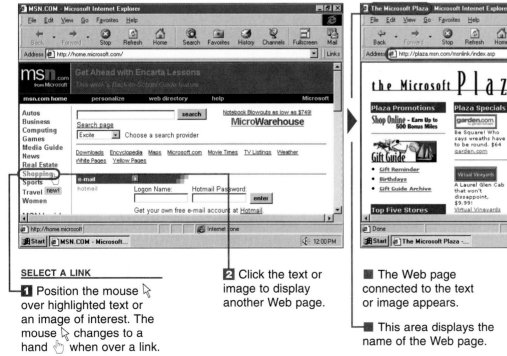

SELECT A LINK

1 Position the mouse over highlighted text or an image of interest. The mouse changes to a hand when over a link.

2 Click the text or image to display another Web page.

■ The Web page connected to the text or image appears.

■ This area displays the name of the Web page.

■ This icon is animated as the Web page transfers to your computer.

■ This area displays the address of the Web page.

DISPLAY A SPECIFIC WEB PAGE

You can easily display a page on the Web that you have heard or read about.

You need to know the address of the Web page you want to view. Each page on the Web has a unique address, called a Uniform Resource Locator (URL).

DISPLAY A SPECIFIC WEB PAGE

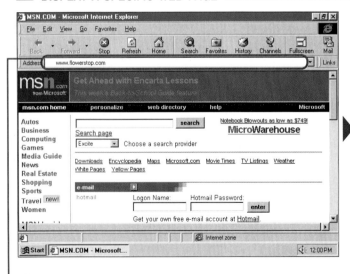

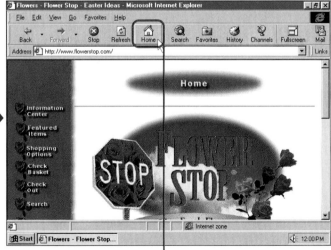

■1 Click this area to highlight the current Web page address.

■2 Type the address of the Web page you want to view and then press the Enter key.

■ When you start typing the address of a Web page you have previously typed, Internet Explorer completes the address for you.

■ The Web page appears on your screen.

DISPLAY YOUR HOME PAGE

■1 Click **Home** to display your home page at any time.

CHANGE YOUR HOME PAGE

You can specify which Web page you want to appear each time you start Internet Explorer. This page is called your home page.

CHANGE YOUR HOME PAGE

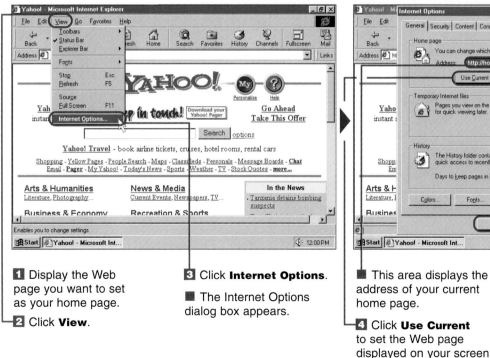

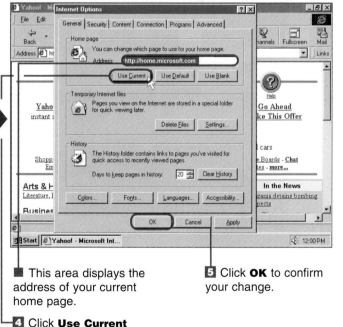

1 Display the Web page you want to set as your home page.

2 Click **View**.

3 Click **Internet Options**.

■ The Internet Options dialog box appears.

■ This area displays the address of your current home page.

4 Click **Use Current** to set the Web page displayed on your screen as your new home page.

5 Click **OK** to confirm your change.

STOP TRANSFER OF INFORMATION

If a Web page is taking a long time to appear on your screen, you can stop transferring the page and try connecting again later.

STOP TRANSFER OF INFORMATION

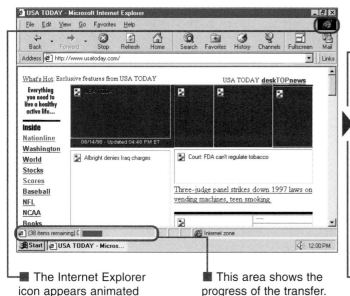

■ The Internet Explorer icon appears animated when information is transferring to your computer.

■ This area shows the progress of the transfer.

1 Click **Stop** to stop the transfer of information.

■ You may also want to stop the transfer of information when you realize a Web page does not interest you.

MOVE THROUGH WEB PAGES

You can move back and forth through Web pages you have viewed since you last started Internet Explorer.

MOVE THROUGH WEB PAGES

1 Click **Back** to display the last Web page you viewed.

■ Click **Forward** to move forward through the Web pages you have viewed.

You can display a list of the Web pages you have viewed.

1 Click ▼ beside **Back** or **Forward** to display a list of Web pages you have viewed. A menu appears.

2 Click the Web page you want to view.

ADD A WEB PAGE TO FAVORITES

You can use the Favorites feature to create a list of Web pages you frequently visit. You can quickly return to any Web page in the list.

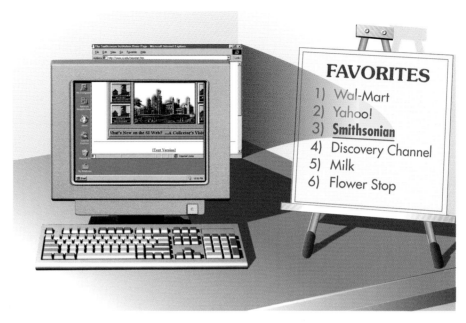

FAVORITES
1) Wal-Mart
2) Yahoo!
3) **Smithsonian**
4) Discovery Channel
5) Milk
6) Flower Stop

ADD A WEB PAGE TO FAVORITES

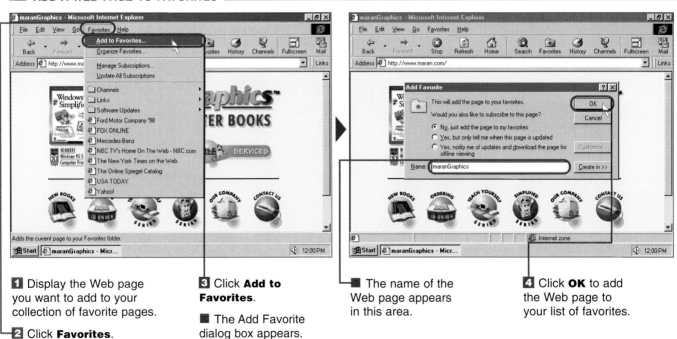

1 Display the Web page you want to add to your collection of favorite pages.

2 Click **Favorites**.

3 Click **Add to Favorites**.

■ The Add Favorite dialog box appears.

■ The name of the Web page appears in this area.

4 Click **OK** to add the Web page to your list of favorites.

What is the benefit of adding Web pages to my list of favorites?

Web page addresses can be long and complex. Selecting Web pages from your list of favorites saves you from having to remember and constantly retype the same addresses.

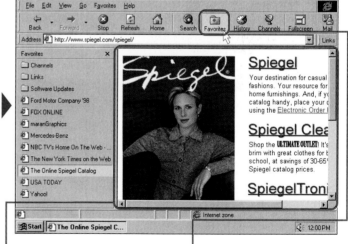

VIEW A FAVORITE WEB PAGE

1 Click **Favorites** to display a list of your favorite Web pages.

■ A list of your favorite Web pages appears in this area.

2 Click the favorite Web page you want to view.

Note: To display the favorite Web pages in a folder, click the folder ( ).

■ The favorite Web page you selected appears in this area.

■ You can repeat step **2** to view another favorite Web page.

3 When you finish viewing your list of favorite Web pages, click **Favorites** to hide the list.

SEARCH THE WEB

You can find pages on the Web that discuss topics of interest to you.

There are search tools available on the Web that catalog information about millions of Web pages. Popular search tools include Lycos, Yahoo! and Excite.

▬▬▬ SEARCH THE WEB ▬▬▬▬▬▬▬▬▬▬▬▬▬▬▬

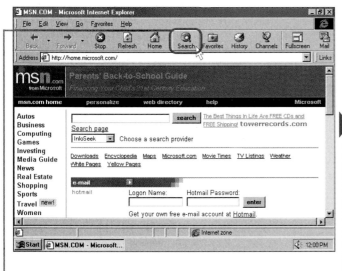

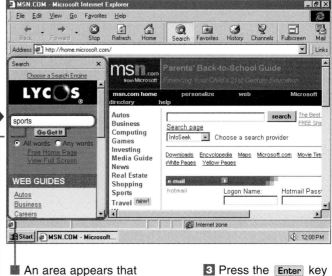

1 Click **Search** to find Web pages of interest.

*Note: The Security Warning dialog box may appear if Microsoft needs to transfer information to your computer. Click **Yes** to transfer the information.*

■ An area appears that allows you to search for Web pages.

2 Click this area and then type a word you want to search for.

3 Press the `Enter` key to start the search.

How do search tools find Web pages?

Some search tools use a program, called a robot, to scan the Web for new and updated pages. Thousands of new Web pages are located and cataloged by robots every day. New pages are also cataloged when people submit information about the pages they have created.

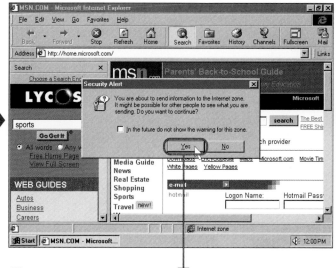

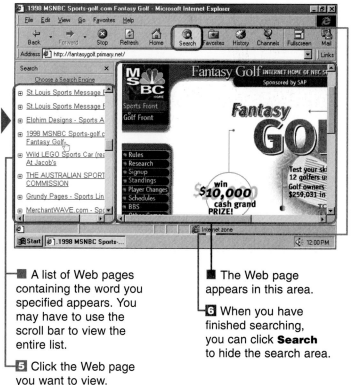

■ The Security Alert dialog box appears.

4 Click **Yes** to continue.

■ A list of Web pages containing the word you specified appears. You may have to use the scroll bar to view the entire list.

5 Click the Web page you want to view.

■ The Web page appears in this area.

6 When you have finished searching, you can click **Search** to hide the search area.

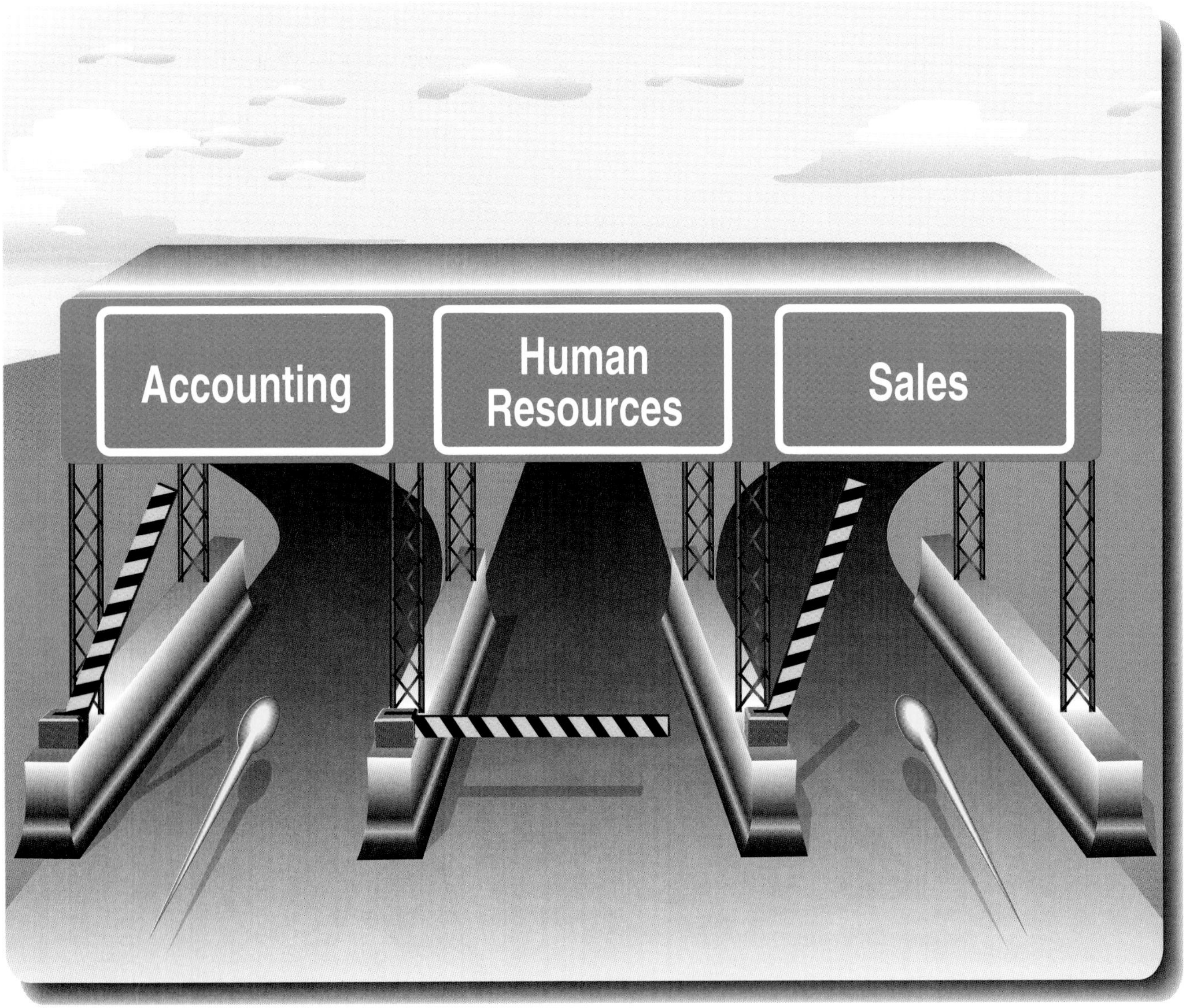
Accounting
Human Resources
Sales

CHAPTER 13

Manage User and Group Accounts

In this chapter you will learn how to use the Windows NT server to manage user and group accounts on a network.

ADD A COMPUTER TO THE NETWORK

Before a new person can access the network, you must add their computer to the network.

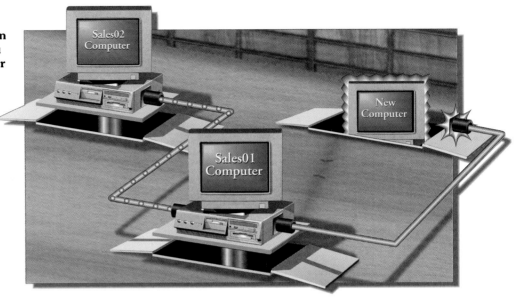

Sales02 Computer

New Computer

Sales01 Computer

ADD A COMPUTER TO THE NETWORK

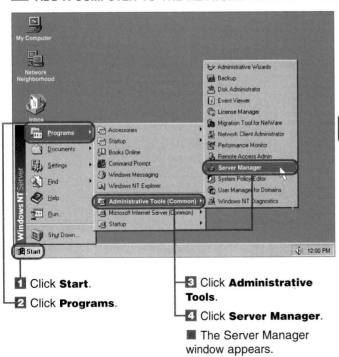

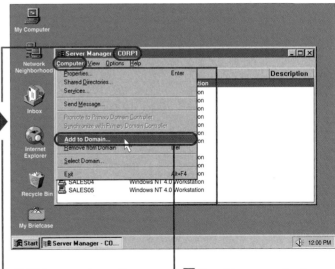

1 Click **Start**.

2 Click **Programs**.

3 Click **Administrative Tools**.

4 Click **Server Manager**.

■ The Server Manager window appears.

■ This area shows the name of the domain the new computer will belong to. A domain is a group of computers on the network that are administered together.

5 To add a computer to the domain, click **Computer**.

6 Click **Add to Domain**.

■ The Add Computer To Domain dialog box appears.

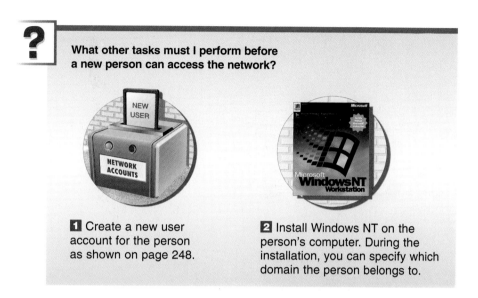

What other tasks must I perform before a new person can access the network?

1 Create a new user account for the person as shown on page 248.

2 Install Windows NT on the person's computer. During the installation, you can specify which domain the person belongs to.

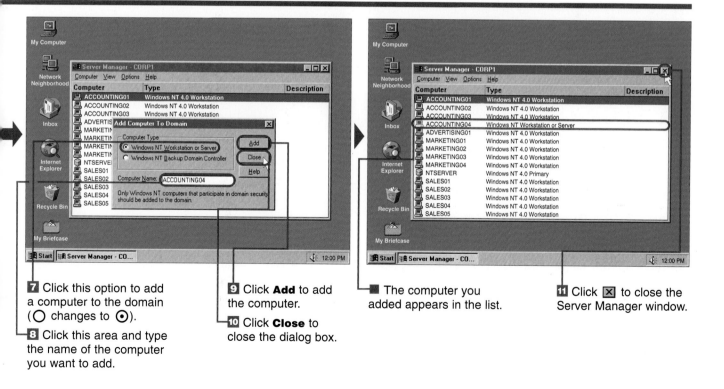

7 Click this option to add a computer to the domain (○ changes to ⊙).

8 Click this area and type the name of the computer you want to add.

9 Click **Add** to add the computer.

10 Click **Close** to close the dialog box.

■ The computer you added appears in the list.

11 Click ☒ to close the Server Manager window.

CREATE A NEW USER ACCOUNT

Before a new person can access information on the network, you must create a new user account for the person.

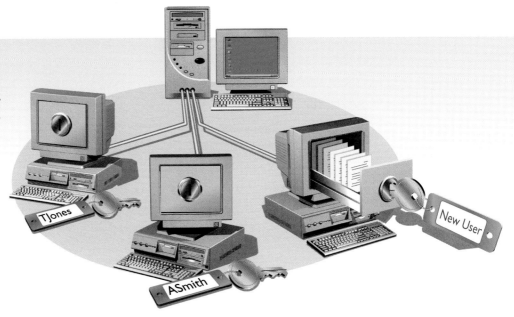

CREATE A NEW USER ACCOUNT

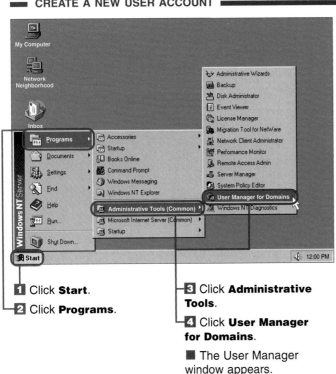

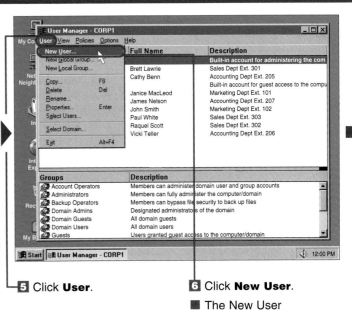

1 Click **Start**.

2 Click **Programs**.

3 Click **Administrative Tools**.

4 Click **User Manager for Domains**.

■ The User Manager window appears.

5 Click **User**.

6 Click **New User**.

■ The New User dialog box appears.

? What password should I use?

When choosing a password, do not use
words that people can easily associate
with the user, such as their name or
favorite sport. The most effective
password connects two words or
number sequences with a special
character (example: easy@123).
To increase security, make sure the
user memorizes the password and
does not write it down.

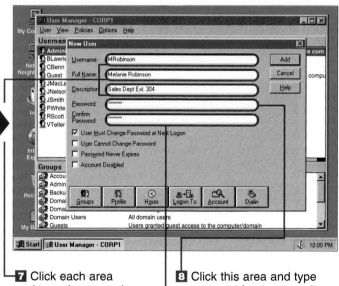

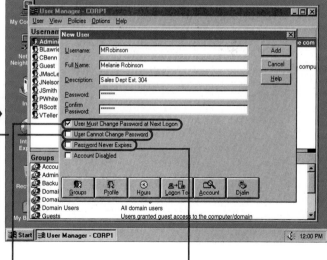

7 Click each area
and type the person's
user name, full name
and description.

8 Click this area and type
a password for the user. An
asterisk (*) appears for each
character you type to protect
the password.

9 Click this area and retype
the password to confirm the
password.

■ This option instructs the
user to change the password
the next time the user
connects to the network.

■ This option prevents
the user from changing
the password.

■ This option prevents the
password from expiring.

10 You can click an option
to turn the option on (☑)
or off (☐).

CONTINUED ▶

CREATE A NEW USER ACCOUNT

You can specify which groups you want a new user to belong to. The user will have the same access to information on the network that is granted to each group.

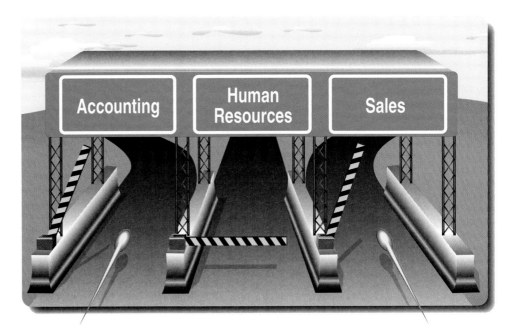

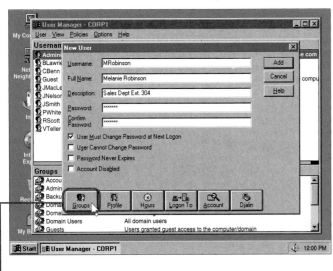

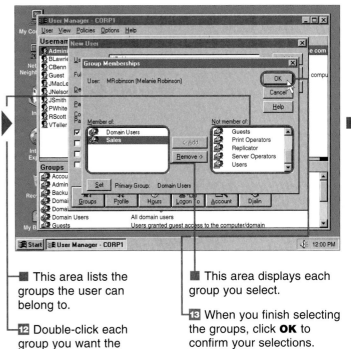

11 To specify which groups you want the new user to belong to, click **Groups**.

■ The Group Memberships dialog box appears.

■ This area lists the groups the user can belong to.

12 Double-click each group you want the user to belong to.

■ This area displays each group you select.

13 When you finish selecting the groups, click **OK** to confirm your selections.

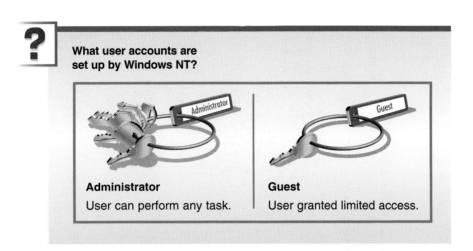

**What user accounts are
set up by Windows NT?**

Administrator
User can perform any task.

Guest
User granted limited access.

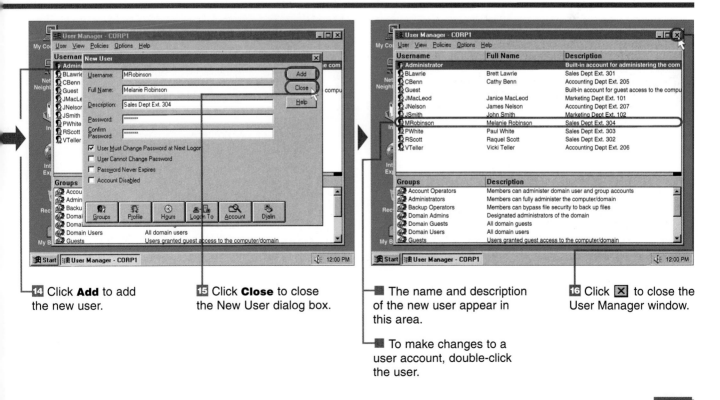

14 Click **Add** to add
the new user.

15 Click **Close** to close
the New User dialog box.

■ The name and description
of the new user appear in
this area.

16 Click **X** to close the
User Manager window.

■ To make changes to a
user account, double-click
the user.

CREATE A NEW GROUP ACCOUNT

You can create a new group account. Each member of the group will have the same access to information on the network.

Creating a new group account is useful when people working on a project need to share the same information and equipment.

CREATE A NEW GROUP ACCOUNT

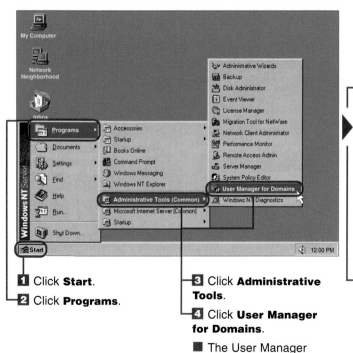

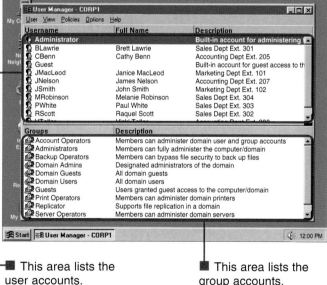

1 Click **Start**.

2 Click **Programs**.

3 Click **Administrative Tools**.

4 Click **User Manager for Domains**.

■ The User Manager window appears.

■ This area lists the user accounts.

■ This area lists the group accounts.

? **What are some of the group accounts set up by Windows NT?**

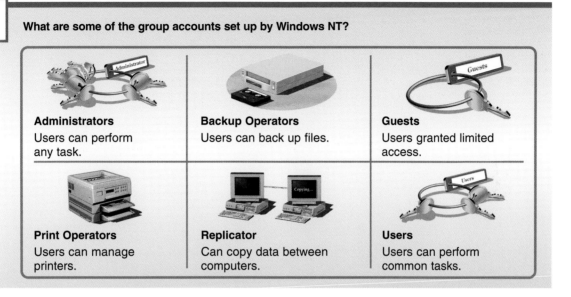

Administrators
Users can perform any task.

Backup Operators
Users can back up files.

Guests
Users granted limited access.

Print Operators
Users can manage printers.

Replicator
Can copy data between computers.

Users
Users can perform common tasks.

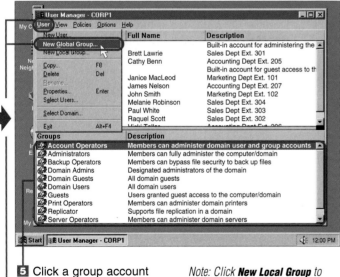

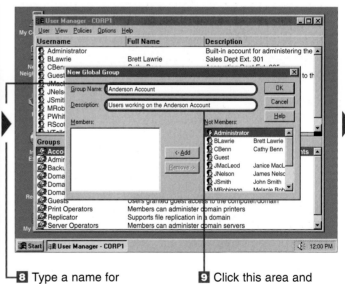

5 Click a group account in this area.

6 Click **User**.

7 Click **New Global Group** to create a group that can be used by all computers on the network.

*Note: Click **New Local Group** to create a group that can only be used by computers within the same domain. A domain is a group of computers on a network that are administered together.*

■ The New Global Group dialog box appears.

8 Type a name for the group.

9 Click this area and type a description for the group.

CONTINUED

CREATE A NEW GROUP ACCOUNT

You can specify
which users you
want to belong
to a new group
account.

SALES GROUP

■ CREATE A NEW GROUP ACCOUNT (CONTINUED)

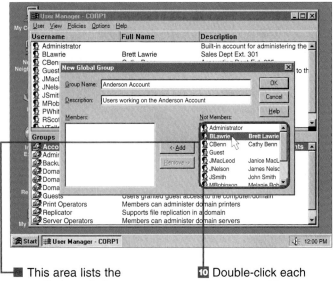

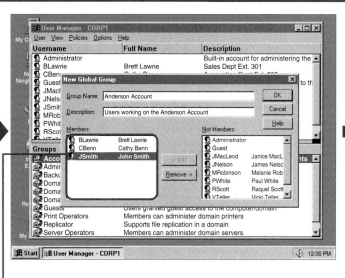

■ This area lists the
users that can belong
to the group.

10 Double-click each
user you want to
belong to the group.

■ This area displays
each user you select.

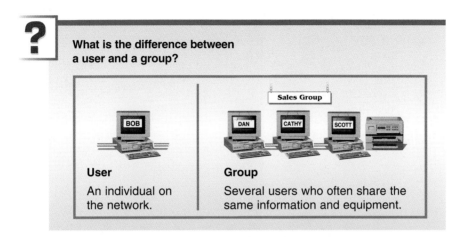

What is the difference between a user and a group?

User
An individual on the network.

Group
Several users who often share the same information and equipment.

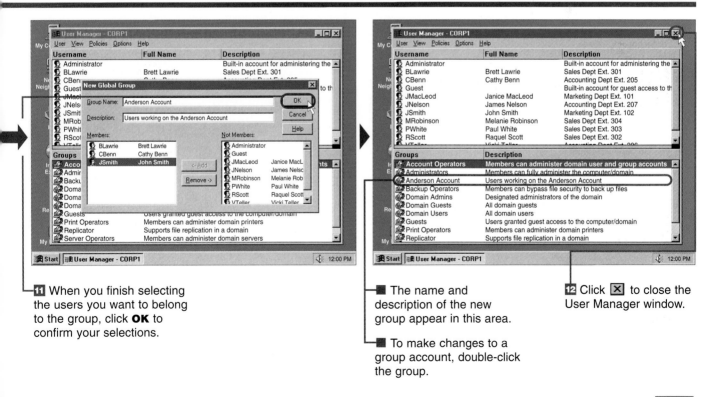

■11 When you finish selecting the users you want to belong to the group, click **OK** to confirm your selections.

■ The name and description of the new group appear in this area.

■ To make changes to a group account, double-click the group.

■12 Click ✖ to close the User Manager window.

DELETE A USER OR GROUP ACCOUNT

You can delete a user or group account you no longer need.

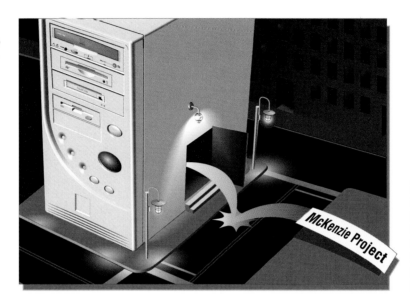

For example, you may have created a group account to allow colleagues working on a project to share information. When the project is complete, you can delete the group account.

■■ DELETE A USER OR GROUP ACCOUNT ■■

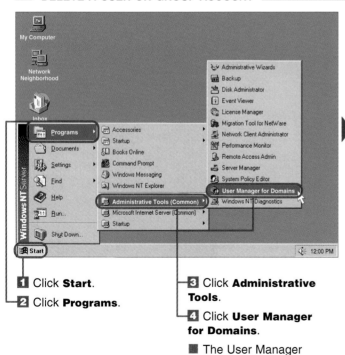

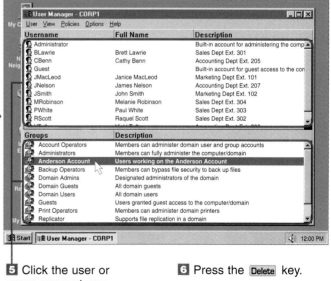

1 Click **Start**.

2 Click **Programs**.

3 Click **Administrative Tools**.

4 Click **User Manager for Domains**.

■ The User Manager window appears.

5 Click the user or group account you want to delete.

6 Press the Delete key.

? What should I consider when deleting a user or group account?

■ You cannot recover deleted user or group accounts.

■ You cannot delete user or group accounts set up by Windows NT.

■ If you delete a group account and then create a new group with the same name, the new group will not have the permissions of the old group.

■ Deleting a group account removes only the group, not the users that were members of the group.

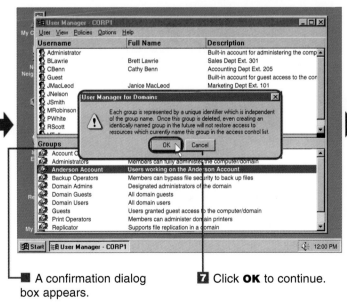

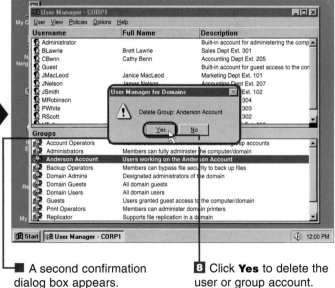

■ A confirmation dialog box appears.

7 Click **OK** to continue.

■ A second confirmation dialog box appears.

8 Click **Yes** to delete the user or group account.

■ The user or group account disappears from the User Manager window.

ASSIGN USER AND GROUP RIGHTS

You can change the rights granted to users and groups. Rights determine what a user or group can do on a computer.

ASSIGN USER AND GROUP RIGHTS

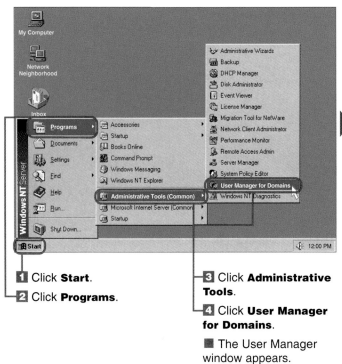

1 Click **Start**.

2 Click **Programs**.

3 Click **Administrative Tools**.

4 Click **User Manager for Domains**.

■ The User Manager window appears.

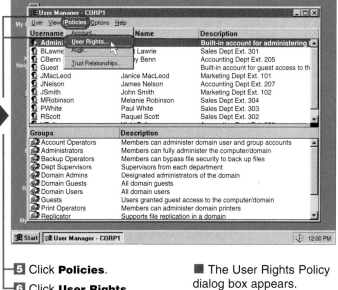

5 Click **Policies**.

6 Click **User Rights**.

■ The User Rights Policy dialog box appears.

What rights can I assign to users and groups?

RIGHTS

• Access this computer from network
• Add workstations to domain
• Back up files and directories
• Change the system time
• Force shutdown from a remote system
• Load and unload device drivers
• Log on locally
• Manage auditing and security log
• Restore files and directories
• Shut down the system
• Take ownership of files or other objects

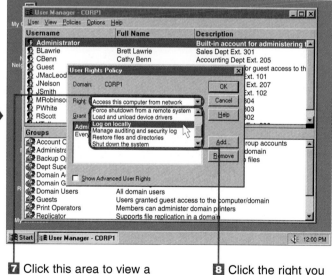

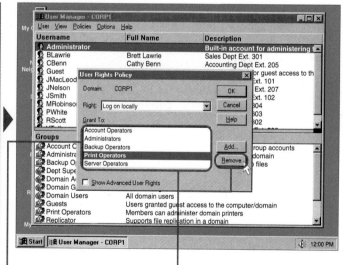

7 Click this area to view a list of rights you can assign to users and groups.

8 Click the right you want to work with.

■ This area lists the groups who have been assigned the right you selected.

REMOVE A GROUP

9 To remove a group you no longer want to have the right, click the group.

10 Click **Remove**. The group disappears from the list.

CONTINUED ▶

ASSIGN USER AND GROUP RIGHTS

Each right allows a
person to perform
certain tasks on a
computer. You can
assign a right to
additional groups
and users.

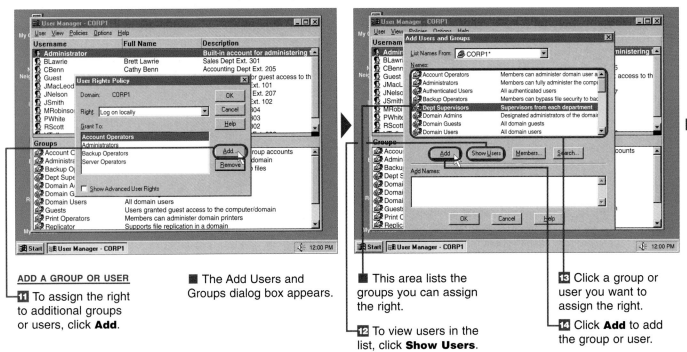

<u>ADD A GROUP OR USER</u>

11 To assign the right
to additional groups
or users, click **Add**.

■ The Add Users and
Groups dialog box appears.

■ This area lists the
groups you can assign
the right.

12 To view users in the
list, click **Show Users**.

13 Click a group or
user you want to
assign the right.

14 Click **Add** to add
the group or user.

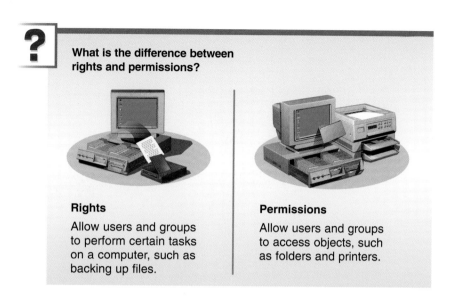

?

What is the difference between rights and permissions?

Rights

Allow users and groups to perform certain tasks on a computer, such as backing up files.

Permissions

Allow users and groups to access objects, such as folders and printers.

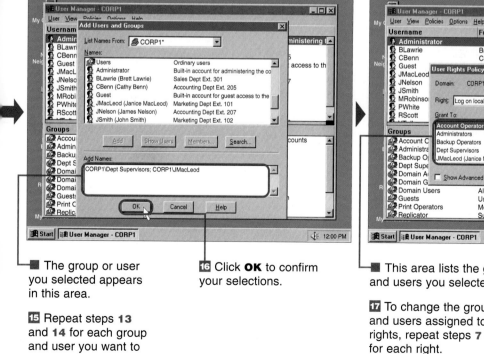

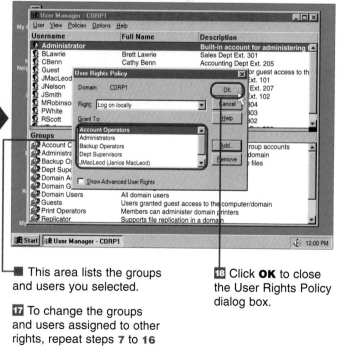

■ The group or user you selected appears in this area.

15 Repeat steps **13** and **14** for each group and user you want to assign the right.

16 Click **OK** to confirm your selections.

■ This area lists the groups and users you selected.

17 To change the groups and users assigned to other rights, repeat steps **7** to **16** for each right.

18 Click **OK** to close the User Rights Policy dialog box.

CHANGE ACCOUNT POLICIES

You can control how passwords are used by everyone on the network.

CHANGE ACCOUNT POLICIES

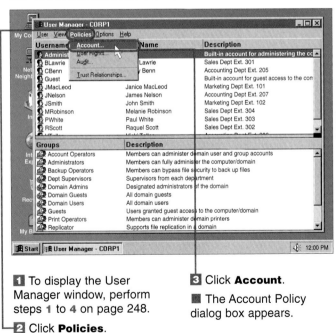

1 To display the User Manager window, perform steps **1** to **4** on page 248.

2 Click **Policies**.

3 Click **Account**.

■ The Account Policy dialog box appears.

4 Click an option to specify a time limit for a password, after which the user must change the password (○ changes to ◉).

5 If you selected the second option, click this area and type the number of days.

?

Why would I want to restrict the way passwords are used?

Restricting the way passwords are used can improve security on the network. For example, you can specify that users must have a password with at least a certain number of characters. Longer passwords are usually more difficult to guess.

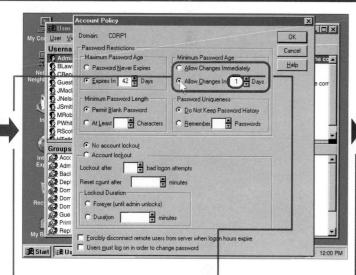

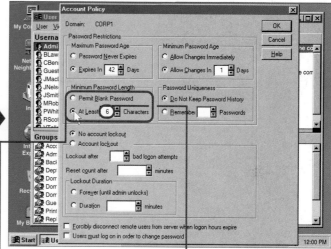

6 Click an option to specify when users can change their passwords (○ changes to ⊙).

7 If you selected the second option, click this area and type the number of days.

8 Click an option to specify the minimum number of characters a password must contain (○ changes to ⊙).

9 If you selected the second option, click this area and type the minimum number of characters.

Note: A password can contain 1 to 14 characters.

CONTINUED ▶

CHANGE ACCOUNT POLICIES

You can stop users from connecting to the network after unsuccessfully attempting to log on.

■ CHANGE ACCOUNT POLICIES (CONTINUED) ■

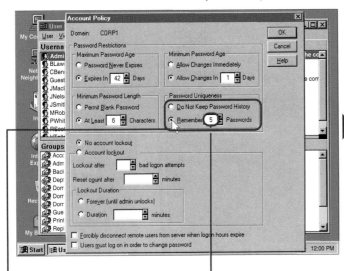

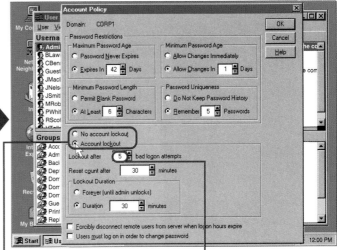

10 Click an option to specify if Windows NT will remember the passwords a user types and not allow the person to reuse them (○ changes to ⊙).

11 If you selected the second option, click this area and type the number of passwords that Windows NT will remember.

Note: Windows NT can remember 1 to 24 passwords.

12 Click an option to specify if you want to lock out accounts after users unsuccessfully attempt to log on to the network (○ changes to ⊙).

*Note: If you selected **No account lockout**, skip to step **17**.*

13 To specify the number of unsuccessful logon attempts that must occur before locking out an account, click this area and type the number of attempts.

?

Why would I want to lock out users from the network?

Locking out users after they unsuccessfully attempt to log on to the network can help prevent unauthorized people from gaining access to the network. If you do not lock out users, an individual could repeatedly enter different passwords to try and gain access to the network.

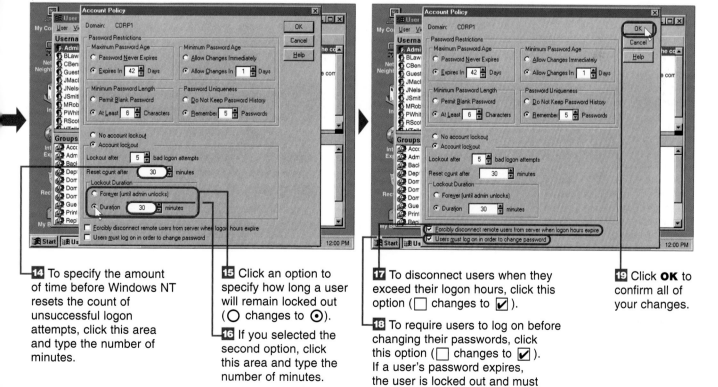

14 To specify the amount of time before Windows NT resets the count of unsuccessful logon attempts, click this area and type the number of minutes.

15 Click an option to specify how long a user will remain locked out (○ changes to ⊙).

16 If you selected the second option, click this area and type the number of minutes.

17 To disconnect users when they exceed their logon hours, click this option (☐ changes to ☑).

18 To require users to log on before changing their passwords, click this option (☐ changes to ☑). If a user's password expires, the user is locked out and must inform the network administrator.

19 Click **OK** to confirm all of your changes.

CHAPTER 14

Manage a Windows NT Server

There are several programs you can use to manage a Windows NT server. In this chapter you will learn how to close a misbehaving program using Task Manager, partition a hard disk using Disk Administrator and much more.

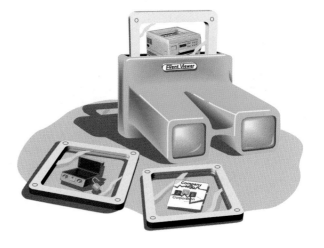

USE TASK MANAGER

You can use Task Manager to control the programs running on a computer and monitor CPU and memory use.

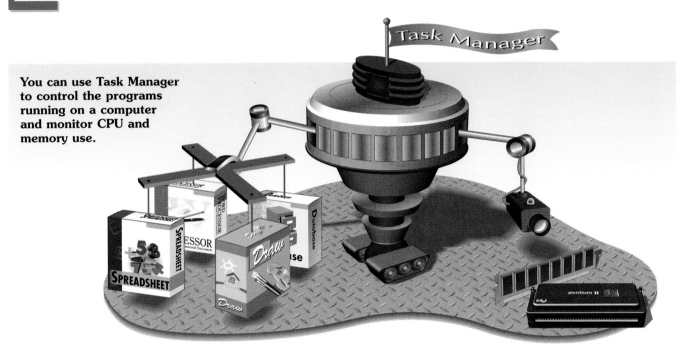

USE TASK MANAGER

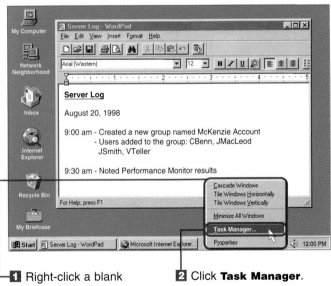

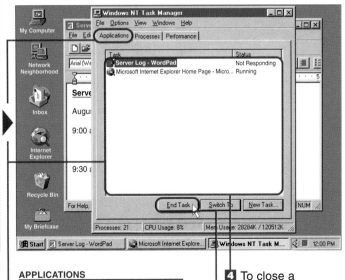

1 Right-click a blank area on the taskbar. A menu appears.

2 Click **Task Manager**.

■ The Windows NT Task Manager window appears.

APPLICATIONS

3 Click the **Applications** tab.

■ This area lists the programs that are currently running and the status of each program.

Note: Misbehaving programs display the phrase "Not Responding".

4 To close a misbehaving program, click the program.

5 Click **End Task**.

*Note: A dialog box may appear. Click **End Task** to close the program.*

? **Why would I use Task Manager to close a misbehaving program?**

If you are unable to use the mouse or keyboard in a program, you can use Task Manager to close the program without shutting down other open programs or Windows NT. When you close a misbehaving program, you lose all the unsaved information in the program.

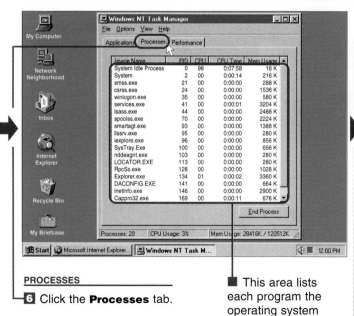

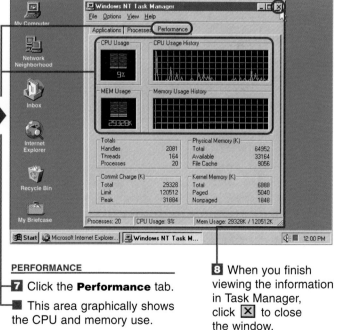

PROCESSES

6 Click the **Processes** tab.

■ This area lists each program the operating system is currently running.

PERFORMANCE

7 Click the **Performance** tab.

■ This area graphically shows the CPU and memory use.

8 When you finish viewing the information in Task Manager, click ☒ to close the window.

USE PERFORMANCE MONITOR

You can use
Performance Monitor
to view information
about the performance
of your computer.

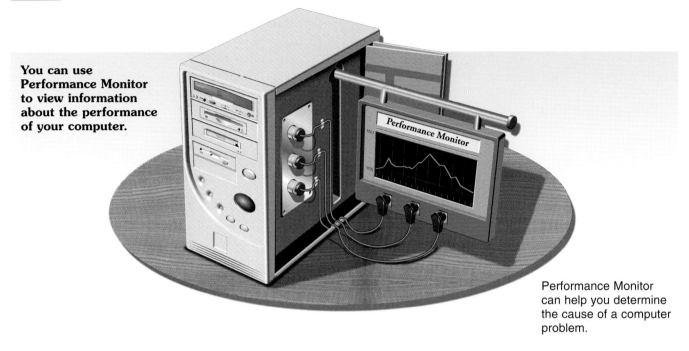

Performance Monitor
can help you determine
the cause of a computer
problem.

■ USE PERFORMANCE MONITOR ■

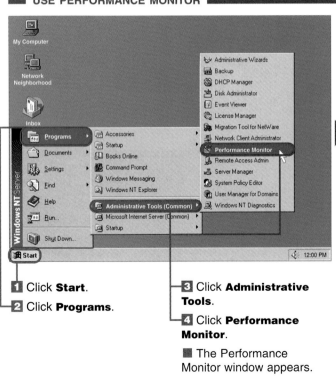

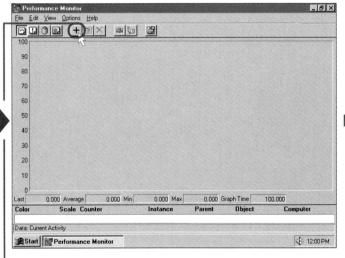

1 Click **Start**.

2 Click **Programs**.

3 Click **Administrative Tools**.

4 Click **Performance Monitor**.

■ The Performance Monitor window appears.

5 Click ⊞ to add an item you want to monitor to the window.

■ The Add to Chart dialog box appears.

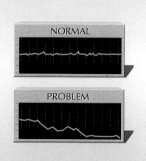

Should I use Performance Monitor even when I do not have a computer problem?

You may want to observe and record information about how your computer performs when there are no problems. If your computer's performance starts to deteriorate, you can compare the recorded information to the new information in Performance Monitor. This can help you find the cause of the problem.

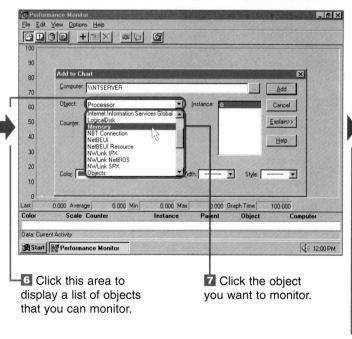

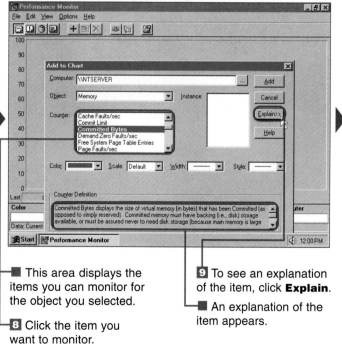

■6 Click this area to display a list of objects that you can monitor.

■7 Click the object you want to monitor.

■ This area displays the items you can monitor for the object you selected.

■8 Click the item you want to monitor.

■9 To see an explanation of the item, click **Explain**.

■ An explanation of the item appears.

CONTINUED

USE PERFORMANCE MONITOR

If you see consistently high values for an item in Performance Monitor, you may need to repair or upgrade your computer hardware.

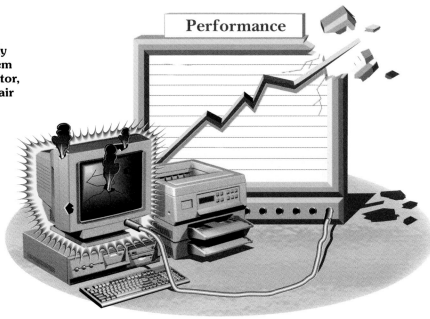

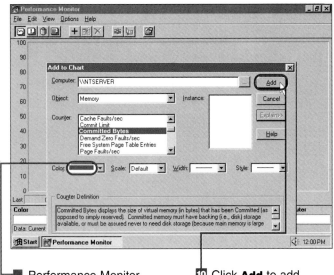

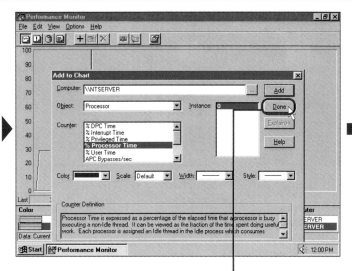

■ Performance Monitor will use this color to show the item you selected.

10 Click **Add** to add the item to the window.

■ To add additional items to the window, repeat steps **6** to **10** for each item.

11 Click **Done** to close the Add to Chart dialog box.

What items should I monitor?

Monitoring these items can provide a good starting point for evaluating the performance of a computer.

Object: Processor

Item: % Processor Time

Percentage of time the processor performs useful work.

Object: Memory

Item: Committed Bytes

Size of virtual memory used by the computer. Virtual memory is a part of the hard disk used to simulate more memory.

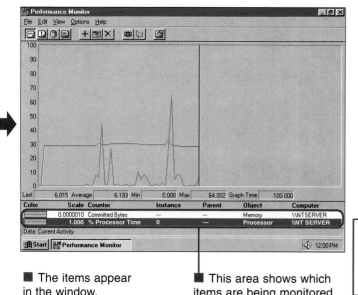

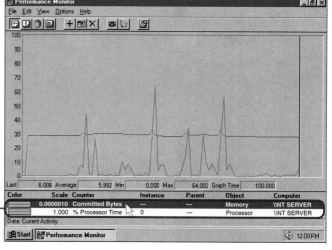

■ The items appear in the window.

■ This area shows which items are being monitored and the colors used to chart the information.

DELETE AN ITEM

1 If you no longer want to show an item in the window, click the item you want to delete.

2 Press the Delete key.

USE EVENT VIEWER

You can use Event Viewer to see a list of events that have occurred on a computer.

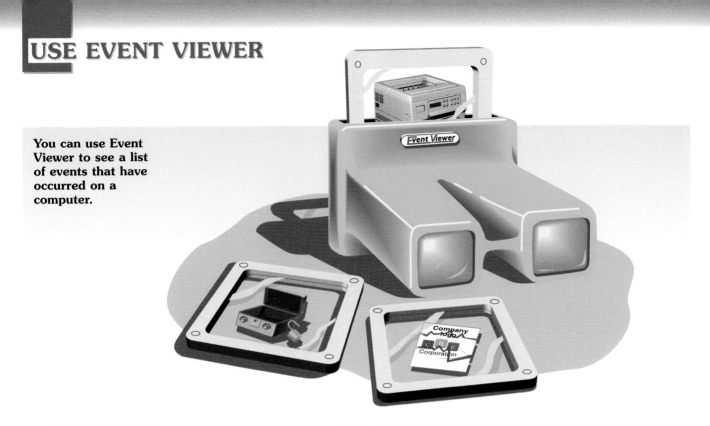

USE EVENT VIEWER

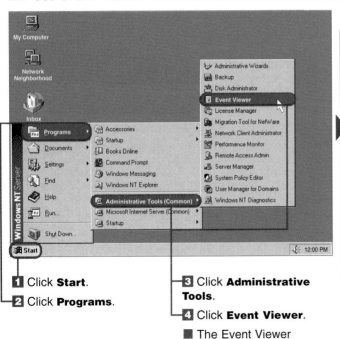

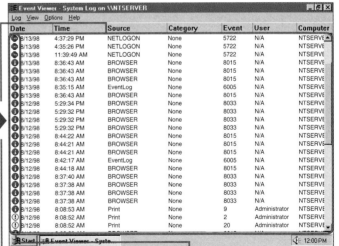

1 Click **Start**.

2 Click **Programs**.

3 Click **Administrative Tools**.

4 Click **Event Viewer**.

■ The Event Viewer window appears.

■ Initially, this area displays the date, time and other information about each system event that has occurred.

■ A symbol appears beside each event to indicate the importance of the event.

ⓘ Normal event

⨀ Noteworthy event

⊘ Problem event

What types of events can I view?

System

Displays system events, such as the installation of a printer.

Security

Displays security events, such as attempts to log on to the computer. Initially, Windows NT does not track security events. To track these events, see page 276.

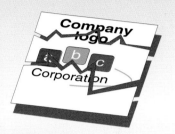

Application

Displays application events, such as a file error.

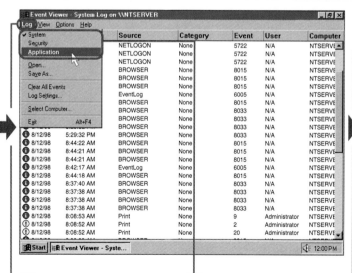

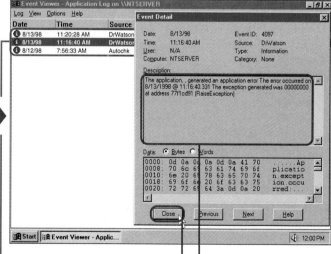

5 To change the type of events that are displayed, click **Log**.

6 Click the type of events you want to view.

■ The Event Viewer window now displays the type of events you selected.

7 To view detailed information about an event, double-click the event.

■ The Event Detail dialog box appears.

■ This area shows a description of the event.

8 When you finish reviewing the information, click **Close**.

You can change the
audit policy to select
which security events
you want to track.

You can track successful and
failed security events. For
example, you can track failed
logon attempts to discover
when an unauthorized user
is trying to connect to the
network.

CHANGE AUDIT POLICY

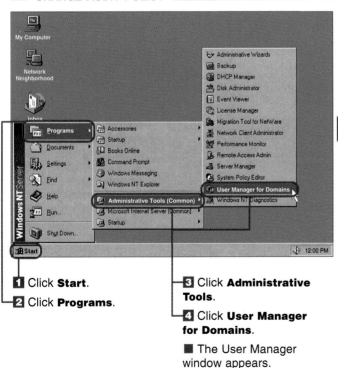

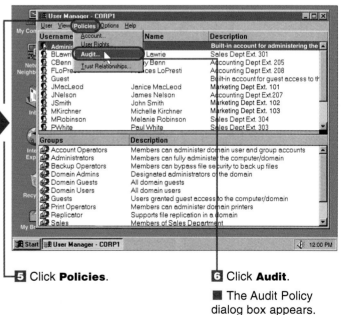

1 Click **Start**.

2 Click **Programs**.

3 Click **Administrative Tools**.

4 Click **User Manager for Domains**.

■ The User Manager window appears.

5 Click **Policies**.

6 Click **Audit**.

■ The Audit Policy dialog box appears.

Which security events can I track?

Logon and Logoff
User logged on or off the network.

File and Object Access
User accessed a folder, file or printer that is set up for auditing.

Use of User Rights
User exercised a user right.

User and Group Management
User created, changed or deleted a user or group account or changed a password.

Security Policy Changes
User changed user rights or audit policies.

Restart, Shutdown, and System
User restarted or shut down the computer or an event occurred that affects system security.

Process Tracking
Tracks certain program events.

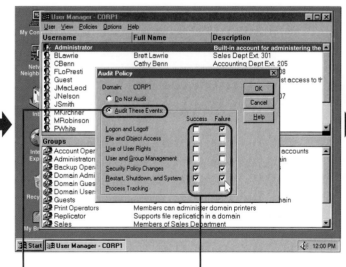

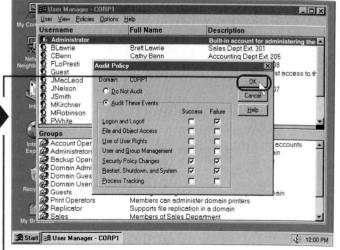

7 Click this option if you want to track security events (○ changes to ◉).

8 You can track successful and failed security events. Click the appropriate option(s) for each event you want to track (□ changes to ☑).

9 Click **OK** to save your changes.

■ You can now use Event Viewer to view security events you chose to track. See page 274 to use Event Viewer.

USE WINDOWS NT DIAGNOSTICS

You can use Windows NT Diagnostics to view information about the hardware and software installed on a computer.

USE WINDOWS NT DIAGNOSTICS

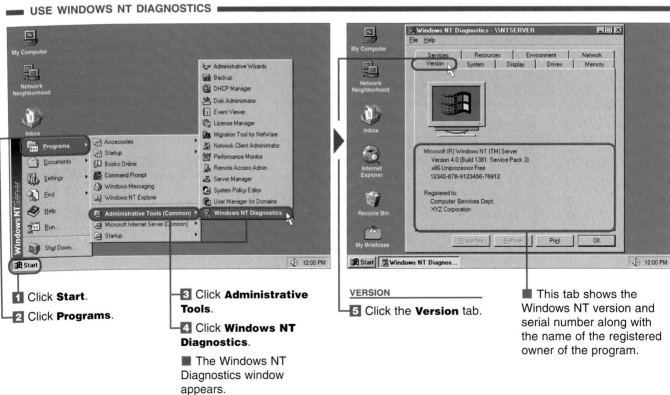

1 Click **Start**.

2 Click **Programs**.

3 Click **Administrative Tools**.

4 Click **Windows NT Diagnostics**.

■ The Windows NT Diagnostics window appears.

VERSION

5 Click the **Version** tab.

■ This tab shows the Windows NT version and serial number along with the name of the registered owner of the program.

Can I use Windows NT Diagnostics to determine if I can upgrade Windows NT?

In the Windows NT Diagnostics window, display the Version tab. This tab indicates if you have installed a service pack for Windows NT. A service pack upgrades features and fixes problems found in software programs. You can get the latest service pack for Windows NT free of charge from the Microsoft Web site at www.microsoft.com

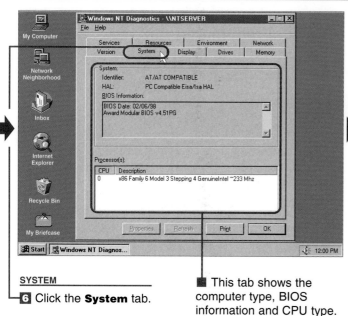

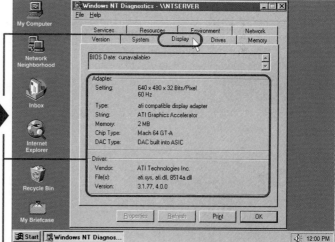

SYSTEM

■6 Click the **System** tab.

■ This tab shows the computer type, BIOS information and CPU type.

Note: The Basic Input/Output System (BIOS) controls the transfer of data between devices inside a computer.

DISPLAY

■7 Click the **Display** tab.

■ This tab shows information about your video card and driver.

Note: The video card generates the images displayed on the monitor. The driver is software that allows the video card and computer to communicate.

CONTINUED ▶

USE WINDOWS NT DIAGNOSTICS

You can view information about your drives, memory, services and hardware resources.

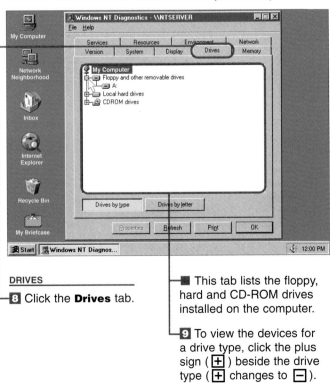

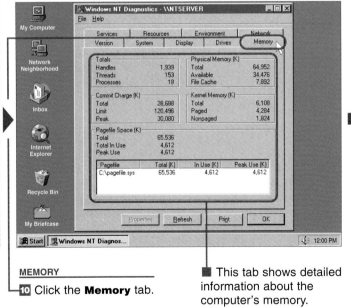

DRIVES

8 Click the **Drives** tab.

■ This tab lists the floppy, hard and CD-ROM drives installed on the computer.

9 To view the devices for a drive type, click the plus sign (⊞) beside the drive type (⊞ changes to ⊟).

MEMORY

10 Click the **Memory** tab.

■ This tab shows detailed information about the computer's memory.

Note: A computer uses memory to temporarily store information.

What information do the Environment and Network tabs show?

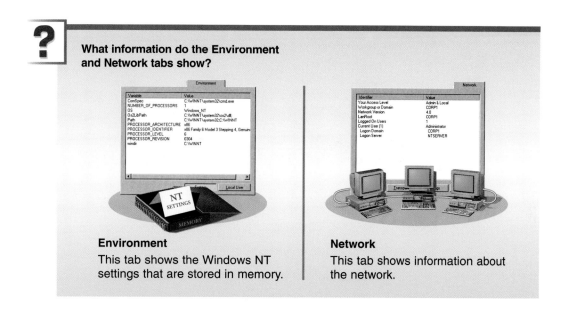

Environment

This tab shows the Windows NT settings that are stored in memory.

Network

This tab shows information about the network.

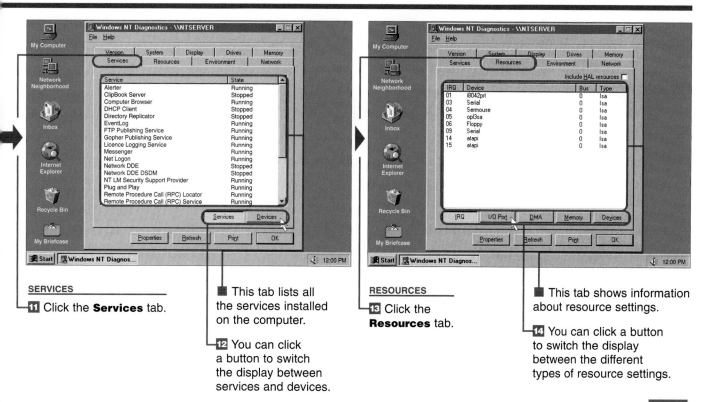

SERVICES

11 Click the **Services** tab.

■ This tab lists all the services installed on the computer.

12 You can click a button to switch the display between services and devices.

RESOURCES

13 Click the **Resources** tab.

■ This tab shows information about resource settings.

14 You can click a button to switch the display between the different types of resource settings.

USE SERVER MANAGER

You can use Server Manager to view the users currently connected to a computer on the network and which resources are in use.

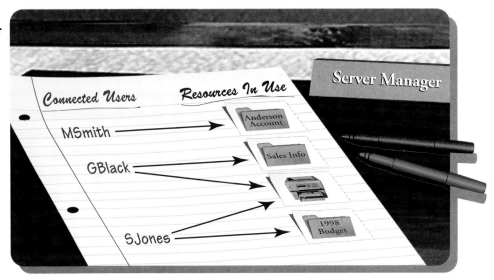

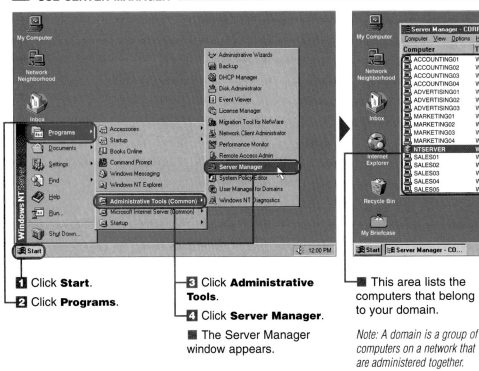

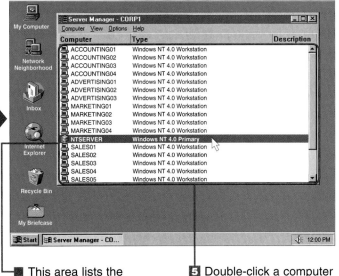

1 Click **Start**.

2 Click **Programs**.

3 Click **Administrative Tools**.

4 Click **Server Manager**.

■ The Server Manager window appears.

■ This area lists the computers that belong to your domain.

Note: A domain is a group of computers on a network that are administered together.

5 Double-click a computer you want to manage.

■ The Properties dialog box appears.

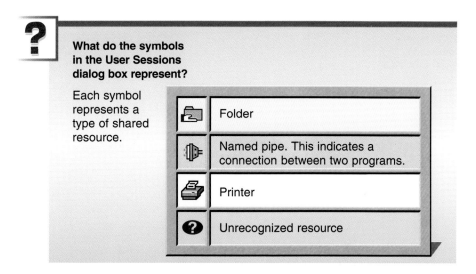

?

What do the symbols in the User Sessions dialog box represent?

Each symbol represents a type of shared resource.

📁	Folder
🔌	Named pipe. This indicates a connection between two programs.
🖨	Printer
❓	Unrecognized resource

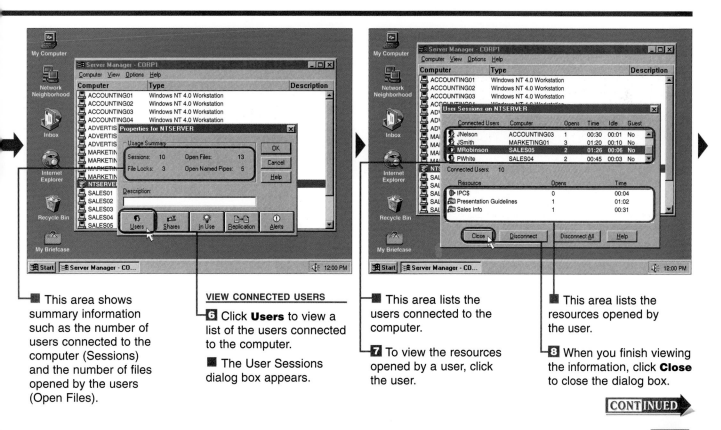

■ This area shows summary information such as the number of users connected to the computer (Sessions) and the number of files opened by the users (Open Files).

VIEW CONNECTED USERS

6 Click **Users** to view a list of the users connected to the computer.

■ The User Sessions dialog box appears.

■ This area lists the users connected to the computer.

7 To view the resources opened by a user, click the user.

■ This area lists the resources opened by the user.

8 When you finish viewing the information, click **Close** to close the dialog box.

CONTINUED

USE SERVER MANAGER

You can use Server Manager to view a list of all the shared resources on a computer and which users are working with the resources.

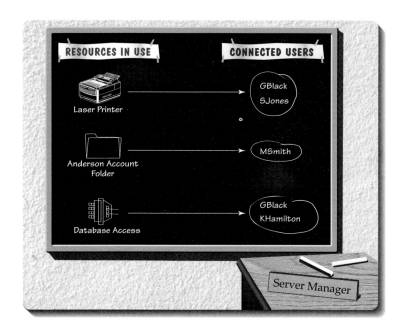

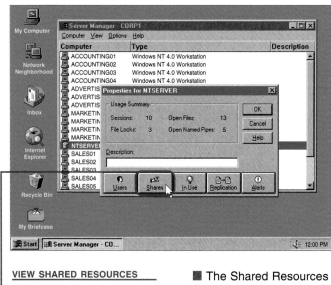

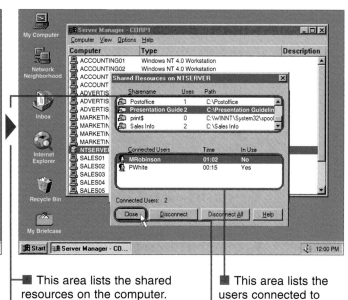

VIEW SHARED RESOURCES

■9 Click **Shares** to view a list of the shared resources on the computer.

■ The Shared Resources dialog box appears.

■ This area lists the shared resources on the computer.

■10 To view the users connected to a shared resource, click the resource.

Note: Shared resources that display the $ symbol are created by Windows NT.

■ This area lists the users connected to the shared resource.

■11 When you finish viewing the information, click **Close** to close the dialog box.

?

How do I disconnect a user from all shared resources?

You may need to disconnect a user from all shared resources to access files the user is working with. Make sure you warn users before disconnecting them.

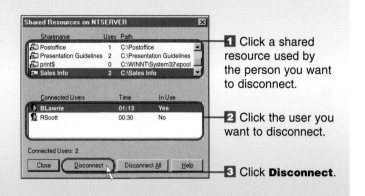

1 Click a shared resource used by the person you want to disconnect.

2 Click the user you want to disconnect.

3 Click **Disconnect**.

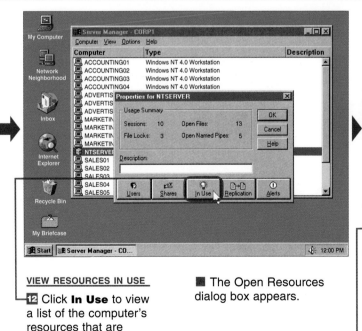

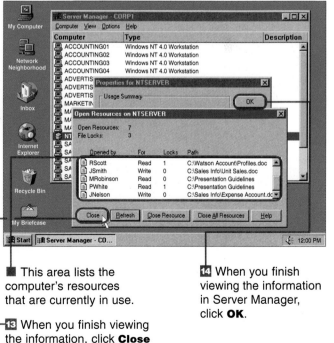

VIEW RESOURCES IN USE

12 Click **In Use** to view a list of the computer's resources that are currently in use.

■ The Open Resources dialog box appears.

■ This area lists the computer's resources that are currently in use.

13 When you finish viewing the information, click **Close** to close the dialog box.

14 When you finish viewing the information in Server Manager, click **OK**.

USE DISK ADMINISTRATOR

You can use Disk Administrator to manage hard disks installed on a computer.

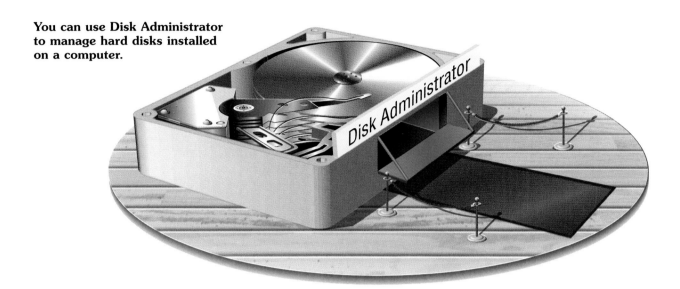

VIEW DISK INFORMATION

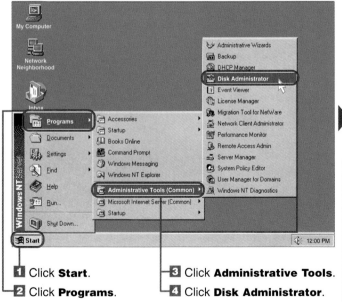

1 Click **Start**.

2 Click **Programs**.

3 Click **Administrative Tools**.

4 Click **Disk Administrator**.

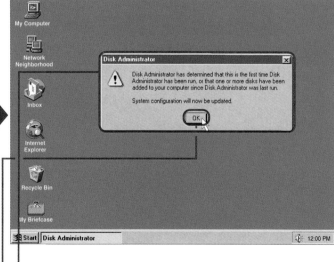

■ This dialog box appears the first time you start Disk Administrator or if you have added a hard disk to the computer.

5 Click **OK** to continue.

■ A second dialog box may appear, stating that no signature was found on the disk. Click **Yes** to write a signature on the disk.

■ The Disk Administrator window appears.

What is a partition?

A partition is a portion of a hard disk that functions as a physically separate unit. A hard disk can have up to 4 partitions. One or more partitions can be grouped together to create a volume.

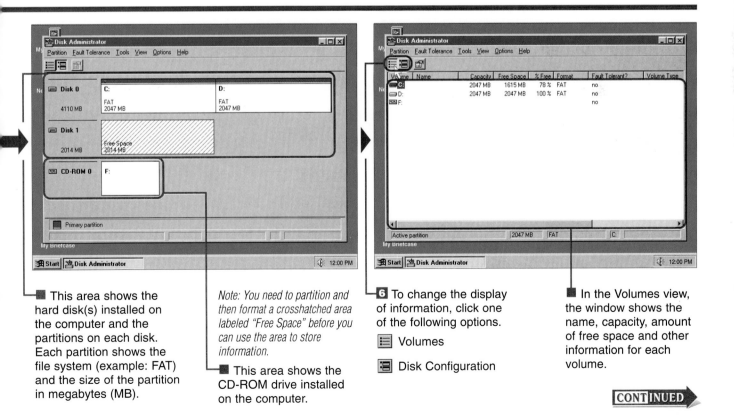

■ This area shows the hard disk(s) installed on the computer and the partitions on each disk. Each partition shows the file system (example: FAT) and the size of the partition in megabytes (MB).

Note: You need to partition and then format a crosshatched area labeled "Free Space" before you can use the area to store information.

■ This area shows the CD-ROM drive installed on the computer.

⬛ To change the display of information, click one of the following options.

⊟ Volumes

⊟ Disk Configuration

■ In the Volumes view, the window shows the name, capacity, amount of free space and other information for each volume.

CONTINUED ▶

USE DISK ADMINISTRATOR

When you add a new hard disk to a computer, you need to partition the disk before you can use the disk to store information.

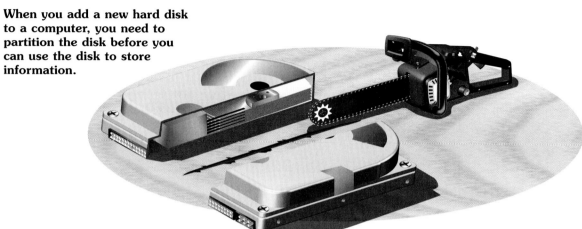

CREATE A PARTITION

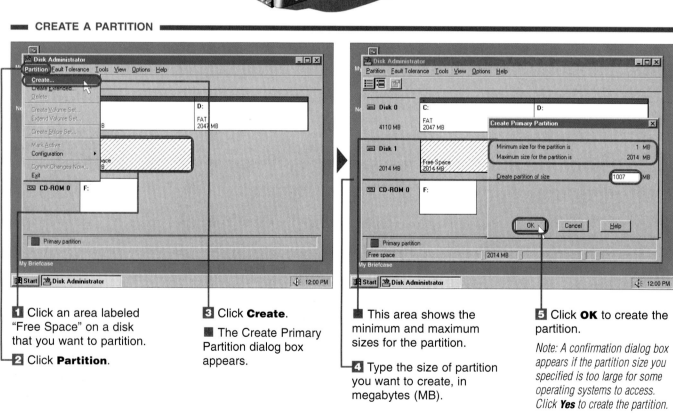

1 Click an area labeled "Free Space" on a disk that you want to partition.

2 Click **Partition**.

3 Click **Create**.

■ The Create Primary Partition dialog box appears.

■ This area shows the minimum and maximum sizes for the partition.

4 Type the size of partition you want to create, in megabytes (MB).

5 Click **OK** to create the partition.

*Note: A confirmation dialog box appears if the partition size you specified is too large for some operating systems to access. Click **Yes** to create the partition.*

What size should I use for a new partition?

If you use the maximum partition size, you can create only one partition. If you use a smaller value, you can create two or more partitions. For example, you can create one partition to store programs and another partition to store documents.

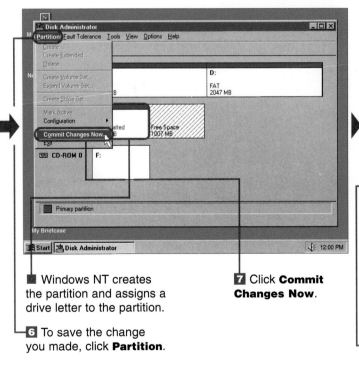

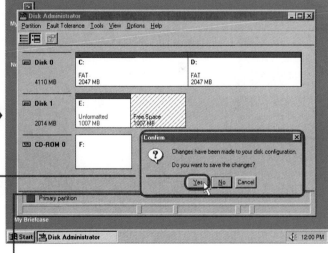

■ Windows NT creates the partition and assigns a drive letter to the partition.

6 To save the change you made, click **Partition**.

7 Click **Commit Changes Now**.

■ A confirmation dialog box appears, asking if you want to save the changes you made.

8 Click **Yes** to save the changes.

■ A second confirmation dialog box will appear, indicating that the disks were updated successfully. Click **OK** to close the dialog box.

Note: To format the partition so you can use the partition to store information, see page 290.

CONTINUED

USE DISK ADMINISTRATOR

Before you can use a new hard disk, you need to format the disk to prepare the disk to store information.

You must partition a hard disk before you can format the disk. To partition a disk, see page 288.

FORMAT A PARTITION

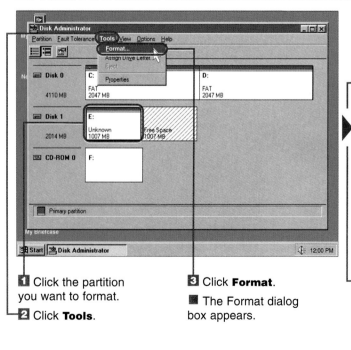

1 Click the partition you want to format.

2 Click **Tools**.

3 Click **Format**.

■ The Format dialog box appears.

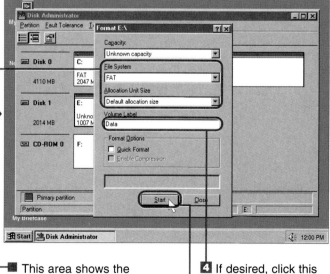

■ This area shows the file system and allocation unit size for the partition.

Note: An allocation unit is the smallest storage area on a disk.

4 If desired, click this area and type a label for the partition.

5 Click **Start** to start the format.

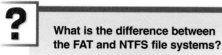

What is the difference between the FAT and NTFS file systems?

FAT

The File Allocation Table (FAT) is a list maintained by Windows NT that keeps track of where files are stored on a hard disk. FAT is widely accepted and is the default file system for Windows NT.

NTFS

The NT File System (NTFS) is specifically designed for Windows NT. This file system provides better security and can work with larger hard disks.

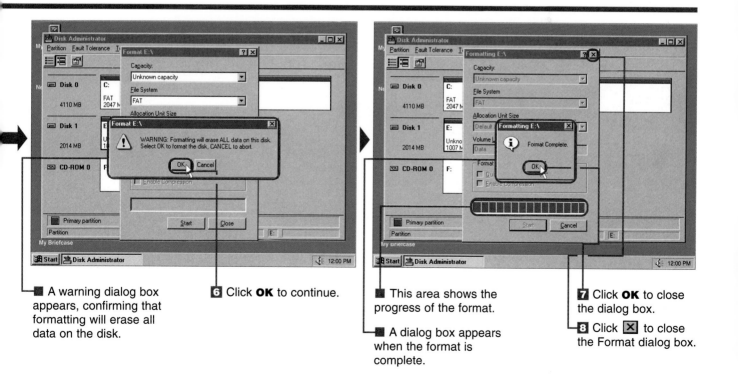

■ A warning dialog box appears, confirming that formatting will erase all data on the disk.

6 Click **OK** to continue.

■ This area shows the progress of the format.

■ A dialog box appears when the format is complete.

7 Click **OK** to close the dialog box.

8 Click **X** to close the Format dialog box.

ADD A NETWORK SERVICE OR PROTOCOL

You can add a network service or protocol to a computer. This gives the computer additional capabilities.

Service

A service lets you share and access information and equipment on a network.

Protocol

A protocol is a language that computers and equipment on a network use to communicate. Computers and equipment must use the same protocol to exchange information.

■ ADD A NETWORK SERVICE OR PROTOCOL ■

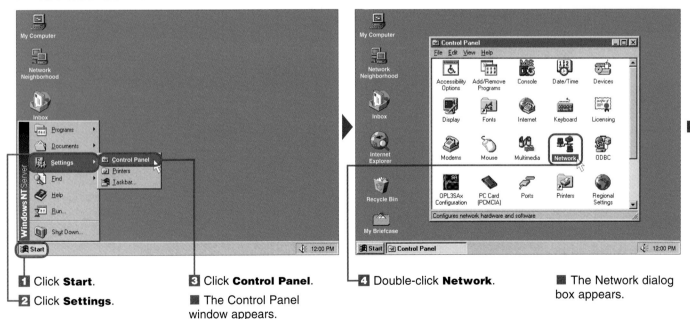

1 Click **Start**.

2 Click **Settings**.

3 Click **Control Panel**.

■ The Control Panel window appears.

4 Double-click **Network**.

■ The Network dialog box appears.

? **What services does Windows NT provide?**

Here are three popular services that
Windows NT provides.

Microsoft DHCP Server

Automatically assigns
IP addresses to computers
on a network. A computer
needs an IP address to
access the Internet.

NetBIOS Interface

Allows computers on
a Microsoft network
to communicate.

Services for Macintosh

Allows PC and Macintosh
computers to share files
and printers.

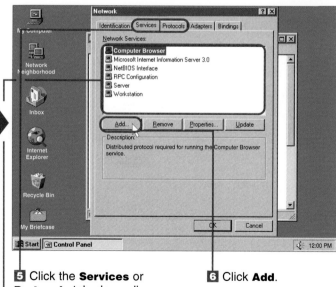

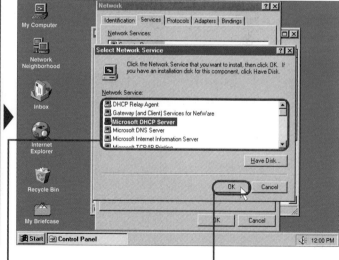

5 Click the **Services** or
Protocols tab, depending
on what you want to add.

■ This area lists the services
or protocols currently installed
on your computer.

6 Click **Add**.

■ The Select Network
dialog box appears.

7 Click the service or
protocol you want to add.

8 Click **OK** to confirm
your selection.

CONTINUED ▶

ADD A NETWORK SERVICE OR PROTOCOL

You will need your Windows NT Server CD-ROM disc to add a network service or protocol to a computer.

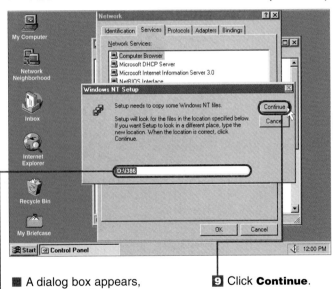

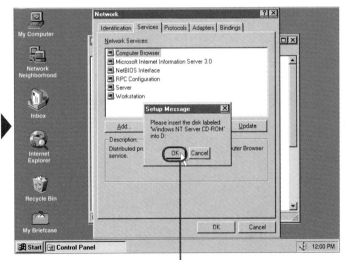

■ A dialog box appears, indicating that Setup needs to copy some Windows NT files.

■ This area shows where Setup will look for the files.

9 Click **Continue**.

■ A dialog box appears, asking you to insert the Windows NT Server CD-ROM disc into the drive.

10 Insert the CD-ROM disc into the drive.

Note: If the Windows NT CD-ROM window appears after you insert the CD-ROM disc, click ☒ to close the window.

11 Click **OK** to continue.

■ Windows NT copies the necessary files to the computer.

What protocols does Windows NT provide?

Here are three popular protocols that Windows NT provides.

NetBEUI Protocol

Used to exchange information between Windows computers set up on a small network.

NWLink IPX/SPX Compatible Transport

Used to communicate with a NetWare network.

TCP/IP Protocol

Used to connect to large networks, such as the Internet.

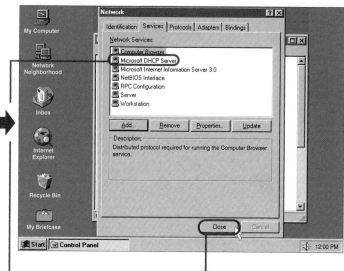

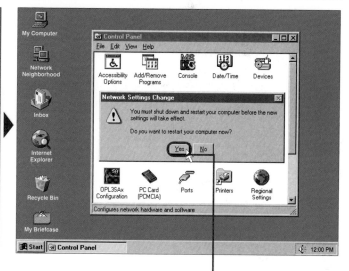

■ The service or protocol you added appears in the list.

12 Click **Close** to close the Network dialog box.

■ A dialog box appears, stating that Windows NT needs to restart the computer before the new settings will take effect.

13 Click **Yes** to restart the computer.

INDEX

INDEX

INDEX

INDEX

OVER 6 MILLION

OTHER 3-D Visual SERIES

SIMPLIFIED SERIES

Windows 98 Simplified
ISBN 0-7645-6030-1
$24.99 USA/£23.99 UK

Windows 95 Simplified
ISBN 1-56884-662-2
$19.99 USA/£18.99 UK

More Windows 95 Simplified
ISBN 1-56884-689-4
$19.99 USA/£18.99 UK

Windows 3.1 Simplified
ISBN 1-56884-654-1
$19.99 USA/£18.99 UK

Word 97 Simplified
ISBN 0-7645-6011-5
$24.99 USA/£23.99 UK

Office 97 Simplified
ISBN 0-7645-6009-3
$29.99 USA/£28.99 UK

Microsoft Office 4.2 For Windows Simplified
ISBN 1-56884-673-8
$27.99 USA/£26.99 UK

Creating Web Pages Simplified
ISBN 0-7645-6007-7
$24.99 USA/£23.99 UK

World Wide Web Color Yellow Pages Simplified
ISBN 0-7645-6005-0
$29.99 USA/£28.99 UK

Internet and World Wide Web Simplified, 2nd Edi
ISBN 0-7645-6029-8
$24.99 USA/£23.99 UK

POCKETGUIDES

The Proven 3-D Visual Approach To Learning Computers In A Handy Pocket Size.

Windows 98 Visual PocketGuide
ISBN 0-7645-6035-2
$14.99 USA/£13.99 UK

Windows 95 Visual PocketGuide
ISBN 1-56884-661-4
$14.99 USA/£13.99 UK

Word 6 For Window Visual PocketGuide
ISBN 1-56884-666-5
$14.99 USA/£13.99 UK

FOR CORPORATE ORDERS, PLEASE CALL: 800-469-6616

S A T I S F I E D   U S E R S !

from:
maranGraphics™ & **IDG BOOKS**

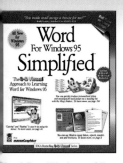

Word For Windows 95 Simplified
ISBN 1-56884-681-9
$19.99 USA/£18.99 UK

Word 6 For Windows Simplified
ISBN 1-56884-660-6
$19.99 USA/£18.99 UK

Excel 97 Simplified
ISBN 0-7645-6022-0
$24.99 USA/£23.99 UK

Excel For Windows 95 Simplified
ISBN 1-56884-682-7
$19.99 USA/£18.99 UK

Excel 5 For Windows Simplified
ISBN 1-56884-664-9
$19.99 USA/£18.99 UK

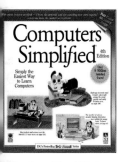

Computers Simplified, Fourth Edition
ISBN 0-7645-6042-5
$24.99 USA/£23.99 UK

America Online Simplified
ISBN 0-7645-6033-6
$24.99 USA/£23.99 UK

PC Upgrade and Repair Simplified
ISBN 0-7645-6049-2
$24.99 USA/£23.99 UK

The 3-D Visual Dictionary of Computing
ISBN 1-56884-678-9
$19.99 USA/£18.99 UK

WordPerfect 6.1 For Windows Simplified
ISBN 1-56884-665-7
$19.99 USA/£18.99 UK

ALSO AVAILABLE:

Windows 3.1 Visual PocketGuide
ISBN 1-56884-650-9
$14.99 USA/£13.99 UK

Excel 5 For Windows Visual PocketGuide
ISBN 1-56884-667-3
$14.99 USA/£13.99 UK

WordPerfect 6.1 For Windows Visual PocketGuide
ISBN 1-56884-668-1
$14.99 USA/£13.99 UK

Lotus 1-2-3 R5 For Windows Visual PocketGuide
ISBN 1-56884-671-1
$14.99 USA/£13.99 UK

FOR CORPORATE ORDERS, PLEASE CALL: 800-469-6616

OVER 6 MILLION

OTHER 3-D Visual SERIES

TEACH YOURSELF VISUALLY SERIES

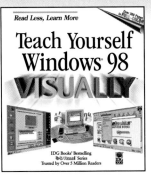

Teach Yourself Windows 98 VISUALLY

ISBN 0-7645-6025-5
$29.99 USA/£28.99 UK

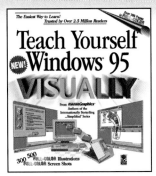

Teach Yourself Windows 95 VISUALLY

ISBN 0-7645-6001-8
$29.99 USA/£28.99 UK

Teach Yourself Computers & the Internet VISUALLY, 2nd Edition

ISBN 0-7645-6041-7
$29.99 USA/£28.99 UK

Teach Yourself Networking VISUALLY

ISBN 0-7645-6023-9
$29.99 USA/£28.99 UK

Teach Yourself Access 97 VISUALLY

ISBN 0-7645-6026-3
$29.99 USA/£28.99 UK

Teach Yourself Netscape Navigator 4 VISUALLY

ISBN 0-7645-6028-X
$29.99 USA/£28.99 UK

Teach Yourself Word 97 VISUALLY

ISBN 0-7645-6032-8
$29.99 USA/£28.99 UK

Teach Yourself the Internet and World Wide Web VISUALLY

ISBN 0-7645-6020-4
$29.99 USA/£28.99 UK

FOR CORPORATE ORDERS, PLEASE CALL: 800-469-6616

S A T I S F I E D U S E R S !

from:
maranGraphics™ & **IDG BOOKS**

MASTER VISUALLY SERIES

Teach Yourself Office 97 VISUALLY

ISBN 0-7645-6018-2
$29.99 USA/£28.99 UK

Master Windows 98 VISUALLY

ISBN 0-7645-6034-4
$39.99 USA/£36.99 UK

Master Windows 95 VISUALLY

ISBN 0-7645-6024-7
$39.99 USA/£36.99 UK

Master Office 97 VISUALLY

ISBN 0-7645-6036-0
$39.99 USA/£36.99 UK

Visit our Web site at:
http://www.maran.com

FOR CORPORATE ORDERS, PLEASE CALL: 800-469-6616